Waynesburg College Library
Waynesburg, Pa. 15370

D1794500

364 T396

Theoretical methods in
 criminology

THEORETICAL METHODS IN CRIMINOLOGY

For Mike

THEORETICAL METHODS IN CRIMINOLOGY

Edited by
ROBERT F. MEIER

 **SAGE** PUBLICATIONS Beverly Hills London New Delhi

Copyright © 1985 by Sage Publications, Inc.

All rights reserved. No part of this book may be reproduced or utilized in any form or by any means, electronic or mechanical, including photocopying, recording, or by any information storage and retrieval system, without permission in writing from the publisher.

For information address:

                SAGE Publications, Inc.
                275 South Beverly Drive
                Beverly Hills, California 90212

SAGE Publications India Pvt. Ltd.  SAGE Publications Ltd
           M-32 Market   28 Banner Street
      Greater Kailash I   London EC1Y 8QE
    New Delhi 110 048 India   England

Printed in the United States of America

Library of Congress Cataloging in Publication Data

Main entry under title:

Theoretical methods in criminology.

   Bibliography: p.
   1. Crime and criminals--Addresses, essays, lectures.
I. Meier, Robert F. (Robert Frank), 1944-
HV6028.T49   1985   364   84-27716
ISBN 0-8039-2425-9

FIRST PRINTING

Contents

Acknowledgments 7

PART I. INTRODUCTION

1. An Introduction to Theoretical Methods in Criminology
   ROBERT F. MEIER 11

PART II. GENERAL ISSUES IN CONSTRUCTING CRIMINOLOGICAL THEORIES

2. The Methodology of Theory Construction in Criminology
   JACK P. GIBBS 23

3. The Level of Explanation Problem in Criminology
   JAMES F. SHORT, Jr. 51

PART III. ASSUMPTIONS ABOUT THEORETICAL METHODS

4. The Assumption of Natural Science Methods: Criminological Positivism
   JOHN HAGAN 75

5. The Assumption that General Theories Are Not Possible
   CHARLES R. TITTLE 93

6. The Assumption that Theories Can Be Combined with Increased Explanatory Power: Theoretical Integrations
   DELBERT S. ELLIOTT 123

7. The Assumption of the Efficacy of Middle-Range Explanation: Typologies
   DON C. GIBBONS 151

**PART IV. ASSUMPTIONS ABOUT THE
NATURE OF EXPLANATIONS**

8. The Neoclassical Theory of Crime Control
   ERNEST van den HAAG   177

9. The Assumption that Crime Is a Product of
   Individual Characteristics: A Prime
   Example from Psychiatry
   MICHAEL HAKEEM   197

10. The Assumption that Crime Is a Product of
    Environments: Sociological Approaches
    ALBERT K. COHEN   223

About the Authors   245

Acknowledgments

I would like to thank all of the authors for their very hard, and very good, work. The support services of the Department of Sociology and the Social Research Center at Washington State University are excellent; I would like to acknowledge their contribution to this effort. Finally, for their advice, patience, and understanding, I would like to thank my editors at Sage Publications.

—Robert F. Meier

PART I
INTRODUCTION

1

An Introduction to Theoretical Methods in Criminology

ROBERT F. MEIER

Lytton Strachey begins his biographical approach to Victorian manners in *Eminent Victorians* by observing that "the history of the Victorian Age will never be written: we know too much about it." He continues: "Ignorance is the first requisite of the historian—ignorance, which simplifies and clarifies, which selects and omits, with a placid perfection unattainable by the highest art" (Strachey, 1969: vii). Strachey's comments may go too far with respect to history in general, but they are surely relevant to criminological theory.

Strachey's problem was that he was too close to his subject and, presumably, this is why distance in time and space provide the necessary "ignorance" (or detachment) for that history. That being the case, criminologists should be superb historians, not because we know too much about our theory, but because we are so detached from it.

Many accounts rely on a simple formula for presenting theory. It is portrayed as though it were information (facts) rather than an orientation with which to interpret events and their contexts. Students learn that there are four major theoretical traditions in sociological criminology, and that these traditions contain virtually all sociological theories on the subject. Criminological theory is a body of theory containing identifiable persons (such as Robert K. Merton or Edwin H. Sutherland[1]) and the major ideas or concepts of those persons (for example, anomie and differential association). Each school term, the names of major figures in criminological theory are dutifully paraded out and their ideas discussed. The ideas are then ritually demolished. It is one of the rites of criminology. Seldom are students instructed about the ways these theories developed or the assumptions that underlie them. Students, in short, learn the substance but not the method of criminological theory.

SUBSTANTIVE CRIMINOLOGICAL THEORY

Substantive criminological theory has developed in many different forms, largely following the disciplinary biases of its developers. Thus there is biological, psychological, psychiatric, psychoanalytic, economic, and sociological theory, to name a few. Theory identified with particular disciplines has dominated the study of crime since Lombroso.

Substantive theory is composed of specific ideas that attempt to explain individual offending or patterns of offending. This is the theory that is taught in criminology classes and reproduced in the professional literature in criminology. In the United States, because criminology has most frequently been taught in departments of sociology, most criminologists have come to subscribe to a form of sociological theory. The major perspectives in sociological criminology developed since the 1920s, with those theories that are fairly recent (say, post-1950) having antecedents to earlier views.

Before about 1950, criminologists placed substantial confidence in their ability to generate etiological theories that would explain the origin of all crime. Through the 1940s, the most pressing theoretical questions in criminology seemed to be how some persons, but not others, came to commit crimes and how these crimes were distributed in social space. Thus "Why did they do it?" questions, and "Why is there more crime in this place and in this group than in that place and in that group?" questions produced the major theoretical responses. The usual sociological answers to these theoretical questions included (1) residing in a community that lacked adequate restraints over deviant conduct (Shaw and McKay), (2) residing in a society that pressured people to pursue success goals without providing legitimate means by which to achieve them (Merton), and (3) learning criminal norms (Sutherland).

These general answers are often identified as "basic" approaches to criminological theory and referred to as *control, strain* or anomie, and *learning* approaches to crime (and deviance). A subsequent approach, *labeling*, did not develop fully until later, although some of the ideas associated with that approach can be traced to writers in the 1920s and 1930s.

Post-World War II America signaled a shift in the interests of criminologists and this produced a shift in substantive theory. There was no single intellectual work in 1950 that produced the shift, but it was about that time that different questions began to dominate conventional criminological theory.[2] During the 1950s, the theoretical questions changed to revolve around the origins of criminal and delinquent norms and how some persons came to subscribe to those norms (Cohen, Miller, Cloward and Ohlin). During the 1960s, the issues included the origin of "conventional" norms (both social rules and laws), the process by which some rules became laws while others did not, and the consequences on criminal careers of enforcing these rules (Becker, Kitsuse, Schur). The work in the 1970s was, in part, a reaction against the labeling tradition, with attention turning to the role of sanctions (Gibbs, Tittle) and the effectiveness of crime control agencies (Wilson, van den Haag) in producing compliance with legal norms. The 1980s has so far witnessed a continuation of these concerns, as well as an interest in reconceiving criminological theory into more commonsensical terms, such as the "routine activity approach" of Cohen and Felson, a theoretical perspective that denies a role for such time-honored, traditional theoretical concepts as criminal motivation, socialization, freedom from restraint, elite preferences, and social structural strain.

Most theoretical work after 1950 fell within the same broad approaches identified earlier—control, strain, and learning. While the questions of criminologists changed, the same theoretical frameworks that had served them so well prior to 1950 were continuously applied. For example, in the work on subcultural delinquency, Cohen's strain theory is merely an extension of Merton's; Miller's learning theory applies Sutherland's perspective to subcultural delinquency; and Cloward and Ohlin combine both anomie and differential association traditions. In addition, however, a reactivist conception of deviance and a theory of secondary deviation (both of which are usually identified as *labeling* theory or the "interactionist perspective") developed in the 1960s.

An additional perspective, usually identified as a "conflict" or "radical" alternative, seemed to emphasize slightly different questions, such as the origin of specific laws and the influence of elite preferences on the content and application of those laws. As such, it is not offending that requires explanation, but, rather, how such behavior came to be in conflict with elite interests and how those interests are tied to the political structure of a society.

Although each of the four major sociological traditions has generated much fruitful research that has deepened our understanding of crime, each has also generated a substantial critical literature. The criticisms include a concern about negative cases (crimes and/or criminals that are not explained by a given theory), the inability of a theory to account for the distribution of crime, a lack of attention to causative factors identified by other disciplinary theories (for example, personality traits, biological features), as well as "internal" disputes regarding the adequacy of each theory to be evaluated by empirical test. In fact, the criticisms that have been levied against each theoretical tradition are so extensive that they cannot be conveniently catalogued here. Indeed, whole monographs have been written on the subject. And so extensive are the inadequacies of these theories that it appears there is no body of theory that even most criminologists would identify currently as the "best" we have.

Substantive criminological theory emphasizes the ability of specific persons to become associated with specific ideas. Differential association cannot be mentioned without Sutherland's name, and anomie theory invariably results in a citation to the work of Robert Merton. But there is more to criminological theory than the ideas of a few criminologists. In fact, there is so much more that there is little agreement on the best direction for criminological theory; agreement seems confined to lamentations that criminological theory is stagnant. Such criticisms are not particularly recent (for instance, see Manning, 1973), although more recent observers have advanced similar conclusions (see Meier, 1980). Yet the diagnosis that criminological theory is moribund—which perhaps means simply that it is no longer novel or that it is not generating interesting researchable questions—did not lead to a coherent corrective, either by such critics or by others who agreed with them.

Because of the varied and extensive criticism of all four of the basic approaches in conventional criminological theory, it might be assumed that there is little about which criminologists agree. That conclusion would be premature. There are several assumptions, or key ideas, that orient the theoretical posture of criminologists regardless of their specific ideological or theoretical persuasions. Not all criminologists agree on the the substance of these ideas, but the ideas are reflected, implicitly or explicitly, in all criminological theories at least to some degree.

THEORETICAL METHODS IN CRIMINOLOGY

Dissatisfaction with the content of criminological theory can result in more defensible substantive theory, theory that is more immune to serious criticisms and that serves to explain better the occurrence of crime. But the development of new substantive theory does not take place in an intellectual or theoretical vacuum. It is necessary to discuss two terms in this connection: methods and theoretical methods.

The term "method" is often used in two ways. First, it is almost always used in the context of empirical research to denote the manner in which data are collected. In this context, the term frequently implies a cookbook or formula approach to research so that a researcher can follow a few simple "do's and don'ts" for study design, sampling, and actual data collection. A second meaning of "method" refers more generally to an orientation to scholarly work, an approach that pledges allegiance to the canons of science and logic. In this sense, method is not a list of tasks, but a perspective on knowledge and explanation. I take the term "method" to refer to this latter meaning.

The term "theoretical methods" denotes approaches, assumptions, and techniques of theory construction. As such, references in this book to specific, substantive criminological theories are usually made in the context of building theory, but such references tend to be merely illustrative. What matters is what undergirds substantive theories. In this way, criminologists who are dissatisfied with the substance of criminological theory can follow Strachey's advice to pull back a bit from the subject matter by looking at the intellectual foundations of that theory. By looking critically at the foundations of our theory we might become not only better acquainted with our own theory, but, one hopes, better acquainted with possible alternatives based on those, or other, assumptions.

But criminologists must learn to think theoretically. New insights do not simply come to those who are sufficiently introspective. Rather, what is needed is a stimulus to such ideas. One such stimulus is an examination of basic assumptions and ideas that underlie current theoretical efforts so that new theory can proceed by escaping previous problems. In other words, what may be needed is not a study about the major ideas in substantive criminological theory, but one about the assumptions and basic problems of that theory.

A concern with theoretical methods requires not only a sound familiarity with the general subject matter of criminology (so-called facts to be explained and the nature of previous explanations), but also an awareness of the taken-for-granted bases on which such theories are constructed. Those assumptions are examined too infrequently. Most discussions about criminological theory confine the topic solely to substantive theory (for example, see Gibbons, 1979), even in those publications that are devoted exclusively to criminological theory (see Vold, 1958, 1979). There is usually little consideration of the intellectual grounding of specific theories (but see Kornhauser, 1978; Shoemaker, 1984); rather, what seems to be emphasized much more is how adequate an explanation for crime the specific theory is and perhaps the implications of that theory for crime control policies.

This book is only a preliminary effort to reexamine criminological theory by not focusing exclusively on substantive theory; rather, this book emphasizes theoretical methods. This approach is not standard in criminology, where substantive theory dominates theoretical discussions. The absence of concern over theoretical methods in criminology stems largely, but not exclusively, from our familiarity and comfortableness with substantive theory. Few criminologists have the energy to undertake a major theoretical project of the kind advocated here. There is simply much inertia to be overcome; substantive theory is easier to discuss because that is the vocabulary most criminologists use for the topic of "theory." Substantive theory requires less effort because we have the cognitive categories in place for that kind of theory. Substantive theory is what most of us mean when we use the term "theory"; this is the theory we were taught and, in turn, this is the theory we most often teach our students.

But the promise of theoretical methods offers much (see, for example, Freese, 1980; Stinchcombe, 1978). The ultimate objective of such a reexamination would be the development of new, testable theory that would make sense of known facts about crime and guide research efforts to uncover new facts. The more immediate objective, however, is to provide stimulation to study anew our old theories and to think about them in new and interesting ways.

THE PLAN OF THE BOOK

As should be obvious by now, this book emphasizes not the substance of criminological theory but the methods of constructing such theories. These methods do not constitute a convenient checklist of things to consider in constructing theory; rather, they involve a reconsideration of basic assumptions and understandings that underpin our substantive theories. The two chapters in Part II discuss some general problems in theoretical methods as applied to criminology—the possibility of employing formal theory in identifying independent variables (Gibbs) and the necessity of distinguishing different levels of explanation as they affect the identification of dependent variables (Short).

The chapters in Part III deal with various assumptions concerning alternative methods or models of explanation: positivism (Hagan), eclecticism (Tittle), and the integration of disparate theories (Elliott), and the use of typological approaches (Gibbons). The chapters in Part IV are concerned with different facets of seemingly competing kinds of explanations: neoclassicism, which is based on hedonistic foundations (van den Haag); individualistic explanations (Hakeem); and environmental explanations (Cohen).

Not all such assumptions or problems in criminological theory are examined here, but some of the better known are discussed. One omission is of a chapter on radical theory and the assumptions that underlie that perspective.[3] Because this book is meant to represent only a beginning point in a study of theoretical methods in criminology, subsequent work should not only extend material that is dealt with here, but should also develop topics that are not covered in this volume.

The authors were asked to think about theoretical issues, but not necessarily the substance of criminological theory. The authors of some of the chapters (4-10) were asked to write to an "outline" based on four items. The authors were asked the following questions: (1) What is the perspective/approach? What are the main ideas and principal exemplars in criminology? (2) What are the main advantages and disadvantages of the perspective? Has the assumption helped or hindered criminology (and in what way or ways)? Can you make any other evaluative statements about the approach? (3) What research, if any, is needed to address, disconfirm, or support the perspective? Is research appropriate at all? (4) Speculation: Where do we go from here? What do we need—conceptually, theoretically, empirically—to advance the perspective or assumption? Is any change needed?

The outline is necessarily broad and the result is that the essays here are not standardized. But the goal of the chapters was intellectual stimulation, not standardization. As a result, the reader is likely to encounter some overlap in subject matter (and at times disagreement concerning that subject matter). It should be kept in mind that this is both inevitable and desirable given the nature of the chapters. While each chapter is discrete from the others, they are all related to one another in the sense that they are addressing different facets of criminological theory. Some of the chapters rely on substantive theory more than others (for instance, Hakeem) but all of the chapters here of necessity refer to substantive theory and all raise issues revolving around the explanatory adequacy of that substantive theory without regard to the methods that underlie it.

CONCLUSION

Lytton Strachey's observations regarding the importance of detachment from one's subject do not suggest that if we are too close to a subject that we cannot know it at all. After all, we need to be close to it as well as detached from it to see matters correctly and in perspective. We would do well, however, to remember that sometimes we can see best by not looking directly at something, but by going back and examining it in reference to its beginnings. That is, we can sometimes see better (closer) from afar.

One theme that pervades this collection of essays is that criminological theory can be studied from the viewpoint of "pretheory." That is, our theory is the result of the assumptions (for example, the nature of human conduct) and taken-for-granted understandings (for example, it is better—or easier—to construct theories from everyday language rather than mathematical relations) on which we build our ideas. A better understanding of those assumptions and how we address pretheoretical problems should prove instructive. Such an understanding may, in fact, provide both the necessary closeness and the detachment we need to think better theoretically.

NOTES

1. My assumption here and in the paragraphs to follow is that complete citations to the works of well-known criminologists are not necessary. Of course, if readers are confused as to which specific work is being cited, I can supply the full reference.
2. I have discussed these themes in a paper written in 1979 that was not published until 1983 (Meier, 1983). Some of these ideas are also presented in a subsequent paper; see Short and Meier (1981).
3. I regret that this specific chapter did not materialize.

REFERENCES

FREESE, L. [ed.] (1980) Theoretical Methods in Sociology. Pittsburg: University of Pittsburg Press.
GIBBONS, D. C. (1979) The Criminological Enterprise: Theories and Prospects. Englewood Cliffs, NJ: Prentice-Hall.
KORNHAUSER, R. R. (1978) Social Sources of Delinquency: An Examination of Analytic Models. Chicago: University of Chicago Press.
MANNING, P. K. (1973) "On deviance." Contemporary Sociology 2 (May): 123-128.
MEIER, R. F. (1983) "Criminology in the United States," pp. 267-296 in E. H. Johnson (ed.) International Handbook of Contemporary Developments in Criminology, Vol. I. Westport, CT: Greenwood.
———(1980) "The arrested development of criminological theory." Contemporary Sociology 9 (May): 374-376.
SHOEMAKER, D. J. (1984) Theories of Delinquency: An Examination of Explanations of Delinquent Behavior. New York: Oxford University Press.
SHORT, J. R., Jr. and R. F. MEIER (1981) "Criminology and the study of deviance." American Behavioral Scientist 24 (January/February): 462-478.
STINCHCOMBE, A. L. (1978) Theoretical Methods in Social History. New York: Academic.
STRACHEY, L. (1969) Eminent Victorians. New York: Harcourt Brace Jovanovich.
VOLD, G. B. (1979) Theoretical Criminology (T. Bernard, ed.). New York: Oxford University Press.
———(1958) Theoretical Criminology. New York: Oxford University Press.

PART II

GENERAL ISSUES IN CONSTRUCTING CRIMINOLOGICAL THEORIES

2

The Methodology of Theory Construction in Criminology

JACK P. GIBBS

Systematic tests of criminological theories are precluded as long as criminologists employ the discursive mode of theory construction. Although that mode prevails in most of the social and behavioral sciences, there is a distinct alternative—a formal mode. The two primary goals here are to clarify the discursive-formal distinction and to assess three criminological theories in light of it.

THE DISCURSIVE-FORMAL DISTINCTION

The discursive mode is merely the conventions of a natural language (such as German or English). By contrast, a formal mode comprises rules designed for stating theories, some of which transcend natural language conventions. The rules of mathematics clearly transcend those conventions; but such rules become parts of a formal mode only when someone stipulates how they should be used in stating theories, and specialists in "quantitative" or "mathematical" criminology have yet to undertake those stipulations (see, for example, Fox, 1981; Greenberg, n.d.). For that matter, a *verbal* but nonetheless formal version of a theory is needed prior to stating it mathematically (for what appears to be a contrary view, see Freese and Sell, 1980, especially p. 283).

The discursive-formal distinction is complicated only in that some natural language conventions enter into any mode of theory construction. Contemplate this rule: Some statements in a theory are to be labeled "premises," others "conclusions," and the remainder "definitions." Since the rule is not a natural language convention, it would constitute a formal mode of theory construction. Of course, no actual formal mode comprises only one rule, and in all modes there is some implicit reliance upon natural language conventions. The merits of a particular mode do not necessarily depend on the extent of that reliance; and the relative merit of contending formal modes is secondary for present purposes, because *any* formal mode is superior to the discursive mode.

SOME ELEMENTARY COMPONENTS OF A FORMAL MODE

Although formal modes differ in many respects, there are several similarities. In particular, of nine modes formulated by sociologists since 1964 (see Turner and Beeghley, 1981, for most references), all recognize types of terms and types of statements.

Types of Terms

No one is likely to regard definitions of anomie, differential association, class conflict, or normative consensus as complete; accordingly, those terms are illustrative *constructs*. A construct is a term that a theorist uses in stating a theory and defines, if at all, in such a way that he or she does not claim that the definition is complete (the definition is ambiguous or possibly fails to identify all distinctive features of the phenomenon in question).

Not even a complete definition makes a term empirically applicable if it denotes a quantitative property, in which case the term is empirically applicable to the extent that *independent* observers report the same value for a particular thing or event (for example, as when two or more investigators report the official 1983 burglary rate for a particular city). Empirical applicability is likely to be negligible unless the theorist stipulates (1) a computational formula, (2) the requisite data, and (3) a procedure for gathering or obtaining those data. Those stipulations require a complete definition of the term; hence constructs are not even indirectly empirically applicable.

Concepts. If a theorist regards his or her definition of a term as complete, it is a concept. Suppose a theorist defines the "total crime rate of a territorial unit" as the number of all crimes that occur in a particular territorial unit during a particular year as a ratio to the average daily number of residents of that unit over the year. The theorist might regard that definition as complete, but note again that a quantitative term (one that denotes a quantitative property) is not empirically applicable even indirectly unless linked to a computational formula.

The crime illustration notwithstanding, a complete definition of a quantitative term *does not imply* a computational formula. Consider this definition: "Occupational differentiation" refers to the number of occupations in a population and the uniformity of the distribution of population members among the occupations. Whatever the definition may appear to imply, there are several formulas for expressing the amount of occupational differentiation; and no rules of logic can be substituted for a theorist's judgment of alternatives.

If the link between a concept and a formula is not made explicit *in the theory,* then the theory is simply incomplete and idiosyncratic tests are likely. However, contrary to operationalism, a formula is not a definition, operational or otherwise, of the concept. Like definitions, the formula and related data stipulations do not appear in the premises or conclusions of the theory; but a formula is denoted in those statements by some symbol (such as an acronym), henceforth referred to as a "referential." While the formula can be thought of as a "measure," that term is ambiguous; it may refer to the formula or to a particular value. The ambiguity is avoided here by using the term "referent" to designate a value ostensibly computed by the application of a particular referential formula.

Further observations on empirical applicability. Judgment of the empirical applicability of a referential formula should be based on actual attempts of investigators to apply it, and there are three possible reasons for negligible empirical applicability. First, investigators may regard the referential formula as *unintelligible.* Second, gathering or obtaining data in accordance with the procedural instructions may not be *feasible.* Third, if the referents reported for the same unit differ, the differences indicate *ambiguity* in the formula and/or procedural instructions.

Devising a referential formula and applying it are quite different. Thus a theorist may identify the term "true burglary rate" as a concept (construing its definition as complete) and even think of a referential formula, only to conclude that the formula's application is not feasible because there is no observational procedure for counting burglaries. The term could still be treated as a concept; however, unless linked with a referential, a concept's "position" in a theory is not really different from that of a construct.

Unit terms. "Constructs" and "concepts" are property terms in that they denote particular properties of classes of things or events (for example, the robbery rate of a city, the age of an individual, the seriousness of a crime). Since a property term does not necessarily identify the class of events of things itself, a theoretic statement (a component of a theory) is ambiguous unless it includes a unit term, a term that denotes a class of things or events, such as cities, individuals, or crimes. The theorist regards his or her definition of the unit term as empirically applicable, but no formula is stipulated because the unit term denotes a class of qualitatively distinct *entities* (such as countries).

Although the unit term is obscure in many criminological theories, there is no particular issue. Most criminologists evidently grant that theories about crime may pertain to contrasts among individuals and/or populations. However, criminologists have yet to confront two questions. First, what is the most strategic unit term—cities, states, jurisdictions, countries, or whatever—for theories pertaining to variation in the crime rate? And, second, is "types of crime" a defensible unit term?

Relational terms. Just as an utterance in English without verbs may appear unintelligible, so is a theoretic statement without any relational term, meaning a term that syntactically connects other terms. Consider this italicized illustration: Among cities, the criminal homicide rate *varies directly with* population density.

Since the variety of relational terms in a natural language is enormous, no two relational terms in a discursive theory may be the same. Thus in one premise the relational term may be "based on," in another "varies inversely with," in still another "causes," and so on. The diversity *precludes* genuine rules of deduction.

Although causal terms are relational terms, their use creates problems and issues. Since causation cannot be observed, a causal argument is testable only when translated into an assertion of a space-time association between variables. Such translation requires a definition of causation and criteria of causal evidence, neither of which is provided by so-called causal modeling or by path analysis (see Gibbs, 1982).

Types of Statements

Several conventional labels distinguish types of theoretic statements, notably: premises, principles, assumptions, conclusions, definitions, axioms, postulates, propositions, theorems, and hypotheses. Criminologists occasionally use some of those labels in stating a theory, but they use them uncritically, meaning without explication and a rationale (see, for example, Cohen et al., 1981).

The earliest formal mode of theory construction in sociology, Zetterberg's (1965), does not clarify conventional labels for theoretic statements. Zetterberg speaks primarily only of postulates and theorems. The latter are deduced in Zetterberg's mode, but he writes as though a theorist formulates *all* theoretic statements before labeling some as postulates. His instructions make the selection of postulates arbitrary, and even the rationale for the postulate-theorem distinction is dubious. Zetterberg correctly argues that postulates can be tested *indirectly* by testing theorems, but interpreting indirect tests poses a thicket of problems. To conclude that a theory's postulates are true because tests indicate that the theorems are true is the fallacy of affirming the consequent. Moreover, while negative test findings indicate that some or all of the postulates are false, it may be that the false postulates cannot be identified with confidence. Accordingly, if postulates could be tested directly, it would be folly to test them indirectly.

Yet Zetterberg treats postulates as no less testable than theorems. Any property term in the postulates also appears in at least one theorem; and that practice ignores conspicuous differences among terms—that the meaning of some terms is much clearer than others, that only some terms denote observable phenomena, and so on. If statements differ as to types of constituent terms, they also probably differ as to testability. To illustrate, if all property terms in a statement are constructs, the statement cannot be tested directly.

Some proposed distinctions. The distinction between constructs and concepts facilitates definitions of axioms, postulates, and propositions. An axiom is a synthetic statement in which all property terms are constructs. Consider this illustration: Among countries, the division of labor varies inversely with normative consensus. Should a theorist make that statement, he or she could point to Durkheim's arguments as the rationale; but whether the statement is an axiom depends upon the definitions of "division of labor" and "normative consensus." If the theorist regards both definitions as incomplete or leaves the two property terms undefined, the statement is an axiom.

A postulate is a synthetic statement in which there is a construct and a concept. Consider two illustrations.

Postulate 1: Among countries, the division of labor varies directly with occupational differentiation.

Postulate 2: Among countries, normative consensus varies inversely with the total crime rate.

As before, the identification of statements is not somehow objectively given. The two statements would be postulates only if the theorist (1) treats "division of labor" and "normative consensus" as constructs and (2) regards the definitions of "occupational differentiation" and "total crime rate" as complete.

Given the axiom and two postulates, the sign rule (Gibbs, 1972) can be used to deduce this statement: Among countries, occupational differentiation varies directly with the total crime rate. Since the statement is deduced, it is an *implied* proposition. However, propositions can be arrived at inductively or intuitively; and all of a theory's premises could be propositions (that is, no axioms or postulates). Implied or not, a proposition is a synthetic statement in which all property terms are concepts.

Neither "occupational differentiation" nor "total crime rate" can be considered empirically applicable, even indirectly, until linked to a formula. Suppose that the theorist defines occupational differentiation as previously stated and stipulates this referential formula:

$$RAOD = [1 - (\Sigma X^2/[\Sigma X]^2)]/[1 - (1/Nc)]$$

where X is the number of individuals in an occupational category and Nc is the number of categories. Again, there is no logic by which the definition of occupational differentiation (above) implies that formula or any other, much less the instructions for obtaining the requisite data.

Now suppose that the theorist defines the total crime rate as the number of all crimes that occur in a territorial unit during a year as a ratio to the average daily number of residents of that unit over the year. Finally, suppose that the theorist stipulates this referential formula:

$$ROCR = (C/P)\ 100,000$$

where C is the total number of all crimes reported by the police as having occurred in a particular country during a particular year, and P is the number of residents of that country at any time during the year.

The ROCR formula is in no sense a definition of "total crime rate," operational or otherwise. The concept refers to the *true* number of crimes, but C is the *official* number; and P is not the average daily number of residents. Of course, the theorist will have stipulated the formula with a view to the availability of data, since nothing would be gained by stipulating an empirically inapplicable formula, even if it should appear to correspond more closely to the concept (in this case, the "total crime rate").

Because the link between the concept and the referential formula is *extralogical* (that is, synthetic), it is an untestable empirical assertion (the true amount of occupational differentiation or the true crime rate is unknowable). Accordingly, there are two additional illustrative premises, both designated as a transformational statements because each links a concept and a referential.

Transformational statement 1: Among countries, occupational differentiation varies directly with RAOD.

Transformational statement 2: Among countries, the total crime rate varies directly with ROCR.

In accordance with the sign rule (Gibbs, 1972), the preceding axiom, two postulates, and two transformational statements imply this theorem:

Theorem: Among countries, RAOD varies directly with ROCR.

Observe that all property terms in a theorem are referentials. If the theorist stipulates the corresponding formulas and how the requisite data are to be obtained, then the theorem is as directly testable as any theoretic statement can be.

Rules of Deduction

The conventions of a natural language do not constitute rules of deduction, and that is the principal disadvantage of discursive theory construction. In discursive theories there are long passages ending with a sentence in which the initial word or phrase is "thus," "therefore," "it follows that," or a similar expression. Such terminology suggests that the last sentence in the passage has been deduced; but, typically, it is not even clear what preceding sentences entered into the deduction, let alone what rules of deduction were employed. Even in the case of criminological theories labeled as "formal," the rules of deduction (or derivation) may not be stipulated. Thus, in stating a "formal" theory about opportunity and criminal victimization, Cohen et al. (1981) allude to the derivation of nine propositions from a series of definitions, assumptions, principles, and associated discussions; but they do not identify the rules followed in those derivations, and the rules are by no means obvious.

If some property terms in all theoretic statements are taken as empirically inapplicable, then evidence can be brought to bear on the theory only by deducing testable conclusions. Since it is not the case that any "logic" (such as the classical syllogism, Boolean) will suffice, a mode of theory construction is incomplete if explicit rules of deduction are excluded.

Further comment should be made on the sign rule, if only because there are no conspicuous alternatives when the property terms of a theory denote quantitative phenomena and the premises are not equations. The sign rule requires relational terms in the premises such that a positive sign (+) or negative (-) sign can be used to denote the direction of an asserted association. In the illustration, the sign is positive for "varies directly with" and negative for "varies inversely with."

Only one verbal formula is needed to deduce a theorem from a chain of premises (where each property term appears in at least two premises) in accordance with the sign rule. The sign of the relational term in a theorem is negative if and only if an odd number of the relational terms in the chain of premises have a negative sign.

The sign rule cannot be used justifiably without assumptions about the associations asserted in the premises. The simplest assumption amounts to a *sufficient* condition for the use of the sign rule: All of the associations asserted in the premises are so close that if each is in the direction asserted it would be mathematically impossible for the theorem's sign to be other than that deduced.

It is misleading for Freese and Sell (1980: 283) to suggest that the sign rule has been relegated to "decent oblivion" by the work of Turner and Wilcox (1974). Contemplate what Turner and Wilcox (1974: 586) actually say: "The system based on the 'high correlations' assumption lacked the deductive power of the standard system." How could that statement (or any other in their conclusions) be construed as even suggesting that, regardless of the assumptions made, the sign rule is unjustified? Freese and Sell clearly want to relegate the sign rule to oblivion, but a fictitious burial party is not conducive to a decent interment.

Understanding of the sign rule and the illustrative theory can be furthered by an inspection of Figure 2.1, a pictographic representation of the theory. Note two things. First, the diagram does not show the unit term (countries). Second, the theory ends with the theorem, and the remainder of the diagram represents statements that would be made in reporting a test.

Tests of a Theory

A test of the illustrative theory would require that an investigator apply both referential formulas to two or more countries and report the referents in a table. Suppose that an investigator presents such a table (henceforth referred to as Table X but not shown), with countries in the rows, RAOD referents in column 1, and ROCR referents in column 2. Those referents enter into a test by deducing a prediction about them from the theorem and epistemic statements (see Figure 2.1) that connect the referentials in the theorem and the referents. In accordance with the sign rule, the two epistemic statements and the theorem imply this hypothesis: Among the countries in Table X, the values in column 1 vary directly with the values in column 2.

Whether the hypothesis is accepted as true depends upon the measure of association (for example, rho, r) in the descriptive statement (see Figure 2.1). The illustrative hypothesis would be accepted as true if the sign of the association measure is positive. In turn, the theorem would be treated as false if in several tests the hypothesis and the descriptive statement are incongruent.

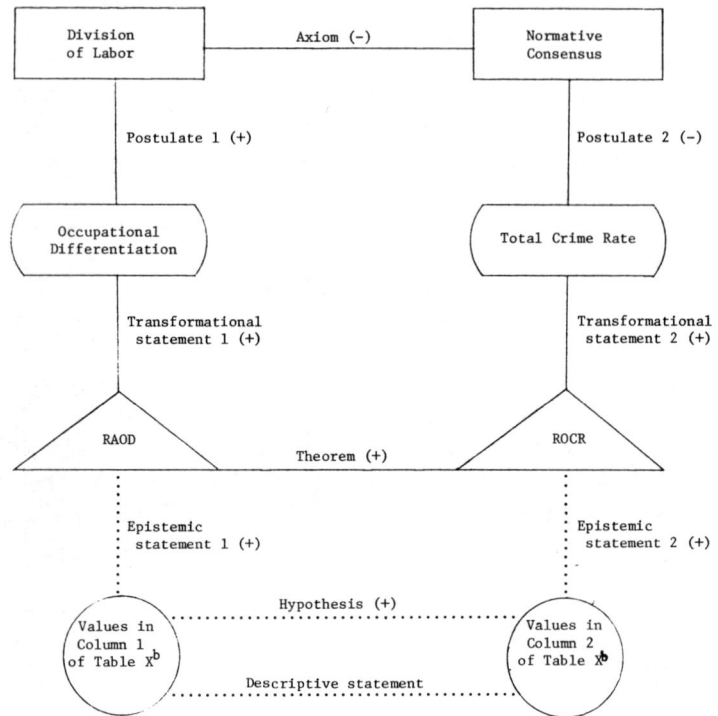

a. The theory pertains to relations among countries (that is, the unit term is "countries"), and the temporal qualifiers of the variables are not shown. The epistemic statements, hypothesis, and descriptive statement enter only into a test of the theory (that is, they are not parts of the theory).
b. Table not shown in the text.

Figure 2.1 Diagram of an Illustrative Theory and Test Statements[a]

Some Qualifications Concerning the Illustrations

No substantive significance should be attributed to the illustrative theory. It is all too simple, and transformational statement 2 is a particularly dubious assertion. Then there is reason to assume that rates for some specific types of crime (such as robbery and homicide) vary independently; hence all rates could not be *closely* associated with normative consensus.

Just as the theory is nothing more than oversimplified illustration, so is that the case for the types of terms, types of statements, and rules of deduction.[1] They are elements of a particular formal mode of theory construction (Gibbs, 1972), but the merits or defects of that mode *are not relevant*. Again, the issue is the relative merits of *any* formal mode and the discursive mode; but, as formal theory is largely alien to criminology (see Short, 1980: 311-312), reference to a particular formal mode is essential for illustrative purposes.

SOME LIMITS OF FORMAL MODES AND CRIMINOLOGICAL QUESTIONS

One great misunderstanding is the belief that a formal mode can be used to "manufacture" theories. No mode can be substituted for a theorist's imagination and judgment; and until a theorist arrives at substantive ideas or arguments, a formal mode has no utility. Since a mode is a set of rules as to a theory's *form,* it does not even suggest the *content* of premises, definitions, or procedures.

Central Questions for Criminology

A formal mode of theory construction neither answers empirical questions nor identifies a field's central questions. The latter limitation takes on special significance because since the 1960s consensus as to criminology's central questions has declined. That decline is reflected in debates, but a fundamental issue has been clearly recognized only rarely.

Although the possibility has received little attention, it could be that since the 1960s criticism of "orthodox" criminological theories has stemmed largely from dissatisfaction with the questions that those theories purport to answer. First, why do individuals differ as to criminality? Or, second, why does the crime rate vary? Both of the questions are "etiological"; and prior to the 1970s criminologists devoted little attention to this "reactive" question: Why does the nature of reactions to behavior vary? The question is worded such that it extends to research and theories not only on criminal law but also on differences in reactions to alleged criminality (for example, the relation between the race of felony defendants and sentences received).

Fifteen years of intense ferment in criminology have had a constructive outcome—acceptance of the reactive question as no less central than etiological questions. But the ferment has not been altogether constructive. Whereas critics have created the impression that they question only the empirical validity of etiological theories, their criticisms commonly suggest a rejection of etiological questions. Such criticism has not been constructive, especially since the critics rarely formulated explicit alternatives to the etiological questions.

Obscure Questions and Unfalsifiable Answers

If a theorist is pursuing a murky question, no mode of theory construction will clarify it; even if the question is clear, a mode has no utility until the theorist can articulate potentially falsifiable generalizations. Accordingly, the following assessment of well-known criminological theories excludes a theory if the questions it purports to answer are obscure or if the answers are not potentially falsifiable. Some examples of such theories follow.

Labeling theory: The reactive conception of deviance. The immediate question about the labeling theory (or perspective or paradigm) is not its empirical validity, but rather: What does the theory purport to explain? The question forces recognition that, far from being unitary, the so-called theory comprises three independent arguments.

One argument is conceptual, *not* empirical. According to the once-conventional normative conception, deviant behavior is behavior contrary to a norm; and a crime is a violation of criminal law. By contrast, according to the reactive conception, deviant behavior is any behavior *so labeled*; and a crime is any act so labeled by a legal official. The two contending conceptions of crime and deviance pose an issue that no mode of theory construction can resolve, and no conception is potentially falsifiable.

Labeling theory: Societal reaction theory. The second component of labeling theory is commonly identified as a theory in itself—the theory of societal reaction to deviance. That identification is misleading. Far from being the product of a particular theorist, the so-called theory is more nearly a vast body of research on reactions to deviance. Even if construed as an argument, there are three versions. The most radical version as it applies to crime: Whether an alleged act is labeled criminal and, if so, the reactions to it depend not upon strictly legal considerations but, rather, on the extralegal characteristics of (1) the suspect, (2) the situation or circumstances, (3) the victim or complainant, (4) the legal reactors, and (5) the operative rules of the reactor's organization. A less radical version asserts that extralegal considerations determine reactions more than do legal considerations. The third version merely claism that reactions to alleged crimes are appreciably contingent on extralegal considerations.

There are so many *possible* determinants of labeling and subsequent reactions that it is difficult to imagine falsification of any version of societal reaction theory. Defenders of the theory can argue that it does not claim that a particular extralegal characteristic (such as race) necessarily determines labeling or other subsequent reactions, but the argument would be an implicit admission that theory does not comprise a potentially falsifiable generalization.

Labeling theory: The theory of secondary deviance. Consider this summary statement: If a deviant act is reacted to punitively, the deviant will engage in further deviance as a consequence. That statement may grossly oversimplify; nonetheless, it is an *empirical proposition* and not a definition. So the theory of secondary deviance and the reactive conception of deviance are logically distinct; and since the theory pertains to the consequences of reactions rather than their determinants, it differs from societal reaction theory.

The theory of secondary deviance is far from incomprehensible; to the contrary, the general assertion is fairly clear: Primary deviance is converted into secondary deviance by reactions. Even primary deviance is a fairly clear notion, for in numerous ways Lemert (1972) suggests that it is behavior contrary to a norm and prior to reactions. However, the notion of secondary deviance (or deviation) is scarcely clarified by Lemert's (1972: 48, 63) explicit definitions. Numerous commentators equate the notion with more deviance, but even that interpretation does not necessarily mean "more of what was originally primary," and it may be a distortion in any case, though one encouraged by Lemert's (1972: ix) assertion that social control leads to deviance.

Whatever the definition of secondary deviance, the theory defies systematic tests because Lemert left two questions unanswered. First, does the theory apply to all primary deviance and all reactions? Second, given a relevant type of primary deviance and a relevant kind of reaction, do all instances of primary deviance become secondary deviance? The theory's plausibility would be diminished by an affirmative answer to either question, but a simple "some" answer would be unfalsifiable.

For present purposes, the immediate shortcoming of the theory is this: the questions that the theory purports to answer are obscure. Surely they are not the conventional etiological questions for criminology (see above); and it would even be disputable to designate this question as central for the theory: Why, ostensibly, do only some individuals become recidivists? Lemert does not purport to identify the conditions that lead to recidivism in some case but not in others.

New, radical, critical, conflict, and Marxist criminology. Even granting that these various camps of criminology can be distinguished (see Bohm, 1982), their putative theories are similar in one respect. It is difficult to identify the question that each theory purports to answer, let alone interpret the ostensible answers as being potentially falsifiable generalizations.

It does not appear that the theories purport to answer the two etiological questions posed above. As for the reactive question, the literature of "unorthodox" criminology does emphasize social class differentials in criminal justice; but there is also a great emphasis on criminal law, and the latter sets the literature apart from societal reaction theory. Even so, the central question about criminal law is debatable. Consider, for example: To what ends do capitalists control criminal law? The literature suggests that capitalists seek protection of the interests of owners of the means of production. While the answer is a generalization, the question presupposes a demonstration that capitalists do control criminal law. Yet prominent theorists in new, critical, radical, conflict, or Marxist criminology (for example, Quinney) have not identified this question as central: *How* do capitalists control criminal law? Indeed, they might reject the question, arguing that the "culture of capitalism" determines criminal law.

JUSTIFICATION OF A FOCUS ON THREE THEORIES

Note particularly that "testability" has not been invoked in the foregoing critiques, all far too brief because of space limitations. If only testable theories can be examined in light of the discursive-formal distinction, the distinction would scarcely have any import for criminology. However, an untestable, discursive theory may have some rudimentary logical form; if so, a formal restatement may be feasible. But when the central question that a discursive theory purports to answer is obscure or the answer is not a potentially falsifiable generalization, the theory is too amorphous to lend itself to a formal restatement.

The purpose of the ensuing observations on the theories of Sutherland, Merton, and Hirschi is to identify some crucial formal and discursive features. The identification is a necessary step toward a formal restatement of those theories, but those restatements are beyond this chapter's scope.

Criminologists should have long since gone beyond Sutherland, Merton, and even Hirschi; but since more recent theories do not treat etiological questions as central, they are not really alternatives. Be that as it may, many of the ensuing arguments would apply to all criminological theories.

Sutherland's Theory of Criminality

The theory is discursive in all but one respect; it comprises nine *numbered* statements (Sutherland and Cressey, 1974: 75-76) that appear to be premises.

(1) Criminal behavior is learned.
(2) Criminal behavior is learned in interaction with other persons in a process of communication.
(3) The principal part of the learning of criminal behavior occurs within intimate personal groups.
(4) When criminal behavior is learned, the learning includes (a) techniques of commiting the crime, which are sometimes very complicated, sometimes very simple; (b) the specific direction of motives, drives, rationalizations, and attitudes.
(5) The specific direction of motives and drives is learned from definitions of the legal codes as favorable or unfavorable.
(6) A person becomes delinquent because of an excess of definitions favorable to violation of law over definitions unfavorable to violation of law.
(7) Differential associations may vary in frequency, duration, priority, and intensity.
(8) The process of learning criminal behavior by association with criminal and anticriminal patterns involves all of the mechanisms that are involved in any other learning.

(9) While criminal behavior is an expression of general needs and values, it is not explained by those general needs and values, since noncriminal behavior is an expression of the same needs and values.

Commentary on the premises. Since many criminologists have reported tests of Sutherland's theory, some readers may question the present argument—that each premise defies a systematic test. Sutherland himself probably did not regard his definitions of his major terms as complete. In any case, many of those terms denote quantitative properties, but Sutherland did not stipulate any formulas. Finally, a set of statements is testable only if one can deduce a prediction from the set about data, which necessarily pertain to particular events or things. Otherwise, how could one argue that the statements are consistent or inconsistent with the data?

There are no rules of logic (for example, the classical syllogism) by which the premises imply a testable generalization about crime rates or individual differences as regards criminality.[2] That is not to deny that the premises are potentially falsifiable or, stated otherwise, to claim that the premises are tautologies. One may find it difficult to imagine premise 1 as being false, but not if one entertains the possibility of genetic determinism in the etiology of crime. Nonetheless, the theory is a far cry from a deductive system. Hence it is pointless to suggest, as numerous criminologists have, that the theory implies a direct relation among juveniles between the number of delinquent friends and number of delinquent acts.

While it can be claimed that only premises 6 and 7 are essential, that claim makes it all the more imperative to clarify "definition" and "differential association," something that Sutherland appeared unable or unwilling to do. Premise 6 is virtually unintelligible unless one assumes that Sutherland used "definition" as an arcane synonym for "experience." However, had he asserted that individuals commit a crime if and only if their life experiences have been such as to determine that behavior, his theory would have appeared to be even more a truism; and the impossibility of systematic tests would have been even more obvious. In any case, Sutherland sowed confusion by switching his terminology from "definitions" to "differential associations."[3]

An illustrative partial restatement. The following definition is the first step: Positive differential association is the ratio of the frequency, duration, priority, and intensity of favorable definitions of a type of crime to which an individual has been exposed to the frequency, duration, priority, and intensity of unfavorable definitions to which the individual has been exposed. Since no amount of elaboration or clarification would enable investigators to compute the ratio for any adult or juvenile, "positive differential association" must be treated as a construct and linked to concepts in two postulates:[4]

> *Postulate I:* Among individuals, positive differential association prior to T_1 varies inversely with the personal disapproval of the type of crime at T_1.
>
> *Postulate II:* Among individuals, positive differential association prior to T_1 varies directly with the self-reported frequency of commission of the type of crime during the subsequent year.

By the sign rule, the postulates imply this proposition: Among individuals, personal disapproval of type of crime at T_1 varies inversely with the self-reported frequency of commissions of the type of crime during the subsequent year. Since investigators are unlikely to employ the same procedure when testing the implied proposition, systematic tests would require statements that link each concept with a referential. Those statements and the two postulates would imply a testable theorem.

The suggestion is not that an extension of the partial restatement of Sutherland would lead to corroborative tests. Although several investigators have reported a negative association among individuals between expressed personal disapproval of a type of crime or delinquency and self-reported commissions, the variance explained is negligible by any reasonable standard.

A well-known restatement. DeFleur and Quinney's (1966) use of set theory, a formal calculus, makes their restatement of Sutherland vulnerable to extensive criticisms. Space limitations dictate a brief treatment of only a few criticisms.

The independent variables in premises 6 and 7 appear to be quantitative at the ratio or interval level; but as DeFleur and Quinney (1966: 5) admit "The level of quantification in our calculus is binary, the *all-or-none* level." Hence they treat the word "excess" in premise 6 as one of two ordinal dichotomies (unfavorable definitions exceed favorable definitions) and dismiss premise 7 as unessential. That dismissal is all the more remarkable because DeFleur and Quinney (1966: 8) characterize premise 7 as both a qualification and an expression of hope for the theory's future. It appears that their mode of theory construction dictated exclusion of some premises, meaning that the tail wagged the dog.

DeFleur and Quinney's relational terms or symbols (for example, →) are extremely questionable. Consider their argument that their restatement of Sutherland's second premise is "a statement of logical relationships between the two factors; it is *not* a statement of a sequence in time" (DeFleur and Quinney, 1966: 5). One must surely wonder how the restatement changed the premise from extralogical (synthetic) to logical. Moreover, if their relational terms or symbols denote *atemporal* relations, how can they be used to interpret a causal argument as an assertion of antecedent association?

DeFleur and Quinney (1966: 1) write as though their major goal is to derive Sutherland's nine premises from underlying postulates. However, what is gained by deriving the premises from a set of ostensibly more general postulates that are no more testable than the premises?

Unless investigators are willing and able to test millions of hypotheses, DeFleur and Quinney restatement is not potentially falsifiable. The composite or summary statement is as follows: $c \rightleftarrows [(m_\wedge a_\wedge t) \rightleftarrows (l \rightarrow e \rightarrow i \rightarrow p]$, where each lowercase letter denotes a superset and the subsets are as follows: for c, types of crime; for m, types of criminal motivation processes; for a, types of criminal attitudinal processes; for t, types of techniques for committing crimes; for l, types of crime-related learning; for e, types of selective patterns of exposure to unfavorable and favorable definitions of a legal code; for i, types of symbolic interaction; and for p, types of primary groups. As DeFleur and Quinney (1966: 20) admit, even if each of the eight supersets (c . . . p) comprises only nine subsets (that is, types), the composite or summary statement would generate over 43 million hypotheses ($9^8 > 43,000,000$). Since the restatement does not enable one to predict which of those millions of hypotheses will be true, it is little more than a fishing license.

Some purported tests. Akers's integration of Sutherland and social learning theory is commendable even though it is no less discursive than Sutherland's original theory. Akers and Burgess (see Akers, 1977: 72-43) reduce Sutherland's nine premises to seven; but no *specific* directions are given as to tests, and the seven statements are no more a deductive system than the original nine.

In a recent report of tests (Akers et al., 1979), social learning theory is described as comprising these five sets of independent variables: imitation, definitions, differential association, social differential reinforcement, and nonsocial differential reinforcement. The connection between some of those sets of variables and Sutherland's theory is debatable; more seriously, the sets are defined by reference to questionnaire data. Perhaps any other kind of definition is bound to be incomplete, meaning that the terms denoting the sets of variables are constructs. However, far from linking the constructs to questionnaire data through concepts and referentials, Akers et al. do not deduce hypotheses by explicit rules.

Akers's strategy is consistent with operationalism, but operationalism perpetuated the discursive mode of theory construction. In particular, questionnaire data do not provide a defensible *measure* of differential association or any other construct, if only because the relevant questions that could be posed are seemingly infinite. Indeed, no value can rightly be construed as a defensible *measure* of differential association. Imagine someone saying in reference to a particular individual: "This value represents the frequency and intensity of all favorable definitions of burglary to which this individual has been exposed since birth." Incredible!

Variables based on questionnaire data may be closely *correlated* with theoretical variables; but variables defined by reference to questionnaire items are not *measures* of those variables, and the correlations are epistemic (unobservable). That is sufficient reason in itself to assert the correlation in a theoretic statement; otherwise, predictions about a body of data cannot be deduced from the theory.

What has been said of Akers's strategy applies to the most recent purported test of Sutherland. Matsueda (1982: 489) recognizes differential association as the critical variable in Sutherland's theory and rightly identifies it as an *unobservable construct*. However, rather than explicitly postulate a relation between differential association and phenomena denoted by a concept, Matsueda (1982: 489) claims to have "operationalized" the construct by "explicitly modeling its measurement error structure." The rationale for that claim is not articulated, and Matsueda's research illustrates how "statistical models" serve to present findings but not to show their bearing on a theory.

Further purported tests of Sutherland without a formal restatement of his theory will waste resources. To be sure, tests are essential for defensible assessments of the theory; but unless the logical bearing of test findings on the theory can be demonstrated, the tests will be counterproductive. However, the suggestion is not that there are real prospects for a defensible formal restatement (see, particularly, Freese and Sell, 1980: 311-325).

Merton's Theory of Anomie and Deviance

Consider this illustrative argument: No adult American is truly puzzled by the typical robbery. The perpetrator pursues a goal (money) that all adult Americans have pursued, and his or her act becomes even more understandable given evidence that he or she had no lawful means to that goal. Given such an illustration, laypersons can comprehend this abstract statement: Deviance stems from a disjunction between culturally approved goals (or cultural goals) and institutionalized means to those goals. However, when one attempts to go beyond that statement, Merton's theory becomes a verbal jungle.

No explicit premises. Merton states his theory (1957) entirely in accordance with the discursive mode; hence the premises are left implicit. However, consider this prime candidate: Among social units, the greater the means-goal disjunction, the greater the total deviance rate. Even if that statement captures the essence of Merton's argument, it is far from testable in any direct sense, and several important features of the theory are ignored.

Computing a total deviance rate is less feasible than computing the total official crime rate. Moreover, ignoring feasibility, no one would be likely to regard total deviance rates as sufficiently reliable. No less serious, the meaning of "means-goal disjunction" is particularly ambiguous in one respect. While Merton clearly indicates that the disjunction is between stress on culturally approved goals and access to institutionalized means, there is no obvious rationale to deny that stress on institutionalized means is also relevant. To illustrate, when an individual becomes unemployed, his or her access to institutionalized means is likely to decline; but *stress* on those means (such as penalties for resorting to illegal means) would not necessarily decline.

The argument is not that Merton should have defined "means-goal disjunction" such that he considered the definition as complete. No definition of that term (or "anomie") is likely to be regarded by anyone as complete; but since Merton never defined the term explicitly, the relevance of "stress on means" is debatable. Moreover, when a construct is left undefined it is difficult for the theorist to link it with concepts.

Expressing the amount of disjunction. Even if it were possible to measure each variable that enters into the notion of a disjunction, Merton does not specify the procedure for combining the values to

TABLE 2.1
Some Alternative Formulas for Expressing the Amount of Means-Goals Disjunction

Social Units	Values for the Three Principal Variables			Formula I $\mid Sg - (Am + Sm) \mid$	Formula II $\mid Sg - [(Am)(Sm)] \mid$	Formula III $\mid (Sg)^2 - [(Am)(Sm)] \mid$	Formula IV $1 - [(Sg)(Am)(Sm)]$
	Sg	Am	Sm				
A	1.00	1.00	1.00	1.000	.000	.000	.000
B	.00	.00	.00	.000	.000	.000	1.000
C	.50	.50	.50	.500	.250	.000	.875
D	.50	.20	.80	.500	.340	.090	.920
E	.50	.80	.20	.500	.340	.090	.920
F	.80	.20	.20	.400	.760	.600	.968
G	.20	.80	.80	1.400	.440	.600	.872
H	.80	.80	.80	.800	.160	.000	.488
J	.20	.20	.20	.200	.160	.000	.992

NOTE: Sg = stress on culturally approved goals; Am = access of members of the social unit to institutional (legitimate) means; Sm = stress on institutional (legitimate) means.

express the amount of disjunction in a particular social unit. Table 2.1 illustrates the difficulty.

When it comes to the total deviance rate, it is irrelevant whether Sg (stress on culturally approved goals) is greater or less than the product or sum of Am (access to institutionalized means) and Sm (stress on those means). Consequently, in all formulas (Table 2.1) the sign of the difference is ignored. Were the sign not ignored, the average of positive and negative values over all culturally approved goals (for example, sexual experience) might be zero and misleadingly suggest "no disjunction."

The assumption is that Sg, Am, and Sm can be measured such that the minimum possible value is .00 and the maximum 1.00, but that simplification does not suggest an appropriate formula. Formula I is unsatisfactory because it produces the next to the highest *disjunction value* for social unit A, the very unit where there appears to be no disjunction. Formula II eliminates that particular anomaly; but it does not distinguish between A and B or between H and J, which suggests that "disjunction" is not the appropriate term. The term suggests *no difference* between Sg and Am or Sm; yet if all three values are very low (as for B and J), there can be no great difference. However, Merton's arguments suggest that deviance would be very common if Sg, Am, and Sm are all low. In any case, social units A, B, C, H, and J make it obvious that even when Sg = Am = Sm the disjunction values may vary considerably. If Formula III is employed, disjunction values are constant where Sg = Am = Sm; but the disjunction value is zero for A, B, C, H, and J, even though that value appears appropriate only for A. Formula IV appears superior, but even in that case the contrast between social units F and G is disconcerting.

The second part of the theory. Although seldom recognized, Merton's theory comprises two parts. The first part pertains to the total deviance rate; the second part pertains to five "modes of adaptation"—conformity and four types of deviance.[5] The second part furthers the theory's scope, but Merton does not clarify its connection with the first part.

Whereas Merton recognizes *five* modes of adaptation, dichotomized combinations of Sg, Am, and Sm (for example, high Sg, low Am, low Sm) indicate that *eight* modes should be recognized; and if Sm is ignored, the dichotomized combinations indicate the need to recognize only *four* modes. In brief, there is an inconsistency between the first and second part of the theory (one not resolved by Dubin's extension, 1959, of Merton's typology of adaptations). Despite the inconsistency, it may appear that premises can be formulated so as to connect the two parts of the theory. Consider two possibilities:

> *Premise I:* Among social units, the greater the ratio of Sg to the product of Am and Sm, the greater the rate of innovative deviance.
> *Premise II:* Among social units, the greater the ratio of Sg to the product of Am and Sm, the less the rate of ritualistic deviance.

If there were no alternative ways of expressing the differences among Sg, Am, and Sm, the two premises would be defensible. However, what are the corresponding premises for retreatism and rebellion? No less serious, it is difficult to collate conventionally recognized types of deviance (such as battery and homosexuality) with Merton's modes. Above all, the means-goal distinction is troublesome. Thus if drug addiction is retreatism (as Merton indicates) because it supposedly represents a rejection of both culturally approved goals and institutionalized means, what of the argument that happiness or contentment is a culturally approved goal and one *perceived* as realizable through drugs? Then what of homosexuality—is it a rejection of institutionalized means, of culturally approved goals, or both?

Now consider what appears indisputable—that robbery is innovative deviance. Even so, the robbery rate could not be used to test the proposition that innovative deviance varies *directly* with the disjunction ratio, $(Sg)^2/[(Am)(Sm)]$. There are numerous alternatives to robbery as innovative deviance (such as burglary and embezzlement), and Merton's theory does not identify their determinants. What has been said about innovation extends to retreatism, ritualism, and rebellion.

Evidential problems. Since space limitations preclude even a brief survey of the research inspired by Merton's theory (see Clinard, 1964), it must suffice to point out that the research has been a far cry from systematic tests. For example, in a putative study of anomie, Lander reported an inverse relation among subareas of Baltimore between official rates of juvenile delinquency and the percentage of owner-occupied homes (see Clinard, 1964: 33). That relation is often described as being consistent with Merton's theory, but it cannot be *deduced* from the theory.

The emphasis on deduction runs contrary to a common belief among criminologists—that explicit deduction is not necessary for systematic tests. Close examination of empirical assessments of Merton's theory will force doubts about that belief. Doubts are particularly likely in contemplating the controversy (see Merton, 1957: 170-176) over the interpretation of Hyman's findings as to social class differentials in the aspirations of American juveniles. The immediate issue is not Merton's claim that the higher arrest or court-appearance rate of lower-class juveniles supports his theory. The claim is diputable because of questions about the reliability of such rates, but Hyman's findings would be controversial even if it were known that the rates are absolutely reliable. Indeed, some responses (see Hirschi, 1969: 8) to the controversy unwittingly suggest that Merton's theory should be construed as a purported explanation of individual differences as well as variation in the deviance rate.

Attempts to modify the theory. A commentary on Merton's theory should recognize attempts to extend or correct it, notably by Cloward and Ohlin (1960), Cohen (1955), and Dubin (1959). No assessment of these works is undertaken here, because they did not solve any of the foregoing problems.

No modification of Merton's theory amounts to a restatement in accordance some explicit formal mode (Merton's failure to identify his premises may have discouraged formal restatements). In the absence of a formal restatement of the theory, general observations are the only empirical basis for modifying Merton; hence a modification may eliminate what is really only a conjectural exception to the theory.

Hirschi's Control Theory

Of the various control theories, Hirschi's (1969) is the best known. However, his version is no less discursive than the others.

Major terms and premises. The general argument underlying Hirschi's theory can be stated readily *only if* conformity is taken as the obverse of deviance (extralegal or legal, including crime and delinquency).[6] If so, the general argument appears to be that attachment to persons, commitment to conformity, involvement in conventional activities, and belief in the moral validity of societal norms are the causes of conformity. That statement poses no logical problems other than questions about tautologies; but serious logical problems arise when Hirschi's premises are stated as explicit assertions about space-time associations. Consider four illustrative versions.

> *Premise 1:* Among individuals, the greater the attachment to persons, the less the frequency of deviant acts.
> *Premise 2:* Among individuals, the greater the commitment to conformity, the less the frequency of deviant acts.
> *Premise 3:* Among individuals, the greater the involvement in conventional activities, the less the frequency of deviant acts.
> *Premise 4:* Among individuals, the greater the belief in the moral validity of societal norms, the less the frequency of deviant acts.

Should Hirschi reject those premises or Caplan's (1978) much more elaborate restatement, it would illustrate how readily discursive theories can be misconstrued. Moreover, to bring evidence to bear on the general causal argument, it must be translated into assertions of space-time associations, such as the four premises. Yet those premises appear to imply that there is a close direct association between any two of the independent variables (attachment, commitment, involvement, and belief). Although Hirschi (1969: 27) appears to accept that interpretation, he stops short of asserting or deducing relations between the independent variables *as part of the theory.* Yet those relations are relevant apart from questions about controlling variables in tests. So there are justifiable doubts at the outset as to what the premises are, how they should be worded, and what they imply.

If the premises are anything like those suggested above, they imply no *additional* statements about the frequency of deviant acts. At most, those premises only imply conclusions about relations between the independent variables; and no one is likely to regard the evidence as particularly relevant even if all of the conclusions are testable. Hence it appears that the foregoing versions of Hirschi's premises would not facilitate tests of his theory.

The methodology of tests. Unlike Sutherland and Merton, Hirschi provides elaborate illustrations of a test procedure. The procedure is objectionable, but not because Hirschi fails to give explicit definitions of his major terms. It is unlikely that even explicit definitions would be construed by anyone as complete, which is to say that the terms are constructs.

A sophisticated criminological theory without constructs is difficult to imagine; but Hirschi leaps from constructs to questionnaire data without intervening concepts or anything akin to postulates, transformational statements, and theorems. Accordingly, his work is subject to all previous criticisms of Akers.

The suggestion that Hirschi's theory is not systematically testable may appear strange in light of numerous purported tests. For example, Jensen and Brownfield (1983) have reported a test of this hypothesis: Attachment to both straight and drug-using parents acts as a barrier to their children's drug use. Since they indicate that the hypothesis is implied by Hirschi's theory and report contradictory findings, they rightly interpret the findings as evidence that Hirschi's theory is at least partially false. However, to show that the theory does imply the hypothesis, Jensen and Brownfield would have to identify the theory's premises and the appropriate rules of deduction. Any such identification is likely to be controversial. Moreover, while the Jensen-Brownfield findings bear directly on the premise about attachment and deviance, its bearing on the other premises is debatable because Hirschi leaves the theory's premises implicit.

A Caveat

Should an imaginative criminologist realize a formal restatement of Sutherland, Merton, or Hirschi that promotes defensible tests, there might be no accolades. Criminologists are so accustomed to assessing theories without reference to systematic tests that many of them may be comfortable with their private criteria. Moreover, formal theory construction cannot resolve a particular issue that hovers over the three theories.

All three reflect insufficient concern with alternative criteria of criminality, whether in computing crime rates or in identifying individual differences. If the theories are construed as explanations of variation in the *true* rate of crime or *real* individual differences, they are forever untestable. Yet if the dependent variable is based on victimization surveys or self-reports, there will be grave doubts about data reliability, and the very idea of *unofficial* criminality is disputable. The only remaining possibility—official crime data—forces recognition of a particular feature of all three theories. None of them emphasizes the problematical character of official reactions to behavior; hence there are no "reactive" variables in the theories (see Gibbs, 1981: 505). That feature may have led criminologists to shift their attention from these and other etiological theories to labeling theory.

SUMMARY AND CONCLUSION

In light of the central argument, that formal theory construction facilitates defensible tests of theories, criminologists should retain the discursive mode of theory construction unless they are truly willing to assess theories primarily by reference to test findings. However, they must also recognize that (1) systematic tests require deductions of predictions about data from the theory and (2) tests are necessary to examine a theory's predictive power.

There are criteria other than predictive power for assessing theories, but they open the door to the anarchy of personal opinion. That point is stressed because positivism has been the whipping boy in criminology for over fifteen years. Not one critic has equated positivism with the argument that predictive power is the ultimate criterion for assessing theories. Nor has any prominent detractor confronted this question: What criterion offers greater prospects for consensus in assessing criminological theories than predictive power? Sooner or later, criminologists will come to recognize that, however desirable, appeals to praxis, liberating themes, and social criticism do not answer the question.

NOTES

1. Whereas the illustration suggests that all theoretic statements are "second order" (the property terms denote only two variables), they may be "first order" (only one variable), "third order" (the relation between two variables is asserted to be contingent on a third variable), or "fourth order" (a relation is assertedly contingent on another relation). For elaboration, see Gibbs (1972).

2. Sutherland's terminology notwithstanding, his theory ostensibly applies to all types of deviance, not just crime and delinquency.

3. The same may be said of the switch to "differential organization" in the second part of the theory, which pertains to rates. That part is too poorly developed to warrant attention (see Gibbs, 1981: 511-512).

4. The symbol "T_1" in the postulates is a *temporal quantifier* that means "any point in time." Space limitations preclude further observations on temporal quantifiers (see Gibbs, 1972) and their use in the illustrative theory. It must suffice to say that the exclusion of temporal quantifiers makes a theoretic statement untestable or vacuously true.

5. Culturally approved goals and institutionalized means are accepted in the case of *conformity*; goals are accepted in the case of *innovation*, but means are rejected in the case of *retreatism*; and both are rejected in the case of *rebellion*, but others are substituted.

6. Contrary to many commentaries, Hirschi's theory applies to all types of deviance, not just juvenile delinquency.

REFERENCES

AKERS, R. L. (1977) Deviant Behavior. Belmont, CA: Wadsworth.
——— et al. (1979) "Social learning and deviant behavior: a specific test of a general theory." American Sociological Review 44 (August): 636-655.
BOHM, R. M. (1982) "Radical criminology: an explication." Criminology 19 (February): 565-589.
CAPLAN, A. (1978) "A formal statement and extension of Hirschi's theory of social control." University of Montreal. (mimeo)
CLINARD, M. B. [ed.] (1964) Anomie and Deviant Behavior. New York: Free Press.
CLOWARD, R. A. and L. E. OHLIN (1960) Delinquency and Opportunity. New York: Free Press.
COHEN, A. K. (1955) Delinquent Boys. New York: Free Press.
COHEN, L. E., J. R. KLUEGEL, and K. C. LAND (1981) "Social inequality and predatory criminal victimization: an exposition and test of a formal theory." American Sociological Review 46 (October): 505-524.
DeFLEUR, M. L. and R. QUINNEY (1966) "A reformulation of Sutherland's differential association theory and a strategy for empirical verification." Journal of Research in Crime and Delinquency 3 (January): 1-22.
DUBIN, R. (1959) "Deviant behavior and social structure." American Sociological Review 24 (April): 147-164.
FOX, J. A. [ed.] (1981) Methods in Quantitative Criminology. New York: Academic.
FREESE, L. and J. SELL (1980) "Constructing axiomatic theories in sociology," pp. 263-368 in L. Freese (ed.) Theoretical Methods in Sociology. Pittsburg: University of Pittsburg Press.
GIBBS, J. P. (1982) "Evidence of causation." Current Perspectives in Social Theory 3: 93-127.
——— (1981) "The sociology of deviance and social control," pp. 483-522 in M. Rosenberg and R. H. Turner (eds.) Social Psychology. New York: Basic Books.
——— (1972) Sociological Theory Construction. Hinsdale, IL: Dryden.
GREENBERG, D. F. (n.d.) Mathematical Criminology. New Brunswick, NJ: Rutgers University Press.
HIRSCHI, T. (1969) Causes of Delinquency. Berkeley: University of California Press.
JENSEN, G. F. and D. BROWNFIELD (1983) "Parents and drugs." Criminology 21 (November): 543-554.
LEMERT, E. M. (1972) Human Deviance, Social Problems, and Social Control. Englewood Cliffs, NJ: Prentice-Hall.
MATSUEDA, R. L. (1982) "Testing control theory and differential association." American Sociological Review 47 (August): 489-504.
MERTON, R. K. (1957) Social Theory and Social Structure. New York: Free Press.
SHORT, J. F. (1980) "Evaluation as knowledge-building—and vice versa," pp. 303-326 in M. W. Klein and K. S. Teilmann (eds.) Handbook of Criminal Justice Evaluation. Beverly Hills, CA: Sage.
SUTHERLAND, E. H. and D. R. CRESSEY (1974) Criminology. Philadelphia: Lippincott.
TURNER, J. H. and L. BEEGHLEY (1981) The Emergence of Sociological Theory. Homewood, IL: Dorsey.
TURNER, S. and W. C. WILCOX (1974) "Getting clear about the 'sign rule.'" Sociological Quarterly 15 (Autumn): 571-588.
ZETTERBERG, H. L. (1965) On Theory and Verification in Sociology. Totowa, NJ: Bedminster.

3

The Level of Explanation Problem in Criminology

JAMES F. SHORT, Jr.

> Ships that pass in the night, and speak
> each other in passing, . . .
> Only a look and a voice; then darkness
> again and a silence.
>
> —Longfellow, *The Theologian's Tale*

How often, after listening to scholarly debate on some contested issue, or even a heated discussion in ordinary conversation, have we concluded that the discussants were really not talking about the same thing. Like Longfellow's "ships that pass in the night," they seemed to be "talking past each other." That, in part, is what levels of explanation are about. But that is not all. Levels of explanation are also implicated in the assumptions we make as we study anything, including criminology. They are important, in short, for what we regard as important, the sorts of theories we construct, and the research we do. As will be explained later, they also have important social policy implications.

This chapter will discuss the relationship of some of the assumptions of theoretical criminology to levels of explanation, with particular reference to crime and delinquency. I make the latter point because the "level of explanation problem" is not unique to criminology, or even to the social and behavioral sciences, though special problems attend each science by virtue of subject matter.

The notion of levels of explanation is not new, though it has not often been described in precisely these words. The idea often has been more implicit than explicit, as, for example, when early sociologists such as Park and Burgess distinguished between biological and social order in human life, and between ecological and social orders (see Turner, 1967). It is found, also, in discussions, by Shaw and McKay, of individual cases ("the boy's own story") on the one hand and, on the other hand, of "delinquency areas" (Shaw, 1966; Shaw and McKay, 1969). Another early example: the distinction noted by Reiss (1951) in the title of his article, "Delinquency as the Failure of Personal and Social Controls."

Sociologists have been chided for not recognizing the importance of levels of explanation other than those upon which they most often focus. Inkeles (1959: 255), for example, distinguishing sociology, "as the study of the structure and functioning of social systems," from psychology ("the study of the structure and functioning of the personal system"), took sociologists to task for neglecting personality in the typical "sociological S-R (state-rate) theory," which attempts to relate social structural variables to behavior. A few years later, based on research with delinquent gangs, I suggested that group processes (GP) should also be added, so that the formulation would read: (S) (P) (GP) = R (Short, 1965). As noted below, however, the R in this formulation (let us say, a crime rate) is not always what we want to explain. In addition, precisely how variables located in different levels of explanation relate to one another is still another problem, one that continues to be much debated, as evidenced in the later chapters in this volume (see, also, the exchange among Elliott et al., 1979; Short, 1979; and Hirschi, 1979).

Levels of explanation, then, refer to the fact that explanation of any phenomenon may be sought in the operation of a variety of components and processes, no one of which is likely to be complete in its explanatory power, the claims of protagonists notwithstanding. Academic disciplines and, even more, subdisciplines tend toward specialization in focus on particular phenomena—problems to be studied—and on particular components and processes, as well as techniques for their study. This is as true of the physical and biological sciences as it is for the social and behavioral sciences (see Judson, 1979). The factor that most clearly distinguishes the social and behavioral sciences from other sciences in this respect is that human beings are *active agents* in a sense quite different from other sciences—even those that deal with animal behavior.

Explanation of any complex phenomenon is likely to require specialized knowledge. In the very nature of scientific specialization, knowledge tends to be generated regarding parts, or aspects, of phenomena under study, rather than regarding all parts or all aspects. This is all part of the division of labor among disciplines.

How, then, should levels of explanation be distinguished? The task is complex, and several classifications have been proposed. When Albert Cohen and I wrote the chapter on juvenile delinquency for the first edition of *Contemporary Social Problems* (Merton and Nisbet, 1961) we distinguished between *sociological* and two levels of *psychological* theory—theories of motivation and of learning or personality development. We retained these distinctions in the second edition. For the third edition (Merton and Nisbet, 1971), however, we collapsed the two psychological levels into one, calling it the *individual* level, and we added a second sociological level, the *microsociological*, as distinct from the *macrosociological*. This bit of history may be helpful to the reader, inasmuch as it reflects the evolution of our thinking regarding the problem of conceptualizing the levels of explanation problem. We stuck with this classification through the fourth edition (1976) and elaborated it.

The individual level of explanation inquires as to what it is about individuals that explains their behavior. It seeks to answer the question most often asked in common discourse: why did this person commit this crime? The question is often asked in terms of motivation (What was the motive for the crime?), but it admits of several other questions and types of analysis. For example, in our 1976 chapter, under this classification Cohen and I discussed biological and psychobiological theories, psychometric approaches, psychiatric theories, and, from a more sociological perspective, role theory and differential association. We might also have discussed other learning theories, but, because of space limitations, we did not.

The point is that each of these types of theories, and variations among them, are focused on the individual criminal or delinquent, on some aspect of the personal characteristics and experiences that might help to explain an individual's involvement in crime or delinquency.

The macro-level of explanation—we had termed it the "macrosociological" level (a misnomer because other disciplines also focus on macro-level explanations, for example, anthropology, economics, geography, history, political science, and psychology)—asks a very different set of questions. This level inquires as to the properties of social systems and cultures, including subcultures, that account for variations in the types and rates of crime. Here the various versions of functionalism, conflict theory, and Marxism are classified. The 1976 Cohen and Short version discussed anomie theory, differential social organization, subcultural theories, and conflict theories under this heading. These types of theories do not explain why a particular individual engaged in a particular act—although the temptation of those who are persuaded by these theories to do so often proves irresistible. Rather, they are concerned to explain why different social systems, cultures, or subcultures produce different types and rates of crime, and why crime in a particular social system, culture, or subculture is patterned in characteristic ways.

In contrast with both the individual and the macro levels of explanation, the micro level, again following Cohen and Short, seeks explanation in the unfolding of events, in the development of situations. The focus is on sequences and patterns of interaction among groups and individuals. "The general theoretical question," we noted in 1971, "would be: What general propositions can we formulate about the structure and the development of interaction situations that produce criminal actions?" (Merton and Nisbet, 1971: 115). We also noted that the types of questions asked at this level of analysis were the least often asked, and that less was known about this level than at other levels.

We now see that "levels of explanation" refers to what is to be explained as well as to how it is to be explained. In the (S) (R) example, explanation is sought of a *crime rate* (R) in terms of social structural variables (S). A classic individual-level explanation, on the other hand, seeks to explain a specific *behavioral response of an individual* (R) in terms of a related stimulus (S). A variety of modifications and elaborations of this elementary relationship have characterized learning theory. In micro-level terms, the phenomenon to be explained is an *event outcome*, which may involve the behavior of one or more individuals. Explanation is sought in terms of interactions that occur in the course of the event.

An additional point should be made with respect to the micro level of explanation. Though the *size* of a group or system is often employed to distinguish micro from macro, that is not the distinguishing criterion in the usage discussed above. My use of the term is to distinguish the outcomes of ongoing processes of interaction among actors from those related to the characteristics of social systems and cultures. The latter are structural and cultural in nature; the micro level, by way of contrast, focuses on events and interactions within systems, structures, and cultures. Groups (for example, gangs and other youth collectivities) are social systems, albeit often small social systems. Group size surely is relevant to interaction and, therefore, to what happens as interaction takes place. But even small social systems are complex, and it is the interaction within and between groups, and between groups and others, that is the focus of the micro level of explanation, as I am employing that term. Interaction within larger systems (for example, within a police bureaucracy) also is the focus of micro-level explanation. But the influence of the group, qua group, and of the bureaucracy, qua bureaucracy—for instance, in terms of norms, roles, and rules—are macro-level phenomena.

These distinctions are not universally recognized or agreed upon. When economists speak of micro- and macroeconomics, for example, they mean something quite different. Microeconomics remains systemic in emphasis, rather than developmental, in the Cohen and Short usage. Similarly, when Longshore and Prager (forthcoming) refer to micro and macro levels of situational analysis, in explaining "the impact of school desegregation," they refer to large-scale systems (metropolitan, state, or national systems) versus small-scale systems (single schools or classrooms). Longshore and Prager add two more dimensions to their analytic scheme: objective/subjective and proximal/distal. The first is reasonably self-explanatory. The comparison is between, for example, "the objective world of institutional constraints" (which in the Cohen and Short classification are macro-level phenomena) and the *meanings* of such institutions and constraints to the people who are affected by them (which are individual-level phenomena). "Proximal" refers to characteristics of the immediate situation, in contrast to characteristics deriving from historical or customary circumstances, and so fit within the micro level, as distinguished above. Longshore and Prager refer to folkways and community climate as distal, for example, in contrast with such characteristics of the immediate situation as the degree of warmth in student-teacher interaction, or whether interaction is characterized by cooperation, competition, or conflict. Regrettably, research in criminology has not employed these distinctions, so it is difficult to evaluate their usefulness. They appear to be quite useful for studying impacts of school desegregation, however.

Another classification is proposed by the new subcultural theories in England, which distinguish among *structure, culture,* and *biography* (see Cohen, 1980). Here structure "refers to those aspects of society which appear beyond individual control, especially those derived from the distribution of power, wealth and differential location in the labor market." Culture is seen as patterned response to structurally imposed conditions, in the form of "traditions, maps of meanings and ideologies" and subculture as "the specific, especially symbolic form through which the subordinate group negotiates its position." Biography refers to "the pattern and sequence of personal circumstances through which the culture and structure are experienced." Or "what the subculture means and how it is actually lived out by its carriers." Here, the distinction between structure and culture is a refinement of what we have called the macro level of explanation, while biography appears to be a more sociologically than psychologically oriented individual level of analysis (Cohen, 1980: v).

WHY A "PROBLEM"?

"Talking past each other" leads to faulty communication and to misunderstanding. Understanding the notion of levels of explanation can help to clarify what is to be explained and which classes of variables and processes are appropriate and relevant. There is ample basis for disagreement concerning the importance of variables and processes at any level of explanation, as between theories of motivation and learning, or structural and cultural variables. We need not further complicate matters by confusing what we are talking about. Agreement on what is to be explained does not necessarily lead to agreement on the appropriate level of explanation, but it seems likely to help and, without it, communication is bound to be faulty.

We tend to give short shrift to levels of explanation other than the one(s) on which our research or theories are focused. Scientists typically adopt either a *ceteris paribus* strategy (specifying that, "other things being equal," this or that is the case), or they make simplifying assumptions with respect to the operation of variables or processes not directly addressed by their research. But the qualifier, "other things being equal," while often a necessary research strategy, does not adequately take into account these other things. Similarly, assumptions regarding the operation of other variables do little to specify the proper role of those variables in an explanatory scheme.

A further problem with respect to levels of explanation—political and social policy implications—is discussed at a later point in this chapter.

THE PROBLEM ILLUSTRATED: GANG DELINQUENCY

The study of delinquent gangs with which I was associated for several years provides good examples of each of the levels of explanation I have noted. A brief "natural history" of this project also serves to illustrate the relationship of traditional research concerns such as theory, research design, techniques of investigation, data analysis, and interpretation to these levels of explanation.

As described more fully elsewhere (Short and Strodtbeck, 1965, 1974), the project began with a request for program evaluation by an agency that had recently initiated an outreach program for male delinquent gangs. For a variety of reasons (see Short, 1980), instead of program evaluation a more extensive program of research was undertaken, with the primary goal of documenting the behavior of the gang boys, individually and collectively, and investigating the applicability of recently advanced theories purporting to account for such behavior. The theories of greatest interest were all couched in macro-level terms, all based on theories of social structure and culture: Cohen's (1955) theory of the delinquent subculture, Cohen and Short's (1958) elaborations of "varieties of delinquent subcultures," Cloward and Ohlin's (1960) theory of delinquent subcultures related to structures of opportunity, and Miller's (1958) theory of "lower-class culture as the generating milieu of gang delinquency" (the project began in late 1958, before all except Cohen's book were published).

While the orienting theories for the research were in important respects competing, they were not sufficiently formalized in common definitions, premises, and conclusions to permit direct comparison by means of a feasible research design. Feasibility was constrained by several factors: funding limitations, the theories, the nature of the research opportunity, and the disciplines of our research team. We could—and did—study the types of delinquent behavior hypothesized by each of the theories to result from operation of etiological variables and processes. But, aside from questions as to the testability of any of the theories (see Gibbs, this volume), a research design based on any one of them was not feasible. We could not test the "reaction formation" hypothesis (Cohen), if indeed it is testable, except by its hypothesized consequent. Comparison of lower-class culture with alternative cultures with respect to delinquent gang-generating capacities (Miller) would have required resources beyond our means, as would identification of communities varying along theoretical dimensions specified by Cloward and Ohlin. In the case of each theory, simply identifying relevant etiological variables would have required a research effort of at least the magnitude of that we were prepared to undertake. The great advantage of the research opportunity—access to several of Chicago's most delinquent gangs—was not well suited to any of these tasks. It was well adapted to the study of particular gangs, *in situ*, and to comparisons of gang members with non-gang members in the communities where the gangs were located. We were able to influence the placement of detached workers with gangs that evidenced the "dependent variable" characteristics in which we were interested, and thus to make the research more relevant to the theories that initially guided the research. The fact that Chicago gangs were at this time mainly all white or all black in composition enabled us to add a racial and ethnic dimension to the research. Beyond this, in order to study social class influences, we decided to study middle-class groups and communities.

Finally, and most relevant to this chapter, the research opportunity enabled us to direct attention to variables and processes at each of the three levels of explanation, by virtue of continuous access to the gangs over a protracted period of time. In saying this, I do not want to give the impression that we deliberately set out to do just that. We added psychologists to our research team, so as to gain additional purchase on individual-level phenomena, and we approached the study on a macro level much as any sociologist might do, by means of observation, interviewing, and study of available records.

Access to the gangs over a long period meant that we were not so restricted as most studies in the types of research techniques we could employ. Through the good offices of the detached workers we could observe the gangs over long periods of time. We could interview them, secure systematic ratings of behaviors, even have them complete instruments of our and others' design. We did all of these things, and from them gathered data on personality (see Cartwright et al., 1975), intelligence, and other personal characteristics, as well as a variety of behaviors, both delinquent and nondelinquent (see Short and Strodtbeck, 1974). Leadership and other gang roles were studied by reports of both detached workers and graduate student observers. Community characteristics were analyzed from both secondary data and field observations.

All of these things were conventional, though their adaptation to the conditions of gang research often required considerable modification. The data thus obtained were rich in implications for theories of interest, and for some theories we had not focused on in the early stages of the project. What began as a project designed initially to examine individual and macro-level phenomena, however, soon began to focus on micro-level processes as well. This was because the nature of the gangs—their size and stability of membership, role and normative structure, and behavior—was not what we had expected it to be. Delinquent behavior was readily observable, and official records confirmed that arrests of gang boys were much more frequent than were arrests of nongang boys. But much else was going on that did not appear in the literature of the day. We began, therefore, to pay closer attention to micro-level processes from the field observations in an effort to understand what was happening to and within the gangs.

Here, then, the micro-level of explanation provided new information that had not previously been described or accounted for. In retrospect—for we did not fully develop the point—group processes emerged as mechanisms that appeared to account for the occurrence of much delinquent behavior (why and when it occurred, and who participated and who did not; see Short and Strodtbeck, 1965: chaps. 8, 9, 10, 12). Certain forms of behavior that had become institutionalized in lower class black communities appeared to account for some of the differences in behavior among black and white youngsters (see Short and Strodtbeck, 1965: chaps. 4 and 5). Analyses of particular episodes were useful in documenting the nature of these institutional forms, as well as for explaining behavioral outcomes of the episodes.

The observational data also permitted us to advance an interpretation of some individual acts of delinquency in terms of a utility-risk paradigm not previously applied to this type of behavior (see Short and Strodtbeck, 1965: chap. 11). Here we were able to combine the three levels of explanation, for the decision of an individual (a gang leader) to commit a crime (a shooting) was shown to be deeply imbedded in characteristics of the local community, as well as the gang, and to result from a particular sequence of interaction involving the gang leader, other members of his gang, and others. Finally, though we did not make the point in the book, we were able to observe the formation and the functioning of a delinquent subculture (chap. 9). Here, too, all three of the levels of explanation I have discussed were operating.

Early in the group process book, we distinguished between four types of influences on the gang boys we were studying: the environment, characteristics of individuals, norms of the group, and group process (Short and Strodtbeck, 1965: 19-20). We noted that, to the extent that theories of gang delinquency treated group variables at all, "they are viewed as resulting from what Homans has called the 'external system' of the group, i.e., relations among group members which solve the problem of survival in the environment" (p. 18). And we observed that we had come to the view that by studying group process we felt we could understand "the processes by which variables at the (other) three levels of explanation . . . become translated into behavior' (p. 20).

The number of levels of explanation one wishes to distinguish is to some extent arbitrary, depending upon both conceptual needs and empirical opportunities. The four "levels" noted above include two at what I have been calling the macro level (the environment and norms of the group). Often it is useful to make distinctions within a given level. In the following example of field observations from our Chicago study, we were particularly concerned to understand the norms of a group we called the "pill poppers" because of their heavy use of drugs in that form. We noted the following:

> The basis of camaraderie among the drug users was their common interest in kicks. Past and present exploits concerned experiences while high, and "crazy" behavior, rather than bravery or toughness. Use of pills and other drugs seemed virtually a way of life with these boys, interspersed with other kicks such as sex, alcohol, and "way out" experiences which distinguished them, individually and collectively. After several observations of this group in their area, a member of the research team reported:
>
> The guys make continual references to dope. They talk about it much as a group of drinkers might talk about liquor. It comes up freely, easily in the conversation, a couple of remarks are made about it, who's taken it recently, how it affected this or that person, etc., and then it is dropped only to come up again before long. Today the guys made comments about dope and baseball. (You get the feeling that whatever the activity of the moment, the guys will talk about it in relation to dope—how taking dope affects their participation in the activity.) A commonly expressed notion was that so and so played baseball better when he was "high" than at any other time. Whether they believed this was hard to tell. It sounded much

like oft-heard remarks that "I play poker better when I'm half drunk or high" (i.e., remarks made in the community at large). The remarks about dope are hard to record because they do not seem to express any attitude toward dope. They just seem to accept it in a matter of fact way—it seems to be so commonplace to them that the attitudes are often assumed and not felt worthy of expression. (At the same time it is true that comments expressing a positive attitude toward dope are not rare. The guys like to talk about their "highs," how much they have taken, how high they were, what they did while high, etc.) Perhaps one attitude is implicitly expressed, though, in these remarks; the attitude of acceptance.

Five months later this same observer reported on a hanging session in which the group related "tales about some of the crazy and humorous things" in which various of the drug users had been involved.

The relating of these tales was greeted by laughter from all. Often the worker or observer would mention an incident and Butch would fill us in or correct us on details. Some of the incidents mentioned:

(1) The time Willie was so high he walked off a roof and fell a story or two and broke his nose. Worker thought he had been on a roof, while Butch maintained he fell from a boxcar. Butch said it was over a week before he went to the doctor. Harry said he walked around the hospital in a crazy looking green coat whenever the guys went to visit him.

(2) The time Snooks, Baby, and Jerry climbed on a roof to wake Elizabeth. One of the guys reached through the window and grabbed what he thought was Elizabeth's leg and shook it to wake her up. It turned out to be her old man's leg and it woke him up.

(3) The more recent incident in which Sonny leaped over the counter to rob a Chinaman, who proceeded to beat him badly. When the police came, Sonny asked that they arrest this man for having beaten him so. He was doped out of his mind and didn't know what was happening.

(4) Walter got into an argument with a woman over whose car it was they were standing by. He insisted they call the police, and waited confidently until the police showed and took him away.

(5) Sonny tried to break into a building and was ripping off a door when the police found him.

(6) Some of the guys slept out in a car and woke the next morning to find the car was being pulled away. They asked the tower to stop just long enough so they could get out.

(7) One of the guys broke into a car and just about tore the door off doing so—this was a car with all the windows broken out—he was too high to notice.

(8) One of the boys tried to start a car but just could not manage it. The car had no motor.

All laughed at these true tales. Butch even noted that he had been with the guy who broke into the car with no windows.

The observer noted, in conclusion, that "these tales may be in the process of becoming legendary within the group. They are so characteristic of this group and describe it so well" (p. 209). We lack sufficient detail of these interactions to permit micro-level analysis that might explain the particular behavioral outcomes that were reported. In this instance, that was not our primary purpose, though such data might have been even more informative toward understanding the emergence of group norms, since the types of behaviors reported were the distinguishing characteristics of the group. And they were being appropriated in the creation of the mythology of the group. We were witness to the emergence of a subculture in some respects peculiar to the group, but a subculture with much in common with other drug-using groups.

These analyses suggest the potential usefulness of the levels of explanation for each other, though we were not able to exploit the data fully in this respect.

The extent to which data and interpretations from our study of Chicago gangs can be generalized to other gangs in other places and at other times we do not, and probably cannot, know. Whether or not the micro level of explanation can serve as a link between the other two levels for any field of inquiry remains to be determined. Regrettably, we did not formalize these relationships, and so they remain relatively undeveloped theoretically. But the prospect of theoretical advance through further and more systematic study of the micro level, and of relationships among the levels, is, I think, attractive.

SPECIAL PROBLEMS POSED BY ORGANIZATIONAL BEHAVIOR

When organizations are the objects of study, level of explanation problems take somewhat different forms. The study of individual behavior within organizations is common enough, as are case studies of organizations; both are types of individual-level inquiry. Similarly, interpersonal and inter- and intraorganizational relationships have been studied extensively, most focused on macro-level description of organizations and organizational systems. When these focus primarily on description of ongoing interaction among organizations, and the outcome of such interaction, as in Vaughan's (1983) study of billing fraud by a major pharmaceutical company, they contribute to micro-level explanation. Such studies are rare, however.

The traditionally person-centered character of the law poses special problems in this respect, as the long-standing controversy over whether white-collar crime is "really" crime testifies (see Sutherland, 1945; Tappan, 1960). As the complexity of organizational life has increased, as organizations have multiplied in number and purpose, the issues in this controversy are exacerbated. Reiss and Biderman's (1980) suggestion that "white-collar lawbreaking" be the focus of attention seems eminently sensible, though it does not solve the semantic problem of white-collar crime as a concept. Study of organizations as victims and as perpetrators of law violation has lagged, for many reasons unrelated to levels of explanation (see Reiss, n.d.).

FORMALIZATION AS A STRATEGY: THE IMPORTANCE OF THEORETICAL WORK

Criminology remains a derivative and largely descriptive discipline, despite ambitious attempts to declare and defend its independent status and to formalize (see for example, Wolfgang and Ferracuti, 1967). The requirements of formalization, as distinct from the discursive mode of theory construction (see Gibbs, this volume), entail rigorous attention to what we are calling the level of explanation. Note that the specific questions asked by criminological theories, in Gibbs's phrasing, address the individual and macro levels, but not the micro level of explanation: "First, why do individuals differ as to criminality? Or, second, why does the crime rate vary?" These etiological questions are contrasted with a "reactive" question: "Why does the nature of reactions to behavior vary?" As discussed, below, that question has most often been approached at the macro level, though reactive questions may also be phrased and studied at the individual and macro levels of explanation.

Whether or not one agrees with Gibbs's criteria for the development of formal theory or his predictive criterion for assessing theory, the need for greater rigor in how theories are stated in order to guide empirical inquiry can hardly be disputed. The goal of a science, some would maintain, is to become a theoretical science. The goal of a theoretical science is the cumulation of knowledge. These goals are not inconsistent with Gibbs's views. How, then, are they related to levels of explanation problems?

A truly theoretical science would specify definitions, premises, and conclusions regarding phenomena which are themselves well defined. In Gibbs's discussion, the phenomena to be explained (as expressed in the questions asked) in effect *prescribe* a particular level of explanation. It is possible, however, to phrase a theoretical question in terms requiring more than one level of explanation. Thus, for example: "What types of interactions among members of youth groups (both individual members and groups specified as to type or characteristics, such as psychobiological characteristics of individual members and organizational characteristics of groups) produce what types of behavior?" It would be necessary, of course, to define very carefully all of these terms, including the behavior to be explained. In the "reactions to status threat" examples noted from the Chicago gang research project, while all of the responses might be characterized as aggressive, some involved predatory behavior as well as physical aggression, and some were verbally rather than physically aggressive behaviors. What types of aggressive behavior might be theoretically generalizable is, of course, an important theoretical and empirical question.

This question requires analysis at each of the three levels of explanation we have been discussing: generalization as to "types of interaction" (micro), characteristics of individuals (individual level), and group characteristics (macro). The social and behavioral sciences are far from being able to answer such a complex question, or even to specify the premises upon which its answer might be based. And this sort of question can never be answered without formal theory at each level of explanation.

Theories grow in different ways. Wagner and Berger (1983) have recently examined a variety of theoretical activities in an effort to determine whether and how theoretical growth occurs. They conclude that a great deal of theoretical growth has occurred and that more is possible. They discuss three "primary types of theory relations"—theory elaboration, theory proliferations, and theory competition—and they argue that each of these generates a different form of growth of knowledge. Wagner and Berger also discuss theory variation and theory integration as types of theory relations.

Several examples of theoretical growth are provided by Wagner and Berger. Unfortunately, none of them comes directly from criminology, though distributive justice theory and exchange theory, which are discussed, have applications in criminology. It is clear from these examples, however, that productive theoretical work requires formal rigor in statement and in definition. It appears from Wagner and Berger's examples that theoretical growth tends to occur primarily at a particular level of explanation, rather than involving more than one level.

For this reason, I conclude this section with the suggestion that research concerning relationships between levels of explanation might advance knowledge in a systematic way. For example, it might be hypothesized that, to the extent that behavior is rational and calculated, as much crime surely is, it will be less attributable to personal pathology and other individual-level characteristics in more homogeneous, more rigidly structured, and better integrated societies than will be the case in less homogeneous, less structured, and less integrated societies. Similarly, the micro level of explanation is expected to be less important to the explanation of behavior in societies in which traditions governing interpersonal and institutional relationships remain strong, compared to societies in which such traditions are less well developed and less binding and constraining. Thus we would expect both personal pathology and micro-level processes to be less relevant to the explanation of crime (and other types of behavior) in a society such as Japan, in which, despite rapid social change, traditions governing interpersonal and institutional relationships have remained strong (see Nakane, 1970), than in the United States, where traditions are less binding and constraining on individuals.

These hypotheses have analogues within societies, as well. Micro-level processes probably are more important to the explanation of the behavior of gang members, individually and collectively, than they are for young people who are more involved in more formally and effectively structured, adult-sponsored, institutions. Gangs, lacking formal rules and traditions of enforcing them, and without effective adult sponsorship, are relatively more free to respond to the demands of group process, and to what we called "aleatory" elements, lower-class culture and the risks associated with that culture (see Short and

Strodtbeck, 1965, 1974: chap. 11). In turn, this has consequences for the experiences of gangs that have attempted to "go conservative," the expression used during the 1960s to convey the efforts of gangs to engage in legitimate social and, in some instances, economic and political activities. These efforts were fraught with great difficulty, because of both individual and macro-level constraints, such as lack of necessary skills on the part of many gang members on the one hand and entrenched political opposition, suspicion and resentment by some community residents, and harsh economic realities on the other (see Short, 1979). Only by combining elements from different levels of explanation can such complex matters be fully explained or understood.

The stakes of theoretical work are high, with respect to both the development and the application of knowledge. Without cumulative knowledge, as many of us who have attempted upon occasion to wrestle with the beast of social policy and program implementation can testify, "the welter of observations and facts becomes more confusing than enlightening, particularly to the policy maker, politician, community leader, or concerned citizen who must 'make sense' of them as a basis for decisions" (Short, 1980: 311).

THE ORGANIZATION OF KNOWLEDGE IN CRIMINOLOGY AS A PROBLEM OF LEVELS OF EXPLANATION

Recognizing that crime is, by definition, a political phenomenon, the organization of textbooks in criminology and juvenile delinquency has long struck me as anomalous. Etiological factors and processes related to crime and delinquent behavior are customarily discussed prior to discussion of the nature of systems of law enforcement and justice. The "invention" of crime and delinquency as a product of the state is noted early in the textbook literature, but the nature of these systems is not treated until after discussion of theory and research concerning the etiology of crime and/or delinquency. Yet the operation of justice systems and other institutions clearly is involved in the etiology of crime and delinquency: The behaviors of law enforcement officers and court officials, and of actors in other institutions, and the relationships among these actors and systems are critical to the understanding of both etiology and control of crime and delinquency. Yet these topics often are treated as though they bear little relationship to each other.

Even the statistical systems that have been invented to record the incidence and prevalence of delinquent behaviors are problematic with respect to levels of explanation. They largely ignore organizational behavior—a critical matter with respect to white-collar violations (see Reiss and Biderman, 1980)—and they are totally inadequate for micro-level analysis.

Note that "reactive questions"—why and how reactions to crimes vary—may be, and have been, addressed at different levels of explanation. And here the meaning of official statistics is an issue of great importance; that is, whether, or the extent to which, the data reflect the behavior of violators of law or of law enforcers. Each position has its defenders.

Studies of social control institutions, their organizational and normative structure (macro-level phenomena), and of the personal characteristics of persons functioning in these institutions (at the individual level) abound, for example. As is the case with questions of the etiology of crime, however, micro-level studies of "reactors" rely more upon exemplification than upon systematic study. There are good examples of each level of explanation, however: For example, Sarri and Hasenfeld's *Brought to Justice? Juveniles, the Courts, and the Law* (1976) is a national, macro-level study of the structure and practices of a large sample of juvenile courts; many studies have detailed personal characteristics of police (McNamara, 1967); and a variety of observational studies report encounters between police, probation officers, and judges and suspected offenders and other citizens (Emerson, 1969).

Policy Implications

The framing of problems often prejudges how they will be defined and what will be done about them. As Louis Wirth used to print out to students in his theory classes, "A way of seeing is also a way of not seeing." If crime is defined as a problem residing within individuals, other levels of explanation and amelioration are likely to be neglected, if perceived at all. Social policies and programs, whether based on assumptions that crime is properly explained as a quality of individuals, or on systematic evidence in this regard, often lead to neglect of other levels of explanation. As Caplan and Nelson (1973: 201) note, "Problem definitions take on a life of their own; they set in motion a variety of social and psychological forces which give them important functional significance." Further, "to *question* established definitions is to challenge important institutions and belief systems that have their origins in those definitions."

Caplan and Nelson focus on the consequences of "person-blame" interpretations of social problems, suggesting the following:

(1) Such interpretations offer a convenient apology for freeing the government and primary cultural institutions from blame for the problem.
(2) Since those institutions are apparently not the cause of the problem, it may be legitimately contended that they cannot be held responsible for amelioration. If they do provide such help, they are credited with being exceedingly humane, while gaining control over those being helped, through the manipulation of problem definitions in exchange for treatment resources.
(3) Such interpretations provide and legitimate the right to initiate person-change rather than system-change treatment programs. This in turn has the following functions: (a) It serves as a publicly acceptable device to control troublesome segments of the population, (b) it distracts attention from possible systemic causes, and (c) it discredits system-oriented criticism.
(4) The loyalty of large numbers of the well-educated, melioristic-minded nonneedy is cemented to the national structure by means of occupational involvement in "socially relevant" managerial, treatment, and custodial roles required to deal with those persons designated as needing person-centered correction.
(5) Person-blame interpretations reinforce social myths about one's degree of control over one's own fate, thus rewarding the members of the great middle class by flattering their self-esteem for having "made it on their own." This in turn increases public complacency about the plight of those who have not "made it on their own."

The major conclusion that can be drawn from the above is that person-blame interpretations are in everyone's interests—except those subjected to analysis.

Lest this analysis be misinterpreted as "antipsychological," I must reiterate my position that each level of explanation is important and, without attention to each level, complete explanation and understanding are impossible. Cultures and social systems may produce criminals and delinquents, but criminals and delinquents are persons. Individual characteristics are important, and social policies designed to alter criminogenic conditions do not necessarily address the immediate, individual, and micro-level questions: Why did he or she do it and what can be done about it?

An additional point should be made. It has become fashionable, in some circles, to adopt individual-level focused policies and programs to "combat crime," not because macro-level forces are assumed to be unimportant, but because it is believed that social policy can do little about them. This "new behaviorism," as Cohen (1983) describes it, regards the causes of crime as irrelevant, focusing instead on the threat and the reality of incarceration to control crime. In so doing, it reduces the study of the etiology of crime to an academic exercise, of knowledge for its own sake. Without denying deterrent effects, I reject this position unequivocally.

**Levels of Explanation
and Modes of Thinking**

The social and behavioral sciences are not so different from the physical and biological sciences as often has been assumed. Equally important, in some respects the sciences are not so terribly different from the humanities. Creativity takes many forms, and the forms customarily associated with different scientific and humanities disciplines are not exclusive to those disciplines. Thus the Cartesian model of science that has dominated science since Descartes is being questioned, and in some cases supplemented by models that are more flexible. An excellent example is provided by the work of Barbara McClintock, Nobel laureate for her work in molecular genetics.

Reviewer Stephen Jay Gould notes that McClintock's genius lies in her ability to combine the approaches of the naturalist and the experimentalist in her research, and in her holistic approach to thinking about problems. The experimental, essentially reductionist, approach has been much preferred in McClintock's field. McClintock, however, has not restricted her efforts to the standard approach of experimenting with simple organisms and at the level of the physiochemical properties of molecules. Instead, she chose a very complex organism, maize, one that has the additional disadvantage—for experimental purposes—that it produces only one generation each year. And she insists on studying each plant, focusing on its individuality, rather than on the properties of large numbers of cloned groups, as is customary in the search for fundamental processes of genetic systems. McClintock told her biographer that an organism "isn't just a piece of plastic, it's something that is constantly being affected by the environment, constantly showing attributes or disabilities in its growth. . . . No two plants are exactly alike. . . . I start with the seedling, and I don't want to leave it. I don't feel I really know the story if I don't watch the plant all the way along. So I know every plant in the field. I know them intimately, and I find it a great pleasure to know them" (quoted in Gould, 1984: 6).

McClintock's style of thinking, which Gould describes as the "simultaneous integration of many pieces into single structures," is also unconventional, for it "does not follow the style of logical and sequential thinking often taken as a canonical mode of reasoning in science" (p. 4). Instead, "she works by a kind of global, intuitive insight. If she is stuck on a problem, she will not set it out in rigorous order, write down the deduced consequences and work her way through step by step, but will take a long walk or sit down in the woods and try to think of something else, utterly confident that a solution will eventually come to her in *extenso*" (p. 4).

Gould observes that this mode of thinking is not unusual, but it is "perhaps rare (and certainly not generally appreciated) in science." Among scientists it tends to be regarded as mysterious, even mystical, "because we have neither good words nor concepts in our largely linear language to express such a modality" (p. 4).

If there is an analogue to Barbara McClintock's combination of methods and style of thinking for the social sciences, it may lie in somehow combining insights and data that result from different methods of inquiry applied to different levels of explanation. More is required, the analogy suggests, than simply accumulating cases to be treated statistically, as Shaw felt might eventually be done with case studies (Rice, 1931). Gould notes that, while McClintock's major discovery (of transposable genetic elements) was made via her "different manner of working" (and in pursuit of quite another problem), "the discovery that proved her right and elevated her to heights of peer and public recognition came from molecular biologists working with simple unicellular organisms as physical objects" (p. 6). The observational methods employed in the course of one level of inquiry may provide insights to other levels as well. In this way, for example, micro-level inquiry may suggest mechanisms and properties that can be more systematically measured, formalized, and even manipulated by experimental means, in later study.

We do not often approach our disciplines in this way, though there have been calls for "transitive or bridging concepts" between levels of explanation (Finestone, 1976) and for examination of the assumptions of disciplines by other disciplines, such as those of economics, which are of special interest to criminologists (Short, 1980). Perhaps we require a Barbara McClintock to carry it off. While genius of her type would certainly help, we can surely do better simply by recognizing the problem and turning our attention to it.

REFERENCES

CAPLAN, N. and S. D. NELSON (1973) "On being useful: the nature and consequences of psychological research on social problems." American Psychologist 28 (March): 199-211.

CARTWRIGHT, D. S., B. TOMSON, and H. SCHWARTZ (1975) Gang Delinquency. Monterey, CA: Brooks/Cole.

CLOWARD, R. and L. E. OHLIN (1960) Delinquency and Opportunity. New York: Free Press.

COHEN, A. K. (1955) Delinquent Boys: The Culture of the Gang. New York: Free Press.
——— and J. F. SHORT, Jr. (1958) "Research in delinquent subcultures." Journal of Social Issues 14: 20-27.

COHEN, S. (1983) "Social-control talk: telling stories about correctional change," pp. 101-129 in D. Garland and P. Young (eds.) The Power to Punish. London: Heinemann.
———(1980) Folk Devils and Moral Panics: The Creation of the Mods and Rockers. New York: St. Martin's.

COTTRELL, L. S., Jr., A. HUNTER, and J. F. SHORT, Jr. [eds.] (1973) Ernest W. Burgess on Community, Family, and Delinquency: Selected Writings. Chicago: University of Chicago Press.

ELLIOTT, D. S., S. S. AGETON, and R. J. CANTER (1979) "An integrated theoretical perspective on delinquent behavior." Journal of Research in Crime and Delinquency 16 (January): 3-27.

EMERSON, R. M. (1969) Judging Delinquents. Chicago: Aldine.

FINESTONE, H. (1976) "The delinquent and society: the Shaw and McKay tradition," pp. 23-49 in James F. Short, Jr. (ed.) Delinquency, Crime and Society. Chicago: University of Chicago Press.

GOULD, S. J. (1984) "Triumph of a naturalist" (review of *A Feeling for the Organism: The Life and Work of Barbara McClintock*, by Evelyn Fox Kellers). New York Review of Books 31 (March 29): 3-6.

HIRSCHI, T. (1979) "Separate and unequal is better." Journal of Research in Crime and Delinquency 16 (January): 34-38.

INKELES, A. (1959) "Personality and social structure," pp. 249-276 in Robert K. Merton et al. (eds.) Sociology Today: Problems and Prospects. New York: Basic Books.

JUDSON, H. F. (1979) The Eighth Day of Creation: Makers of the Revolution in Biology. New York: Simon & Schuster.

LONGSHORE, D. and J. PRAGER (forthcoming) "The impact of school desegregation: a situational analysis," in Ralph H. Turner and James F. Short, Jr. (eds.) Annual Review of Sociology, Vol. 11. Palo Alto: Annual Reviews Inc.

McNAMARA, J. H. (1967) "Uncertainties in police work: the relevance of police recruits' backgrounds and training," pp. 163-252 in David J. Bordua (ed.) The Police: Six Sociological Essays. New York: John Wiley.
MERTON, R. K. and R. A. NISBET [eds.] (1961, 1971, 1976) Contemporary Social Problems: An Introduction to the Sociology of Deviant Behavior and Social Disorganization (1st, 3rd, and 4th eds., respectively). New York: Harcourt Brace Jovanovich.
MILLER, W. B. (1958) "Lower class culture as a generating milieu of gang delinquency." Journal of Social Issues 14 (Summer): 5-19.
NAKANE, C. (1970) Japanese Society. Berkeley: University of California Press.
REISS, A. J. (1951) "Delinquency as the failure of personal and social controls." American Sociological Review 16 (April): 196-208.
——— (n.d.) "Person-centered perspective on law-breaking." (unpublished).
——— and A. D. BIDERMAN (1980) Data Sources on White-Collar Law-Breaking. Washington, DC: U.S. Department of Justice, National Institute of Justice.
RICE, S. A. (1931) "Hypotheses and verifications in Clifford R. Shaw's studies of juvenile delinquency," pp. 549-565 in Stuart A. Rice (ed.) Methods in Social Science: A Case Book. Chicago: University of Chicago Press.
SARRI, R. and Y. HASENFELD [eds.] (1976) Brought to Justice? Juveniles, the Courts, and the Law. Ann Arbor, MI: National Assessment of Juvenile Corrections.
SHAW, C. R. (1966) The Jack-Roller: A Delinquent Boy's Own Story. Chicago: University of Chicago Press. (Originally published in 1930.)
——— and H. D. McKAY (1969) Juvenile Delinquency and Urban Areas. Chicago: University of Chicago Press. (Originally published in 1942.)
——— (1960) The Jack-Roller: A Delinquent Boy's Own Story. Chicago: University of Chicago Press.
SHORT, J. F., Jr. (1980) "Evaluation as knowledge-building and vice versa," pp. 303-326 in M. W. Klein and K. S. Teilmann (eds.) Handbook of Criminal Justice Evaluation. Beverly Hills, CA: Sage.
——— (1979) "On the etiology of delinquent behavior." Journal of Research in Crime and Delinquency 16 (January): 28-33.
——— (1965) "Social structure and group process in gang delinquency," pp. 155-188 in M. Sherif and C. W. Sherif (eds.) Problems of Youth: Transition to Adulthood in a Changing World. Chicago: Aldine.
——— and F. L. STRODTBECK (1965, 1974) Group Process and Gang Delinquency (1st and 2nd eds., respectively). Chicago: University of Chicago Press.
TURNER, R. H. [ed.] (1967) Robert E. Park on Social Control and Collective Behavior: Selected Papers. Chicago: University of Chicago Press.
VAUGHAN, D. (1983) Controlling Unlawful Organizational Behavior: Social Structure and Corporate Misconduct. Chicago: University of Chicago Press.
WAGNER, D. G. and J. BERGER (1983) Do Sociological Theories Grow? Technical Report 91. Stanford, CA: Laboratory for Social Research.
WOLFGANG, M. E. and F. FERRACUTI (1967) The Subculture of Violence: Towards an Integrated Theory in Criminology. London: Tavistock.
SUTHERLAND, E. H. (1945) "Is 'white collar crime' crime?" American Sociological Review 10: 132-139.
TAPPAN, P. W. (1960) Crime, Justice, and Correction. New York: McGraw-Hill.

PART III

ASSUMPTIONS ABOUT THEORETICAL METHODS

4

The Assumption of Natural Science Methods:
Criminological Positivism

JOHN HAGAN

While criminological positivism is a subject of recurrent debate (see Matza, 1964; Quinney, 1974; Taylor et al., 1973), this debate recently has receded into the criminological closet. It is unlikely to stay there. Positivists are fond of noting the accuracy with which past occurrences predict future occurrences of the same or similar kind. On this basis, there is reason to assume that the old issues will take on new life.

In its crudest form, the issue of criminological positivism reduces to whether quantitative techniques constitute a central part of the work we should do. But the issue is broader than this. It involves the way topics are selected for study, research questions are posed, evidence is generated and assessed, findings are accumulated, and theories are built. At issue is the way crime writ large is approached as a subject for serious scholarly attention. Criminological positivism is a clearly conceived position from which all these things are done.

What exactly is criminological positivism? Why is criminological positivism an issue? Why is this issue today in the closet, and why in the past has it divided criminologists? What are the advantages and disadvantages of this perspective? What kind of knowledge results from the application of positivistic principles? Where is criminological positivism taking us? These are the questions addressed in this chapter.

WHAT AND WHO ARE
THE CRIMINOLOGICAL POSITIVISTS?

Although criminological positivism usually is traced to the Italian School—including the work of Cesar Lombroso (1910), Raffaele Garofalo (1914), and Enrico Ferri (1900)—it might as reasonably be traced to the work of Adophe Jacques Quetelet (1842) or William Bonger (1916). What these early positivists had in common has nothing to do with specific causal theories of crime, and everything to do with the way these causes are studied. All of these early criminologists began with the assumption that natural science methods should be used to study criminal behavior. That Bonger and Quetelet are today rarely identified as early positivists, while Lombroso, Garofalo, and Ferri are the focal points of most textbook discussions of positivism, probably says more about an American fascination with the Italian School's application of evolutionary principles than it does about the scientific study of crime.

So the Italian School captured the American imagination, while Quetelet and Bonger did not. Were we starting over, as many think we should, just the opposite would probably be the case. Were this the case, criminological positivism might be a more popular position than it is today. I will make this point by comparing briefly the work of Lombroso (1895) and Bonger (1916). Both of these authors were translated and published in the United States early in this century by the Modern Criminal Science Series of the American Institute of Criminal Law and Criminology. For purposes of illustration, a brief discussion of how these two criminological positivists address the topic of gender and crime is presented.

With the advantage of hindsight, it is easy to see why the Italian School stole the show. Lombroso (1895) captured the biological imagination of America, which was highly developed during the early part of this century. Lombroso's thesis was that criminals could be distinguished from non-criminals by the presence of physical anomalies that represented a reversion to a primitive or subhuman type of being. In other words, Lombroso saw criminals as biological "throwbacks" to an earlier, primitive, or "atavistic" stage of evolution. One might have expected Lombroso to have argued that men are more criminal than women because they are more atavistic. He did not, arguing instead that woman was "atavistically nearer to her origin than the male" (Lombroso, 1895: 107). Lombroso therefore needed to posit something that restrained woman's atavistic inclinations. His answer was that, "in ordinary cases these defects are neutralized by piety, maternity, want of passion, sexual coldness, weakness and an undeveloped intelligence" (p. 151). Lombroso went so far as to trace woman's passivity to the "immobility of the ovule compared with the zoosperm" (p. 109). It is tempting to speculate that Lombroso's theory of female criminality gained currency because it both asserted woman's biological inferiority and warned of the dangers of arousing her passions or developing her intelligence. In any case, Lombroso's *The Female Offender* was published originally in 1895. In 1913, only four years following Lombroso's death, Charles Goring published *The English Convict*, the most important refutation of Lombroso's theory.

In another era, Bonger (1916) might have captured the sociological imagination of America. Bonger was very much aware of biological explanations of sex differences in crime. However, he placed little stock in these explanations, arguing that "the smaller criminality of woman is not to be sought in innate qualities, but rather in the social environment" (Bonger, 1916: 477). Bonger reasoned that as class position declines, so too do differences in the social circumstances of the sexes, and therefore their relative rates of crime. Assuming this was the case, Bonger believed there was a straightforward way of demonstrating the social basis of sex differences in crime:

> A very conclusive proof of the thesis that the social position of woman is what explains her lower criminality is as follows. The difference in the manner of life of the two sexes decreases as we descend the social scale. If the social position of woman is then an important determinant of her lower criminality, the figures ought to show that the criminality of men differs more from that of women in the well-to-do classes than in classes less privileged.

It is the social position of woman, therefore, that determines her relative criminality. More generally, then, "if the life of women were like that of men their criminality would hardly differ at all as to quantity, though perhaps somewhat as to quality" (Bonger, 1916: 478).

Lombroso and Bonger's theories could hardly differ more in their identification of the causes of crime, and therefore in their explanation of sex differences in crime. Where Bonger places causal emphasis on structural position, Lombroso places the emphasis on biological predisposition. What makes both of these theorists criminological positivists, and what would have allowed them to do more than simply talk at or past one another, was their common way of addressing the issue and its resolution. Both begin with the fact of an observed correlation: Men are more criminal than women. In their day, Lombroso and Bonger could observe this correlation between being male and being criminal only with official data. Today we do so with victim and self-report surveys as well. Regardless of data source, what is important here is the initial framing of the topic of interest in terms of variables (sex and crime) and the observation of their covariation. That criminological positivists have continued to monitor this covariation across time and in many places, for adults as well as adolescents, with alternative measures and data sources, reflects an enduring commitment to measurement. Among other things, the interest has been in determining whether criminal behavior can be measured in a reliable and valid fashion. To the extent that it can, we are encouraged that the observed correlation is real.

Assuming the correlation was real, as most criminologists continue to assume today, Lombroso and Bonger sought explanations. Although their results were entirely different, they proceeded in similar ways. Each specified other variables that could account for the observed correlation. Lombroso looked for what he believed to be innate qualities that distinguished the sexes; Bonger looked for differences in their social lives. The variables Lombroso wound up emphasizing were "want of passion" and "undeveloped intelligence," while Bonger emphasized class position and conditions of work. Yet both assumed that a test of their respective theories was to see how sex and crime covaried with the other explanatory variables introduced in their explanations. Lombroso sought to confirm that criminal women possessed similar levels of intelligence and passion as criminal men, while Bonger sought to demonstrate that women formed a larger part of the indigent as compared to "well-to-do" criminal populations. These tests were admittedly crude, and even misleading, in part because of a dependence on official data. Nonetheless, both anticipated a logic of causal analysis that persists to this day: examination of the joint variation of an independent variable (sex) and a dependent variable (criminality) while taking into account values of a third explanatory variable (passion/intelligence/class position). So each theory can be formulated as a testable causal proposition predicting that the observed correlation of sex and crime will disappear within categories of an explanatory variable. While today nobody takes Lombroso's biogenetic theory seriously enough to test it, Bonger's theory has been tested with positive results (Hagan et al., forthcoming). This kind of formulation and test of predictive propositions, using data derived from efforts at the objective measurement of variables, is the hallmark of criminological positivism. Why is this strategy so little discussed today?

WHY IS CRIMINOLOGICAL POSITIVISM A CLOSET ISSUE?

The disjuncture between what many criminologists do in their research and what they do in their teaching is worthy of note. Criminology is a growth area in undergraduate as well as graduate instruction. It is doubtful that this growth is attributable to an emphasis on the methodological principles of criminological positivism. These principles are everywhere in evidence in the publication of criminological research in prestigious journals, and they are rarely or only briefly in evidence in undergraduate teaching. The results are some dramatic disjunctures in the socialization experiences of most professionally successful academic criminologists: They go from undergraduate courses that give only passing attention to the methods of criminological research, to graduate programs that culminate in sophisticated pieces of dissertation research guided by positivistic principles, to academic appointments that often require a continuation of positivistic research to satisfy promotion and tenure demands, combined with a program of undergraduate teaching that is tangential if not antithetical to this research.

Within this context, it should not be surprising that criminological positivism is an issue that only episodically bursts out of the closet and into dispute. The tensions that lie behind this issue are no doubt aggravated by the fact that the more undergraduate teaching practicing criminologists do, and the more they are freed from the demands for research through the process of promotion, the more distant they become from the methodological principles that once guided their work. For many criminologists, the methods of criminological positivism become distant and abstract principles that conflict with the everyday demands of getting through the professorial day. These principles remain central to the prestige-conferring process of getting published and cited in the criminological literature, but eventually this too becomes a threat or an irritant for many practicing criminologists. The skills become tarnished, and the rewards become obscure. Some become professional critics, others become professionally apathetic. Few continue to do the research that distinguishes criminological positivism. Why should criminological research be done in the positivist tradition?

THE BENEFITS AND LIABILITIES OF CRIMINOLOGICAL POSITIVISM

We do criminology for a variety of reasons: in response to the anxiety, anger, and fear that are common responses to crime; in the desire to prevent and control crime; in the hope of preventing crime through individual and social reform; in the effort to understand and explain crime and societal reactions to it; and because of the simple desire to learn more about crime and what it can tell us about our society. These "reasons for doing criminology" mix a desire for knowledge with a desire for action. It conventionally is assumed that knowledge is the only sound basis for action. This assumption is encouraged by the success of the natural sciences and the contributions they have made to the modern world. The open question is whether the social sciences, and more specifically criminology, can do the same.

The answer to this question may depend upon the level at which the issue is addressed. Consider the desire to prevent and control crime. At the most general level, there may be no issue to be researched. Most criminologists probably agree that a *much* more draconian criminal justice system and/or a *much* less stratified social structure would likely produce lower levels of crime. However, the interesting issue here is not empirical, but political, for we are as a society unlikely to move very far in either of the above directions. To do so would be to redefine the kind of society in which we live: a society that prides itself in avoiding totalitarian governmental restraints, and simultaneously accepts high levels of social and economic inequality. Such a society seems likely to endure much crime, and we do.

Meanwhile, we look for modest revisions in the social order, including the use of penal sanctions, individual treatment, and social reforms, that will produce marginal reductions in crime. Examples of such revisions include determinate sentencing statutes, drug therapy programs, various prison reforms, and subsidized employment schemes.

Criminological positivism provides a framework in which such innovations can be evaluated. Experimental and quasi-experimental designs are particularly well suited to tell us when such programs do *not* work, as well as sometimes telling us when and why they do (see Campbell, 1969). However, as well suited as criminological positivism may be to this task, it is a task that brings its own problems.

These problems were signaled in some of the earliest efforts made to guide criminal law reforms through the use of empirical research. One of the first of these efforts involved the National Commission on Law Observance and Enforcement, which became known as the Wickersham Commission. In 1930, the Commission funded a large-scale study of the criminal courts to test "the efficiency of our rules of procedure and our general methods of administering justice" (Schlegel, 1979: 501). The study was in large part a response to a perception that problems of "court congestion" and "breakdowns in the system" were leading, according to President Hoover, to "a general lawlessness of which the lack of enforcement of prohibition was only a single example" (p. 501). The research was conducted through the Yale Law School, under the direction of William O. Douglas, and others, in thirteen federal district courts.

What Douglas and his colleagues found was in many ways surprising. The background concerns of the study suggested a criminal justice system that was plagued by technicalities, delays and continuances, irrational juries, a cumbersome grand jury system, long trials, appeals on obsolete doctrinal points and related problems. Early results suggested something quite different: If anything, the system was *too* efficient. A total of 70 percent of defendants pleaded guilty when they were arraigned, usually on the same day the indictment or information was filed. In the end, 90 percent of the defendants pleaded guilty, with only 1 percent going to jury trial, which usually lasted less than a day. Fines were the most frequent disposition, almost all of which ultimately were paid. Only 15 percent of the cases took longer than two mmoths to complete.

Schlegel (1979) has described in detail the discomfort these findings produced. The Wickersham Commission was displeased with the results and suppressed some of the findings. It was many years before the full results were published. Two aspects of the study were most disconcerting: (1) Despite improved techniques, larger samples, and much funding, little new was found following the early results described above; (2) the findings seldom encouraged the procedural reforms that initially were proposed. This pattern of disappointment is not confined to the distant past. It is repeated, for example, in Moynihan's (1969) chronicle of the efforts to translate ideas about delinquency prevention into the War on Poverty of the 1960s. Here, as elsewhere, negative research findings came into conflict with the goals of preconceived political programs.

These examples underline a feature of criminological (as well as other kinds of) positivism. Positivism is nonpartisan. That is, it has no loyalty to political programs or ideologies. This in part explains how criminologists as different as Lombroso and Bonger could be considered positivists. The principles of positivism are indifferent to political or theoretical claims. This feature makes positivism attractive to some and unattractive to others. It is attractive to those who appreciate the possibility of putting ideas to a kind of test that is relatively independent of their prejudices, preferences, or preconceptions. The formation of testable propositions becomes a common medium through which rival theoretical and/or political claims can be asserted and assessed. For the positivist, science consists of the use of public procedures to test predictive propositions in a replicable fashion. The distinctiveness and usefulness of these principles gives positivism a strong claim to the hearts and minds of criminologists. They are, I believe, our best claim to being a science.

Yet such principles are unattractive to some. For one thing, the principles themselves seem to some *un*principled. That is, the detachment from, indeed the disinterest in, any preconceived theoretical or political position betrays to some a lack of commitment. Some positivists have attempted to mitigate this criticism by suggesting that they would not make public results that were not compatible with their political goals (for example, see Wolfgang, 1963). Others are so sure that the data will and do confirm their theoretical and political positions that they see no real problem (see McDonald, 1976). I prefer to view the issue differently: to see positivism as an opportunity to be as open-minded as is humanly possible—let the data fall where they may. Positivism is a system of thought that gives us our best chance to find out about things as they are, independent of how we might wish them to be. This is the soundest foundation on which theories and policies can be built.

It remains to be said that none of this happens very fast. Positivists are forever recommending "further research." The emphasis is on the *cumulation* of research techniques and findings. For some, this comes too slowly. Part of the frustration with positivism is not only that it lacks political or theoretical commitment, but that the findings are seldom in time to direct clearly the formation of specific policies. The kind of policy changes we spoke of at the outset of this section rarely occur within the timetable of careful and complete empirical research. A recent and dramatic example of this involved the suppression of Robert Martinson's (1974) findings on prison reform. The State of New York proceeded to reform its prisons in advance of the completion of a comprehensive review of the prison research literature Martinson was commissioned to conduct, and then suppressed the results of his study when it came to conclusions that conflicted with reforms already implemented. Related examples were noted above. The process of cumulation is one that is hard for policymakers to appreciate.

Do these examples mean that criminological positivism is a failure and that the process of cumulation is futile? Below, I argue the contrary by reviewing the development of one criminological research literature: that consisting of studies of race and sentencing. Consideration of this literature addresses by counterexample the problem of cumulaltion, and some additional common criticisms of criminological positivism.

Three additional criticisms of criminological positivism are that it focuses too much attention on criminal actors, that it is too deterministic, and that it deflects attention from criminal law (see Matza, 1964). The research literature on race and sentencing is one of the largest in American criminology, and has one of the longest histories. Yet none of the above criticisms accurately characterizes it. Rather than focusing on criminal actors, it focuses on *re*actors: the judges who sentence. This research literature cannot be said to be deterministic. As we will see, no variable is found to control or is expected to control fully the decision making of judges. And, by focusing on judges and the variables that influence their decision making, this literature makes the criminal law and its application the center of its attention. The remaining issue is whether a meaningful cumulation has occurred in this research literature that warrants the efforts invested and the attention of policymakers.

THE CUMULATION OF
ONE RESEARCH LITERATURE

Early sentencing research observed bivariate relationships between race and sentencing outcomes (that is, type and length of sentence). These studies (for example, Johnson, 1951) were particularly concerned with demonstrating the differential use of the death penalty against blacks in the southern United States. These studies are important today as a significant source of historical-comparative data; however, legitimate questions have been raised about their tendency to equate correlation with cause in imputing sentencing differentials to discrimination, without controlling relevant "legal" variables (see Green, 1961; Wolfgang and Riedal, 1973). As subsequent studies began to take additional variables into account, initially with tabular techniques, what we will call an individual-processual approach to sentencing research began to take form.

In the 1960s this research largely used contingency tables to test whether attributes such as race remained significantly correlated with sentence outcome when type of offense and prior record were held constant. Although this research labored under the inherent liabilities of tabular techniques, particularly problems of controlling for more than one or two variables simultaneously, it served the important function (at least implicitly) of encouraging researchers to develop models of the sentencing process. For example, the burden of Edward Green's (1961, 1964) early and important work on sentencing was to argue that when "legal" variables such as offense type and prior record are taken into account, the relationship between race and sentence disappears. Implicit in this argument is the assumption that prior record and current offense mediate (in a causal and sequential sense) the race-sentence relationship. Later arguments have focused on whether race-linked patterns of offense type and prior record should be taken as reflecting differences in criminal *behavior* or as reflecting earlier experiences of differential *treatment* by legal authorities (for example, see Farrell and Swigert, 1978). Both positions could be correct; what is important for our immediate purposes is that in either case it is assumed that offense type and prior record play a causally intervening role in the process by which judges reach sentencing decisions. Two different processes are involved, but each is an example of an individual-processual approach to the analysis and understanding of sentencing data.

Much of the sentencing research of the 1970s involved variations and elaborations of individual-processual models of the sentencing process. Most significant in the development of this approach was the introduction of a number of important "case-processing variables" into these models and the application of more sophisticated multivariate techniques in the effort to test the fit of these models with actual case data. Among the new variables considered were pretrial bail decisions (see, for example, Bernstein et al., 1977), plea and charging decisions (Hagan, 1975c), and the presentence recommendations of probation officers and prosecutors (Hagan, 1975b; Hagan et al., 1979). These studies made increasingly explicit the premise that sentencing is an end result of a decision-making process that involves offenders moving through a series of potentially important stages in a complex criminal justice system. Farrell and Swigert (1978: 442) make this point well: "The highly structured nature of the judicial system lends itself to a systematic analysis of legal processing. The discrete ordering of events—the social characteristics of the defendants prior to their entry into the system, their accumulated criminal histories, the type of legal representation, pretrial release, the mode of adjudication, and final disposition—constitutes a series of stages that allows the researcher to assert the causal sequence of relationships." Structural equation models and log-linear techniques have provided the technology for modeling this complicated process.

But criminal sentencing is not only a matter of processing individuals through a criminal justice system. Both the individuals and the system occupy variable positions or locations within a social structure; so individual processing decisions can vary by social context. This point has been recognized implicitly in some past sentencing research, and it is made increasingly explicit in recent work. For example, early studies of capital punishment often attempted to measure variation in the use of capital punishment against individuals across periods of time (Johnson, 1951), in different jurisdictions (Bedau, 1964, 1965), and according to whether the crime was inter- or intraracial (Wolfgang and Riedel, 1973) in character (that is, interracial crimes represent a conflict across assumed status positions in American society). These studies also suffered from the limitations we have associated with the application of tabular techniques, and they were undertaken with little awareness of one another, thus limiting the full development of their contextual implications.

Since 1977, a number of studies have begun to exploit the possibilities of what I will call a structural-contextual approach. Combining data sets from several jurisdictions, Eisenstein and Jacob (1977), Levin (1977), and Balbus (1973) have linked variations in the political environment to sentencing behavior. Lizotte (1978) has identified the class as well as racial positions of individuals in the social structure and linked those to sentencing outcomes. More recently, Hagan et al. (1980) have distinguished proactive and reactive court organizations and considered their impact on the sentencing of white-collar offenders in ten federal district courts, while Hagan (1982) has examined the consequences of corporate entities compared with individuals acting as victim-complainants in the criminal justice process. All of these studies add some feature of structural and contextual variation to their consideration of the individual processing that leads to sentencing decisions.

Studies with data sets drawn over the last decade have identified a number of structural contexts in which racial discrimination seems to persist. A number of these studies reveal racial discrimination, for example: in rural but not in urban settings (Pope, 1975a; Hagan, 1977); among judges with culturally linked prejudicial attitudes (Gibson, 1978; Hagan, 1975a); for crimes such as rape (LaFree, 1980) and robbery (Thomson and Zingraff, 1981) that are interracial (see also Myers, 1979); among highly politicized crimes (such as drug felonies, Clark and Koch, 1977; Peterson and Hagan, 1984) and settings (for instance, draft evasion during the antiwar movement; Hagan and Bernstein, 1979); in cases in which probation officers offer presentence recommendations (Myers, 1979; Unnever et al., 1980; Hagan, 1975b); and in conditions that mark the intersection of race and class positions in American society (Lizotte, 1978). In contrast, studies of the last decade that have not found discrimination have focused frequently on settings in which discrimination by race may be least likely to be expected, for example, in large urban jurisdictions (see Bernstein et al., 1977; Hagan et al., 1980; Eisenstein and Jacob, 1977; Hagan, Hewit, and Alwin, 1979) and/or in courts that handle large numbers of misdemeanor cases (see Feeley, 1979). These large-volume, highly bureaucratized settings, very characteristic of the American practice of criminal justice, may simply be too constrained by their high visibility, lack of time, and strained resources to allow direct discrimination by race. Said differently, these court settings may be too important symbolically and too bureaucratic organizationally to allow overt discrimination as a frequent occurrence.

Several caveats should be added to our discussion of the significance of structural context in sentencing research. First, it is important to note that the strength of the relationships reported in the recent studies is often not large, in spite of differences in statistical significance. While a few recent studies under specified conditions estimate that black offenders receive sentences of as much as six months to a year longer than white offenders (Lizotte, 1978; Clark and Koch, 1977), and while some recent research suggests continuing disparities involving use of the death penalty (for example, see Radlet, 1981), there is also much work indicating that when racial differences are found, they are small.

The weakness of these race-sentence relationships is not necessarily surprising. An important feature of the individual-processual approach is its conceptualization of race as an exogenous variable exercising its influence through an extended causal chain that includes such intervening variables as offense type, prior record, bail status, and recommendations by various control agents. Since we ordinarily expect that the largest correlations will occur between adjacent variables in such a chain, and since all of these correlations are assumed to be less than perfect, we should therefore expect that the smallest correlations will occur between those variables that are furthest from each other in the causal chain (Blalock, 1964): race and sentence. It is also important to note that the influence that race may have on earlier decisions such as pretrial detention may be even more punishing than the final sentence imposed (see Feeley, 1979). Meanwhile, the increasing attention that has been given to this causal chain has confirmed that other variables do have a regular and important impact on sentence. In fact, there is considerable evidence to confirm that the closer one gets to sentence in such causal chains, the stronger the observed correlations become. Thus it has been noted that presentence recommendations by probation officers and prosecutors exhibit a substantial relationship to sentence (Hagan, 1975b, 1977; Hagan, Hewit, and Alwin, 1979; Myers, 1979; Unnever et al., 1980) and that judges' perceptions of offense seriousness and offender culpability are very strongly related to sentence (Hogarth, 1971). Indeed, in the latter case the relationships are so strong that one may reasonably begin to question the conceptual and methodological separateness of the independent and dependent variables. Nonetheless, the pattern of relationships is consistent with the type of causal chains implied by the individual-processual approach.

The important research on race and sentencing of the future will involve individual-processual analyses of the sentencing process that are also able to take the types of structural and contextual variation we have discussed into account. The importance of this work is reflected in the continuing controversy that surrounds use of the death penalty. We have reviewed historical evidence that the death penalty has been applied disproportionately to black offenders in America. Such evidence was responsible in part for the U.S. Supreme Court deciding in 1972, in *Furman* v. *Georgia* (408 U.S. 238 [1972]), that the application of all death penalty statutes then in existence was arbitrary and capricious, and therefore "cruel and unusual punishment," in violation of the Eighth Amendment. Since that ruling, numerous states and the federal government have enacted new capital punishment statutes. Research is again questioning the constitutionality of this legislation by pointing, in some states, with the kind of increasing sophistication outlined above, to the disproportionate impact of such statutes on black Americans (see, for example, Radlet, 1981; Bowers and Pierce, 1980). This evidence would not be persuasive without the kind of accumulation of technique and findings described here. This kind of accumulation is a key characteristic of positivist inquiry.

THE NEW ETIOLOGY

Ironically, where criminological positivists were once criticized for being too concerned with the study of criminal behavior, research on such issues as race and sentencing has substantially shifted the balance. Today, criminologists are as much or more involved in studying the police, prosecutors, defense lawyers, probation and parole officers, and judges as they are in studying criminal offenders. Labeling and deterrence theorists argue, albeit in diametrically different ways, that the actions of these control agents influence the development of criminal careers. However, no one argues that the actions taken by these agents are the only causes of crime. It is against this background that a renewed interest in etiological theory is emerging.

It may be too soon to say what exact forms the new etiology will take. Nonetheless, the broad outlines of this new research agenda can be seen, or at least speculated about. We expect that there will be a mixture of the new and the old in this work, making sense of old findings in new ways. One new component of this work will involve a reconceptualization of class structure in criminological theory. Traditional etiological theories of crime have substituted consideration of socioeconomic status for class structure. Operationalizations have focused on the measurement of occupational prestige rather than on class position. These are gradational rather than relational measures of class (Wright and Perrone, 1977). However, new neo-Marxian measures of class position, focusing on structural relations, are now available (Wright et al., 1982). These measures locate individuals in the class structure in a categorical fashion that opens up important new avenues of research. Where past research could find only weak and uncertain relationships between socioeconomic status and criminal or delinquent behavior on which to base class theories (Hindelang, 1979; Tittle et al., 1978; Braithwaite, 1981; Thornberry and Farnsworth, 1982; Elliot and Ageton, 1980), new studies using neo-Marxian measures will now attempt to reestablish that a relationship between class position and criminality exists.

Regardless of whether a new class-crime relationship is established, another kind of etiological work is likely to emerge. It will be concerned with reconceiving the ways in which schools and the family are involved in the causal explanation of criminal and delinquent behavior. That school and family experiences play a causal role is difficult to refute (Hirschi, 1969). However, while the older theories conceptualized this causal role in terms of the internalization of values and beliefs, and the socialization of attachments and commitments, the new etiology is more likely to rely on such concepts as the "reproduction of order." The new etiologists will be concerned with the ways in which the family and the school mediate the effects of age and gender, as well as class position. New gender- and class-specific theories are likely to emerge. Whether these theories will do more than reinterpret old findings is as yet unclear. However, the possibility of very different kinds of understandings is apparent (see Greenberg, 1981; Spitzer, 1975; Colvin and Pauly, 1983).

Consider the possibilities for class-specific theories. The traditional focus on socioeconomic status allowed no means of clearly demarcating class divisions. Divisions could be imposed on the status continuum only arbitrarily. The point was that status was continuous rather than discrete. However, the new measures of class position divide the classes in categorical terms. It will now be possible to develop and test class-specific conceptualizations, and to answer the question of whether the causes of crime vary with class categories.

It is important to reemphasize that the new etiology is unlikely to be a wholesale departure from the old etiology. There will be commonalities that reflect the cumulative form of criminological positivism. Some may find the commonalities disturbing reinventions of the past. However, to the extent that the explanatory power of our theories is increased, the efforts will be proven worthwhile.

WHERE IS CRIMINOLOGICAL POSITIVISM TAKING US?

Where are the above kinds of research taking us? It has been suggested here that the hallmark of criminological positivism is the formulation and test of predictive propositions, using data derived from efforts at the objective measurement of variables. Whether the variables are class, gender, and criminal behavior or race and sentencing outcomes, the principles are the same. So, unfortunately, is the pace. The crystallization of propositions into theories, the development of techniques to be used in testing propositions, the collection of relevant data, and the accumulation of findings are time-consuming. Yet criminological knowledge is slowly and steadily expanding as a result of such efforts. Comparisons of the best criminological research done today with work done even one or two decades ago are striking. This process makes it all the more important that we recognize the place of positivistic principles in contemporary criminological work. These principles, and the resulting work, hold the promise of criminology as a science. This is a point that is too often lost in the teaching of undergraduate criminology.

REFERENCES

BALBUS, I. (1973) The Dialectics of Legal Repression: Black Rebels Before the American Criminal Courts. New York: Russell Sage Foundation.
BEDAU, H. A. (1965) "Capital punishment in Oregon, 1903-64." Oregon Law Review 45: 1-39.
———(1964) "Death sentences in New Jersey." Rutgers Law Review 19: 1-2.
BERNSTEIN, I. N., W. KELLY, and P. DOYLE (1977) "Societal reaction to deviants: the case of criminal defendants." American Sociological Review 42: 743-755.
BLALOCK, H. (1964) Causal Inferences in Nonexperimental Research. New York: Norton.
BONGER, W. (1916) Criminality and Economic Conditions. Boston: Little, Brown.
BOWERS, W. and G. PIERCE (1980) "Arbitrariness and discrimination in post-Furman capital cases." Crime and Delinquency 26: 563-635.
BRAITHWAITE, J. (1981) "The myth of social class and criminality reconsidered." American Sociological Review 46: 36-57.
CAMPBELL, D. T. (1969) "Reforms as experiments." American Psychologist 24: 409-429.
CLARK, S. and G. KOCH (1977) "The influence of income and other factors on whether criminal defendants go to prison." Law and Society Review 11: 57-92.
COLVIN, M. and J. PAULY (1983) "A critique of criminology: toward an integrated structural-Marxist theory of delinquency production." American Journal of Sociology 89: 513-552.
EISENSTEIN, J. and H. JACOB (1977) Felony Justice. Boston: Little, Brown.
ELLIOT, D. S. and S. S. AGETON (1980) "Reconciling race and class differences in self-reported and official estimates of delinquency." American Sociological Review 45: 95-110.

FARRELL, R. and V. SWIGERT (1978) "Prior offense as a self-fulfilling prophecy." Law and Society Review 12: 437-453.
FEELEY, M. (1979) The Process Is the Punishment. New York: Russell Sage Foundation.
FERRI, E. (1900) Criminal Sociology. New York: Appleton-Century-Crofts.
GAROFALO, R. (1914) Criminology. Boston: Little, Brown. (Originally published in 1885.)
GIBSON, J. (1978) "Race as a determinant of criminal sentences: a methodological critique and a case study." Law and Society Review 12: 455-478.
GREEN, E. (1964) "Inter- and intra-racial crime relative to sentencing." Journal of Criminal Law, Criminology and Police Science 55: 348-358.
———(1961) Judicial Attitudes in Sentencing. London: Macmillan.
GREENBERG, D. (1981) Crime and Capitalism. Palo Alto, CA: Mayfield.
HAGAN, J. (1982) "The corporate advantage: a study of the involvement of corporate and individual victims in the criminal justice system." Social Forces 60: 992-1022.
———(1977) "Criminal justice in rural and urban communities: a study of the bureaucratization of justice." Social Forces 55: 597-612.
———(1975a) "Law, order and sentencing: a study of attitude in action." Sociometry 38: 374-384.
———(1975b) "The social and legal construction of criminal justice: a study of the pre-sentencing process." Social Problems 22: 620-637.
———(1975c) "Parameters of criminal prosecution: an application of path analysis to a problem of criminal justice." Journal of Criminal Law, Criminology and Police Science 65: 536-544.
———and I. BERNSTEIN (1979) "Conflict in context: the sanctioning of draft resisters, 1963-76." Social Problems 27: 109-122.
HAGAN, J., J. HEWIT, and D. ALWIN (1979) "Ceremonial justice: crime and punishment in a loosely coupled system." Social Forces 58: 506-527.
HAGAN, J., I. NAGEL, and G. ALBONETTI (1980) "The differential sentencing of white collar offenders in ten federal district courts." American Sociological Review 45: 802-820.
HAGAN, J., J. SIMPSON, and A. R. GILLIS (forthcoming) "The class structure of gender and delinquency."
———(1979) "The sexual stratification of social control: toward a gender-based perspective on crime and delinquency." British Journal of Sociology 30: 25-38.
HINDELANG, M. (1979) "Correlates of delinquency: the illusion of discrepancy between self-report and official measures." American Sociological Review 44: 995-1014.
HIRSCHI, T. (1969) Causes of Delinquency. Berkeley; University of California Press.
HOGARTH, J. (1971) Sentencing as a Human Process. Toronto: University of Toronto Press.
JOHNSON, T. (1951) "Is the punishment of rape equally administered to Negroes and whites in the state of Louisiana?" pp. 216-228 in W. L. Patterson (ed.) We Charge Genocide. New York: International.
LaFREE, G. (1980) "The effect of sexual stratification by race on official reactions to rape." American Sociological Review 45: 842-854.
LEVIN, M. (1977) Urban Politics and the Criminal Courts. Chicago: University of Chicago Press.

LIZOTTE, A. J. (1978) "Extra-legal factors in Chicago's criminal courts: testing the conflict model of criminal justice." Social Problems 25: 564-580.

LOMBROSO, C. (1910) Crime, Its Causes and Remedies. Boston: Little, Brown. (Originally published in 1876.)

——— (1895) The Female Offender. New York: Fisher Unwin.

McDONALD, L. (1976) The Sociology of Law and Order. London: Faber & Faber.

MARTINSON, R. (1974) "What works? Questions and answers about prison reform." Public Interest 35: 22-54.

MATZA, D. (1964) Delinquency and Drift. New York: John Wiley.

MOYNIHAN, D. (1969) Maximum Feasible Misunderstanding. New York: Free Press.

MYERS, M. (1979) "Offended parties and official reactions: victims and the sentencing of criminal defendants." Sociological Quarterly 20: 529-540.

PETERSON, R. and J. HAGAN (1984) "Changing conceptions of race: towards an account of anomalous findings of sentencing research." American Sociological Review 49: 56-70.

POPE, C. (1975) Sentencing of California Felony Offenders. Washington, DC: Government Printing Office.

QUETELET, A. (1842) A Treatise on Man. Edinburgh: William & Robert Chambers.

QUINNEY, R. (1974) Critique of Legal Order. Boston: Little, Brown.

RADLET, M. (1981) "Racial characteristics and the imposition of the death penalty." American Sociological Review 46: 918-927.

SCHLEGEL, H. (1979) "American legal realism and empirical social science: from the Yale experience." Buffalo Law Review 28: 459.

SPITZER, S. (1975) "Toward a Marxian theory of deviance." Social Problems 22: 638-651.

TAYLOR, I., P. WALTON, and J. YOUNG (1973) The New Criminology: For a Social Theory of Deviance. London: Routledge & Kegan Paul.

THOMSON, R. and M. ZINGRAFF (1981) "Detecting sentence disparity: some problems and evidence." American Journal of Sociology 86: 869-880.

THORNBERRY, T. and M. FARNSWORTH (1982) "Social correlates of criminal involvement: further evidence on the relationship between social status and criminal behavior." American Sociological Review 47: 505-517.

TITTLE, C., W. WILLEMEZ, and D. SMITH (1978) "The myth of social class and criminality: an empirical assessment of the empirical evidence." American Sociological Review 43: 643-656.

UNNEVER, J. D., C. FRAZIER, and J. HENRETTA (1980) "Race differences in criminal sentencing." Sociological Quarterly 21: 197-207.

WOLFGANG, M. (1963) "Criminology and the criminologist." Journal of Criminal Law, Criminology and Police Science 54: 155-162.

——— and M. RIEDEL (1973) "Race, judicial discretion, and the death penalty." Annals of the American Academy of Political and Social Science 407: 119-133.

WRIGHT, E. and L. PERRONE (1977) "Marxist class categories and income inequality." American Sociological Review 42: 32-55.

WRIGHT, E., C. COSTELLO, D. HACHEN, and J. SPRAGUE (1982) "The American class structure." American Sociological Review 47: 709-726.

5

The Assumption that General Theories Are Not Possible

CHARLES R. TITTLE

This essay addresses issues concerning general theory in criminology, but, given that such terms as "theory," "explanation," and "model" have no consensual meanings and are often interchanged or used to refer to quite disparate ideas (see NcNall, 1983; Quinney, 1974; Walker, 1977), I shall begin by making some conceptual distinctions and declarations to guide the discussion.

"Explanation" is taken here to mean a verbal account of some *specific* phenomenon that answers the question why/how for a particular audience. An explanation attempts to make intellectual sense of observations concerning a *particular* phenomenon by interpreting them within a cognitive scheme in such a way that the quest for comprehension is satisfied. The standards for satisfying intellectual curiosity are more or less demanding, depending upon the audience to which an explanation is addressed. A sophisticated, scientific audience requires, among other things, that the premises of explanation yield predictions about conditions under which particular variables will take on various values. "Prediction" in this sense refers to statements of the type "If A, then B," not to prophecies of future outcomes based on guesses about whether A will or will not be present. The main advantage of such predictions is that they may be tested empirically (if so, they become hypotheses) to measure the power and accuracy of explanations. The greater the empirical potency of predictions derived from an explanation, the greater the confidence scholars can have in that explanation and the more satisfied they are that the phenomenon is understood.

More important, empirical anomalies encountered in tests of hypotheses make it possible to modify explanations for progressive improvement.

"Theory," on the other hand, is a system of interrelated ideas that answers, for *more than one* phenomenon, the question of why/how in a *general, abstract* manner. Theories subsume many explanations of various specific phenomena included in the domain of the theory, explanations that themselves meet the criteria already set forth. Theory is, by definition, *general*, although actual theories may vary in the abstractness of their answers as well as inclusiveness. Although the "generalness" of theories is really a continuous rather than a discrete characteristic, the term "general theory" will be used here to denote a scheme of highly abstract generality designed to account for an *entire domain* of phenomena such as all individual criminal (or socially disapproved) behavior or all variations in the content of criminal laws (or patterns of social disapproval), but it will not be used to signify attempts to account for all criminological phenomena in *all domains*.

Any field of scientific, or positivistic, study has an immediate goal of explaining the specific phenomena within its purview and an ultimate goal of organizing those explanatory principles into theories expressing general processes by which things within the scope of the field operate (Braithwaite, 1960). Since explanations provide answers to why/how questions, they help quench the thirst for understanding, but, because those answers pertain only to narrowly circumscribed areas, they are not totally satisfying. Theories go beyond explanation by pulling together diverse accounts within a unifying scheme, thereby reflecting greater efficiency and generating additional insights that would go unnoticed were knowledge left as a mere collection of separate, ad hoc explanations.

Just as scientific explantions produce predictions that, if translated into specific empirical terms, can be tested, scientific theories produce explanations. By extracting explanations of specific phenomena from theories, deriving predictions from those explanations, and testing those hypotheses, one can assess the credibility of theories and lay the foundation for progressive improvement. Hence the business of science is theory building, research is a means to that end, and the process involves abstract formulation and modification in light of empirical reality (Freese, 1972a, 1972b).

In moving from theory to explanation to prediction to test and back, it is sometimes useful to employ models. A model is a set of hypotheses interrelated and arranged to convey a sequential causal process implied by an explanation or theory. Modelers derive several propositions from a theory or explanation and organize them, usually with the aid of pictorial diagrams, so that simultaneous tests of those hypotheses can be regarded as an evaluation of the causal structure underlying the explanatory scheme. But models are not theories or explanations; they do not themselves answer the question of how/why, they only describe the causal process implied by a given attempt to answer that question.

THE PROBLEM

The predominant style and language of most published work suggest that the criminological community, implicitly at least, has adopted a positivistic approach; that is, there is evidence that the majority of criminologists at least pay lip service to the goal of developing general theory. Yet considerable ambivalence is obvious. There are strong and influential undercurrents declaring that theory is impossible, undesirable, or of only ancillary import. Some of these dyspeptic views stem from conviction that science is inappropriate for studying social phenomena, others flow from faulty perceptions of the scientific process, and a few reflect frustration at slow progress toward general theory. Yet they all share a common assumption: Pursuit of general theory is a fool's errand because of inherent features of criminological phenomena.

I contend that this is an erroneous asumption and that general theory is quite possible, but that it has been impeded mainly by the way criminologists have gone about trying to create it, not by the subject matter itself. This essay (1) describes the most prominent futilitarian positions, (2) argues that the putative barriers they describe can be overcome with specific tactics, and (3) identifies cultural and organizational characteristics of the criminological community that have made appropriate strategies for development of general theory difficult to employ.

FUTILITARIANISM

At least five arguments deriding efforts to construct general theory can be found in the criminological literature: (1) that the subject matter is hopelessly ambiguous; (2) that crime-relevant phenomena are either completely unique or so enormously heterogeneous that theory is unrealistic; (3) that crime-related social processes are situationally problematic rather than recurrent, orderly, and concrete, thus precluding generalization; (4) that crime-relevant phenomena are produced by too many diverse causal factors to permit general theory; and (5) that repeated failure of theoretical effort has proven the hopelessness of the task. Although these five positions are not completely distinct, their core tenets can be differentiated; therefore, the arguments will be presented separately and evaluated individually.

Ambiguous Subject Matter

It is now widely acknowledged that crime, criminal behavior, and the like are inherently relative, time and place bound, arbitrary, and ephemeral. What is included within the criminal code of any particular society is the product of social processes. Consequently, and literally, any behavior or class of behaviors whatsoever may at one time or another, or in one place or another, be designated as crime. Acts that are at one time designated crime in a given society are sometimes later redefined as heroic, while completely legal behaviors may later be declared criminal (Higgins and Butler, 1982). And even when a class of acts is prohibited in the criminal codes of a particular society at a given point in time, the decision as to whether a specific instance of behavior qualifies as commission of that crime is subject to an imprecise interpretive process (Schur, 1979) so that neither crime and noncrime nor criminals and noncriminals are clearly distinguishable (Turk, 1964). Moreover, the concept of law is itself so ambiguous that it is difficult to determine even if law exists in a given social group, much less whether a given act or class of behaviors is illegal (Friedman, 1977; MacNaughton-Smith, 1968; Schur, 1968).

Although the fact of relativity is rarely in dispute (but see Wellford, 1975), the consequences of that condition are perceived to be quite different by various criminologists. Some believe that this precludes any chance of science or general theory. They assume that phenomena to be included within a general account must have concrete, essential, inherent characteristics that permit them to be empirically differentiated from other phenomena. The following statements illustrate variations on this theme:

Any attempt to construct a theory of crime without an adequate foundation is doomed to failure. The field cannot be delineated until an analysis of the term "crime" is made and a basic definition established [Jeffery, 1956: 658].

It is vain to seek the causes of crime as such, of crime anywhere and everywhere. . . . Crime then is essentially relative. It has no inherent quality or property attaching to it as such, attaching to crime of all categories under all conditions [Maciver, 1962: 73].

Finally, it is worth reemphasizing that a recognition of the cultural and temporal relativity of the definition of crime and the reactions to crime calls into question the entire approach of traditional criminology and its assumptions and thus requires an abandonment of the naive search for universal causes of criminality [Phillipson, 1974: 13].

Uniqueness

Some criminologists eschew the effort to build general theory in favor of ethnographic descriptions of specific crime-relevant phenomena or construction of a large number of separate explanations of particular, demonstrably homogeneous, behaviors or situations. The main assumption is that empirical similarity is necessary for broad explanation and that such homogeneity is limited in criminology because it deals with phenomena that are so diverse as to be almost unique.

This diversity is often illustrated by individual criminal conduct. Behaviors to be studied include cross-societal vagaries such as diluting drinks by tavern keepers in ancient Babylon, killing deer on the king's land in France during the middle ages, and possessing drug paraphernalia in the contemporary United States. Even within a given society at a particular point in time the behaviors to be explained may include such seemingly dissimilar things as witchcraft, adultery, and quarreling (Erikson, 1966). Similarly, in some states in the contemporary United States, legally prohibited acts range from physical assault to gambling and include such acts as oral sex, tax evasion, and driving an automobile while under the influence of alcohol.

Clearly, criminal behaviors may differ in the context within which they typically occur, the manner in which they are performed, the likelihood of a victim, the kind of people who usually do them, the degree of social disapproval associated with them, and almost countless other ways. Even when the focus is narrowed to different instances of the same crime, criminal behaviors are found to differ among themselves in numerous ways. Furthermore, in one fell swoop a state legislature could make some common behavior such as coffee drinking a crime, thereby throwing it into the same basic category as rape, tax evasion, or vandalism.

Thus, given the belief by many that obvious similarity is necessary for generalization, it is no surprise that some have come to regard general theory in criminology as a hopeless and ridiculous pursuit and would therefore retreat to description of the myriad details. For example:

> The dynamics involved in the resulting criminal behavior pattern must be studied in the individual case. However it must be demonstrated that a sizeable group of people who engage in the same type of crime share common personality and background factors [Roebuck, 1963: 478].
>
> As a first step to a better understanding of crime—and its causes—it is well to cease discussing crimes and criminals in any general sense and concentrate solely on individual crime situations and individual crimes. We must build up our knowledge of crime and criminals by studying particular crimes and individual criminals [Barnes and Teeters, 1959: 118].
>
> What do cannibalism, testifying against one's fellow police officers, changing one's sex, and mass murder have in common? We would search in vain for similarities if we tried to understand the motives of the people involved, if we tried to determine the causes of their actions. We would also search in vain for some sort of internal consistency in these actions—if they all harmed others, if they were uniformly self-destructive, or if they broke some religious or natural law [Goode, 1978: 6-7].

Others stop short of declaring general theory impossible, but they do assert that it is a secondary, pie-in-the-sky type of enterprise:

> All the past examples of sociological theories of suicide have demonstrated the dangers involved in constructing theories without a firm foundation of careful, detailed descriptions of real-world events. The immediate goal before us, therefore, must clearly be that of providing such careful, comparative descriptions of many forms of social action. Only then can we get on with the general task of constructing more abstract theories to explain social actions [Douglas, 1967: 340].
>
> Until the criminologist learns to suspend his personal distaste for the values and lifestyles of the untamed savages, until he goes out in the field to the cannibals and headhunters and observes them without trying either

to civilize them or turn them over to colonial officials, he will be only a veranda anthropologist. That is, he will be only a jailhouse or courthouse sociologist, unable to produce anything like a genuinely scientific picture of crime [Polsky, 1967: 147].

A Problematic World

A third critique denies the possibility of general theory by assuming that criminological domains are problematic rather than structured and concrete, that they are nonpredictable products of situationally negotiated meanings and subjective interpretations of events and actions (Garfinkel, 1967; Phillipson, 1974; Wilson, 1970). According to this perspective, all behavior is implicated in an ongoing process of action, meaningful response, interpretation of response, and behavioral adjustment to the interpreted meanings of that response. Hence all behavior and all record keeping about behavior are thought to be produced by processes where meanings are sequentially constructed on the basis of shared but implicit interpretative rules. As such, they resist confinement to categories or reduction to general principles.

For example, behavior that ends up being defined by one or another of the participants in an interaction situation, or later by outsiders, as an act of rape may involve a large number of sequentially ordered, interpretative maneuvers of a tentative nature between a male and female that are behaviorally indistinguishable from courtship. How each move in the process is made depends upon how each actor interprets the other's response, which is in turn dependent upon what that participant thought was intended by the other's move. This attribution of meaning may involve generally shared, although in this case perhaps misinterpreted, cognitive conventions, or it may be a product of unique negotiated meanings or at least of what one party thought was a negotiated meaning. Moreover, the outcome may be classified as a rape rather than a sexual encounter only as a result of reconstructed reality after the interactive sequence has taken place. Whether a given sequence of behaviors constitutes rape or seduction is a matter of essentially problematic subjective decisions. Thus police statistics, investigative reports, survey self-reports, or victimization data concerning rape are nothing more than products of situational processes by which sequences of ambiguous acts came to be so interpreted. Rape, therefore, has no concrete essence; it does not exist in an objective sense. And since it does not, one cannot discover the causes of rape, cannot explain its occurrence, and cannot build a theory that would account for it (see Hirschi, 1980).

From this perspective, the job of social scientists is to *understand* how situational interpretations occur in specific contexts; that is, how social participants make their actions comprehensible to each other. Criminologists are to place themselves in the actors' positions and see the world through the actors' eyes, a process aided by empathic involvement in the everyday life of crime-involved persons. The idea is to develop concepts that correspond to the concepts of people in situations, and thereby learn how reality is constructed in the everyday world. No abstract theoretical constructs can, or ought to, be brought to bear. Indeed, theory is actually undesirable, because it imposes an alien, orderly reality upon what is actually a problematic, constructed reality (Liska, 1981: 169).

> If one is aware of and accepts the above distinctions, one is led to abandon the search for an explanation of a particular category of deviance in terms of its inferred "cause" and to find that deviant behavior is better understood if one allows for such problematic expressions as "drift," "contingency circumstances," "labeling" and "neutralizing" processes, public and private behavior, and/or the operation of "reflexivity," "background expectancies," and "tacit understandings." ... it is suggested that we observe and record the patterns of interaction between members and the foundations of these interaction patterns, i.e., the reciprocal effects of the social meanings of social actions upon the members within different social contexts [Jacobs, 1972: 5].

> Hence it is required of sociological observers, who set for themselves the task of making sense out of human activity, to describe and analyze everyday actors' methods of production—the rules for creating those reality experiences that guide their behavior [Hartjen, 1981: 449].

> The alternative way of "doing science" (alternative to examining a presumably deterministic world populated by elements having intrinsic and fixed meanings and seeking after abstraction) is to base concepts and principles of human behavior on careful and systematic observations of the social world as it is constructed and experienced in terms of everyday life.... It calls for examination of the social origins of meaning, how meanings are evolved and applied to things in the environment, the consequences of applying these meanings, and finally, how meanings change [Pfuhl, 1980: 21-22].

Complexity

A fourth objection to general theory focuses on the supposed complexity of causes for the phenomena included under the criminological umbrella. As noted before, the domains of inquiry of interest to criminologists include a bewildering variety of ostensibly unalike phenomena. For instance, it is not at all obvious what such diverse acts as homicide and failure to stop at a traffic light have in common, much less how they might be explained from one theory. So striking are these apparent differences that many scholars have assumed that various forms of crime must require separate theories. Moreover, some have concluded that even ostensibly similar criminal acts must necessarily evoke multiple theories because any behavioral event involves different causes operating at different junctures in a sequence.

Others maintain that any behavior requires an almost unique combination of different kinds of causal influences, each of which must be implicated in a distinct level of theory. This is the well-known and widely debated multiple-factor/cause approach (see discussion by Cohen, 1962; Gibbons, 1981: 98-104; Glaser, 1979; Hirschi and Selvin, 1967: 179-181; Matza, 1964; Sutherland, 1942; Walker, 1977). The multiple-factor argument recognizes the possible importance of genetic, biological, psychodynamic, psychological, social structural, cultural, and situational influences that may operate individually or collectively in a given instance of criminal behavior. In addition, each of these classes of factors is thought to involve a variety of separate causal variables that may operate continuously or intervene episodically.

In view of such logical possibilities and some evidence suggesting a multiplicity of variables having a direct effect or serving as causal contingencies in various situations, some scholars have concluded that no general theory is possible. Instead, they have advocated one or another of the following: (1) a focus on explanations in terms of unique combinations of causal factors in specific situations; (2) strategies of cataloging various possible influences through research on the strength of effect of each in various kinds of situations; or (3) the development of many distinct, usually discipline-linked, theories that can be integrated, if at all, only as synthetic typologies where they are set back to back. Examples of arguments postulating complexity as an inhibitor of general theory follow:

> No conceivable process of abstraction could produce out of these a statement or set of statements that could plausibly be called a "single" or "integrated" theory [Walker, 1977: 131]. . . . Eclecticism in this context

means involving whatever body of theory seems to offer the most plausible explanation of a particular sub-group of "crime" [p. 131]. . . . The quest for a general theory which will account for all instances of crime or deviance or misbehavior makes no more sense than would a search for a general theory of disease [p. 143].

Delinquency is more complex than any single theory used in its analysis [Ferdinand, 1966: 16]. . . . [Theories represented by various disciplines such as sociology, psychology, and biology] are all independent in the sense that the implications contained in one cannot be inferred from the others, it follows that we cannot construct a general, coherent theory of human behavior [p. 22].

Our analyses of individual cases have revealed that it is clearly unrealistic to try to explain all deviancy by one or another theoretical factor [Lowney et al., 1981: 399]. . . . One resolution to the problem of the limited applicability of one or another theory may be found in the concept of "sequential role model." At different stages in the development of a deviant career, the "causes" may differ [p. 401].

Each step requires explanation, and what may operate as a cause at one step in the sequence may be of negligible importance at another step [Becker, 1963: 23].

Failure

A final argument against general theory is simply that all such efforts in the past have failed. Each of the critics previously discussed has at least implicitly, and sometimes explicitly, claimed the failure of theoretical efforts; and they have sometimes offered what they regard as viable alternatives to theoretical work. And hardly any social scientist would defend the position that criminological theory is successful in doing what theory is supposed to do, no matter what the individual's particular view of the purposes of theory (see Meier, 1980). Shortcomings that have been identified are numerous, including logical defects, narrow focus, too much abstraction, not enough abstraction, inability actually to explain anything, failure to yield testable propositions, and lack of empirical support. Although recognizing that theoretical success must always be judged in relative terms, many criminologists nevertheless assume that if general theory were possible, it would have already been achieved, or at least more progress would be apparent. And from that assumption some have concluded that the effort to construct general theory is futile. Perhaps Walker (1977: 128) has expressed this point of view most succinctly:

> The search for the stone may seem a little passé nowadays; so many megaliths have risen and fallen and so varied are the types of conduct which they have purported to explain.

AN OPTIMISTIC REBUTTAL

Although all of these positions appear to have some validity, careful consideration reveals that they do not actually prevent general theory. Instead, they describe problem areas that must be addressed by criminologists. In the following pages, I will show why that is, and will discuss how these problems can be overcome.

Ambiguous Subject Matter

Although many of the specific phenomena with which criminologists deal have no inherent characteristics distinguishing them from other phenomena and are objects of interest only when socially defined in particular ways, this does not necessarily preclude general theory. Were criminologists to regard themselves simply as social scientists, interested in explaining human behavior and social organization in all its forms, but with particular focus on those acts or those institutions that have at some time or place been implicated in social or legal disapproval, discomfort over so-called ambiguity of subject matter would largely dissipate. The objective of criminological study, so conceived, would be to help construct general theories about human behavior, and the particular task of criminologists would be to make sure that theories constructed for that purpose could accommodate crime-relevant phenomena. Thus, instead of trying to explain homicide only when it is socially (or legally) disapproved, ignoring those instances in which homicide is socially mandated (wars, executions, and the like), criminologists would attempt to construct theories accounting for all human killing, and other behaviors, in such a way that the fact of being socially disapproved would be incorporated within the theory as a variable partially specifying the conditions under which homicide, or any other behavior, could be expected to occur with greater or lesser frequency.

Worry over presumed ambiguity of the subject matter stems largely from a ridiculous notion that criminology is, or can be, a separate discipline concerned with a distinct subject matter requiring special theories. It is clear that the phenomena of interest to criminologists are not inherently different from the phenomena of interest to social and behavioral scientists generally and that the behaviors criminologists study are in no essential way intrinsically novel. Once this is acknowledged, it becomes obvious that criminologists are part of a collective social scientific enterprise but with a specific task—to treat crime-relevant activities as foci for testing and expanding theories about human behavior, not because crime-relevant activities are inherently different, but because they offer interesting variations that may challenge comprehensive explanatory schemes.

But relinquishing claim to a distinct disciplinary status will not alter the fact that much of the subject matter of social science is shaped, defined, and sometimes completely created by social definitions. Social disapproaval or illegality are only two of the many aspects of human affairs that appear capricious. Yet this is no insurmountable barrier to theory. To make a fundamental point that will be repeated several times in the discussion to follow, theories in any field are composed of abstract constructs tied together by ideas that conceptually crystallize disparate-appearing empirical objects (Willer and Webster, 1970). Physicists do not find energy, mass, or force in invariant forms or with essential features; indeed, they cannot find them at all in the sense of being able to observe them directly and record their invariant traits. Nor do they build theories by observing a concrete, determinant entity such as energy in order to discover its essence. In fact, considering the enormous number of situations in which heat alone is found and the multiple forms it takes, one could easily despair of its indeterminancy. But this ambiguity is transformed into concreteness once order has been imposed by abstract categorization, and theory has developed to specify systematically the conditions and principles that unify these empirical manifestations. The point is this: The physical world appears ambiguous until underlying orderliness is revealed by conceptualization and theory. Theory does not merely reflect the obvious order of nature; it constitutes the intellectual vehicle through which order can be perceived. Similarly, the seeming ambiguity of social phenomena is not an impediment to theory;

rather, it underlines the fact that not enough progress in accomplishing the theoretical task has yet been achieved. In particular, criminologists have not learned to use abstract concepts but have bound themselves with the assumption that order must obviously inhere in the social world itself (Gibbons, 1966).

Uniqueness

Few would dispute the point that if you look closely enough you will find all social phenomena to be unique. But this is hardly profound or cause for theoretical inertia; indeed, it is true of all fields of study. No two trees are in every respect identical, nor are two criminal acts. Yet obsession with that fact may well obscure enormous similarities that are identifiable and theoretically potent. Surely the individuality of the trees does not negate the reality of the forest, nor does it prohibit a theory about why and how forests come into being or take the forms they do, nor does it prohibit theories explaining common features of the individual trees as products of forest characteristics or some other set of concepts. And uniqueness does not preclude a theory accounting for general tree characteristics while recognizing the possible effects of contingencies (such as weather fluctuations) that intervene in the normal systematic pattern to produce unique features.

In like manner, uniqueness of specific crime-related phenomena should not prevent concepts reflecting abstract characteristics around which theories can be built; nor should it prohibit a contingent theory that accommodates individual variations that may result when unsystematic situational or other variables intrude into a general process. As previously noted, theory becomes possible when one looks beyond obvious empirical features of phenomena in order to identify abstract, nonapparent similarities, which can be organized by general principles (see Willer and Webster, 1970). Cohen's (1955) well-known explanation of gang delinquency illustrates this technique. He begins with a few empirical observations suggesting that gang delinquency occurs mainly among lower-class boys who live in inner-city areas, and that such gangs apparently promote anomalous nonutilitarian behavior. In trying to understand this, he reasons that lower-class boys are ill equipped to participate successfully in the school system. Because of failure or discomfort in school, such boys develop psychological problems that become interactionally shared because of residential proximity. As a result, gangs emerge to solve collectively the common problem of status failure. Attainable positions within the gang come to substitute for the unachievable statuses represented in middle-class-dominated schools, and the values and norms of the gangs encourage denigration of the middle-class standards by which the boys were judged failures, thereby restoring self-esteem.

Taken at face value, Cohen's formulation appears to be limited and unsatisfactory. It does not explain all delinquency—only gang delinquency; it does not even fully account for variations in the forms of delinquency by different gangs; and it does not predict or account for variations among different gangs in exact norms, values, and statuses (see Jensen and Rojeck, 1980). In short, evaluated strictly in terms of empirical variables—gang, delinquency, lower-class status, males—and precise predictions about form, Cohen's explanation seems to fail because of minute differences from case to case.

But this *explanation* of lower-class gang delinquency can be transformed into a *theory of subcultures* by conceptualizing an abstract process that applies to many situations. Thus, instead of referring to lower-class boys, school failure, gangs, and delinquency, the theory refers to subordinates in a status hierarchy, inability to meet the expectations of higher statuses, subcultures, and violations of the norms of a dominant culture. The theory then specifies a process—inability to meet dominant status criteria—that, no matter what the hierarchical system, produces adjustment problems for subordinates. If the subordinates are in close proximity, these adjustment problems will be shared in interaction and a subculture will emerge that helps them overcome those problems. Such a subculture will be characterized by (1) an alternative status system that provides attainable goals for its members, (2) a value system contrary to that of the dominant culture, and (3) a set of norms that prescribes behavior denigrating norms of the dominant culture. This theory of subcultures accounts for a particular type of delinquency because gang behavior can be regarded as an empirical instance of the abstract categories with which the theory deals; that is, an abstract, general process is postulated to be operative once lower-class boys are logically shown to be subordinates thrown into close proximity. But, more than that, the theory also accounts for prison inmate organization, radical student organizations, underground nationalist movements, and numerous other phenomena that lack obvious similarity with gang delinquency but that logically are embodiments of the abstract categories of the theory.

This is not to say that Cohen's theory is empirically correct, that it qualifies as the general theory we are seeking, or that it is an exemplar of what general theory should be like. Despite its virtues, it does not explain why hierarchical systems exist in the first place; it does not account for deviant behaviors that are not subculturally manifest; it does not spell out the contingencies that might lead to varied features of subcultural groups; and it does not take account of individual characteristics that might allow some subordinates to meet higher status expectations or otherwise avoid subcultural group participation. Furthermore, although the theory generates dozens of predictions, only a handful of studies have actually tested any of these hypotheses. So it is simply not known how well the scheme holds up in empirical test or how it ought to be modified for more accuracy. The point is that Cohen's work illustrates how theories unify disparate, unique-appearing phenomena within single abstract schemes, an accomplishment that is unlikely if scholars immerse themselves too deeply in describing variations in empirical phenomena.

A Problematic World

Interactionists have performed a valuable service in alerting the social scientific community to the uncertain nature of much human interaction. At this point, few scholars would take data, of any kind, at face value, nor would they assume that criminological or other social phenomena have inherent, essential qualities that can be unequivocally confined to categories. But this does not mean that social phenomena are totally unstructured, disorderly, and intractable or that a positivist orientation is unwarranted. There are at least three good reasons to reject the extreme implications of an interactionist approach.

First, much of the research conducted within an interactionist framework can itself be interpreted as demonstrating orderliness in the processes by which reality is constructed, albeit orderliness along different dimensions than were previously recognized. For example, Sudnow's (1965) research clearly suggests patterned decision making in a public defender's office. And Douglas's (1967) study points up various factors that may *systematically* intervene to influence whether deaths are classified as suicides. The gap between recognizing actual, or potentially, orderly processes of reality construction in given situations and formulating generalizations about the conditions across situations where one or another process will prevail is not wide.

Second, remembering that theory is fundamentally an abstractive exercise, even a totally problematic world in the interactionist sense would not necessarily obstruct general theory. Consider rape, which, as discussed before, is often not clearly distinguishable from seduction. Certainly there is little point in investigating rape per se in the hopes of building a theory from empirical instances where interaction came to be classified by observers or participants as rape. It does make sense, however, to conceptualize differences between interaction sequences involving genital contact that are typically approved by a social group (however that is defined) and those not typically approved, provided allowance can be made for variation in perception about what constitutes genital contact (which can be treated as measurement error, indeterminacy, or whatever). How such abstract categories might be named by the theorist is irrelevant; the point is that one can conceptually differentiate typically disapproved physical-contact encounters wherein one of the parties asserts that force was used from those in which no such assertion is made. General theories can then be conceived that attempt to explain cross-group or individual variation in social approval of genital-contact encounters or variations in assertions of the use of force by one of the parties, or even to specify the conditions under which individuals are likely to become involved in socially disapproved genital-contact encounters that end up in assertions of the use of force. And, as usual, if such a theory spells out various contingencies that intervene in the operation of systematic processes, phenomena initially appearing ephemeral and mushy may turn out to be structured, causally interconnected, and predictable.

Finally, despite the skill of interactionists in illuminating the problematics of human behavior and reality construction, they have not proven that all is shifting sand. Granted, much rape is problematic, as are murder, suicide, theft, automobile speeding, and any other offense or behavior. But that indeterminacy resides at the fringes. Any sensible person knows that individuals sometimes use force in defying the wishes of someone else in order to achieve genital contact, financial reward, or any number of other things, and that those situations involve real coercion. Most of the time, everybody can agree that rape, robbery, or tax evasion has occurred, although for self-serving reasons some might deny it. Similarly, there is a core of unequivocal instances in which people intentionally take their own lives. And the reality of most murder cannot be negated by those instances in which responsibility for death is unclear.

The problem is not that the phenomena are all problematic; it is that methods for ascertaining what happened are flawed. This makes it difficult to test theories effectively, but it does not prevent theory building. Only if one mistakenly tries to build theory out of presumed empirical inherencies does the constructionist argument weigh heavily.

Complexity

To most criminologists, the best known and probably most discouraging barrier to general theory is the supposed fact that social phenomena are too complex, involving a multitude of causes, to permit one explanatory scheme. This belief rests on two assumptions: (1) Any theory can conceivably explain only those phenomena that are essentially alike, and (2) a single theory implies a single cause or process. And since most are convinced that criminological phenomena are exceptionally diverse or that, even if similar, they are the products of many different causes, it is concluded that separate theories are necessary for different kinds of phenomena or that there must be separate kinds of theories for any particular phenomenon. Eclecticism has, therefore, come to be regarded as a realistic and necessary pattern for social scientific work.

This pessimistic axiom, however, seriously underestimates the potentialities of theory, and its assumptions are mistaken. First, it is incorrect to assume that all phenomena to be explained by a single theory must be empirically alike. Phenomena have only to be subsumable within a similar causative process. The object of theory building is to rise above the confines of everyday categorization and causal assumptions to grasp the ways in which phenomena are abstractly connected. The first step in that process is conceptualization that captures theoretical commonality in the face of empirical dissimilarity. For example, theft, burglary, rape, homicide, and voyeurism seem quite unalike, each a product of different causal factors, when viewed with the cognitive tools provided by the cultures in which they occur. But on an abstract level all may be perceived as instances of the same act—intrusion into private domains. In most Western societies, at least, individuals are entrusted with control of the properties they use every day, their residential domains, and their lives, and with decisions as to who may observe their performance of bodily functions. Burglary, rape, and other crimes intrude into one of these private domains and are therefore theoretically alike, although not essentially alike in an empirical, culturally defined sense.

Second, all of these intrusions may be encompassed within a similar causal theory that provides explanation for intrusive as well as other behaviors. Such a theory necessarily also rests upon integration of divergent causative variables within unifying conceptual categories. For instance, broken homes, personality disorders, and peer pressures have all been implicated as relevant but desultory and fundamentally different causes, or factors, in various empirically distinct behaviors that are here regarded as conceptually similar instances of intrusion. But they may all reflect a single underlying construct that might be theoretically labeled as *interpersonal insecurity*. This generic concept varies independently of whether a child resides with both parents (Weinberg, 1964), although it might have some general association with family intactness; it subsumes many psychological variables often thought to express personality disorders; and it reflects an antecedent condition allowing peer influences to prevail. Thus what appear to be different causes may really be expressions of a common causal dimension.

Further, a general theory spelling out the causal intricacies of interpersonal insecurity and intrusive behavior as well as other causal dimensions and other abstract patterns of behavior, all of which would be included in the same domain of individual conduct, is logically conceivable. At the risk of being accused of setting forth yet another incomplete and faulty theory, I will continue with a hypothetical example to illustrate the form such a theory might take. Suppose a theorist begins with a general statement that all behavior (deviant or otherwise) involves five variables: (1) motivation (impulse, instigation, utility, desire, drive), (2) competing motivations, (3) constraint (cost, inhibition, restraint, control), (4) opportunity to commit the act, and (5) ability to perform the behavior (see Megargee and Hokanson, 1970: 1-3; Sheley, 1983). The theory then postulates that *any specific behavior* will result whenever there is X amount of opportunity to commit that behavior, the actor has Y degrees of ability to act, the strength of motivation to do it exceeds, by Z degrees, the motivation to do something else, and, by Q degrees, the strength of restraint. Borrowing from others, the theorist contends that one variable in the equation —the degree of *motivation* to do anything—is a product of (1) past differential association with social definitions favorable to doing it (Sutherland and Cressey, 1978), (2) the relationship between culturally defined goals and means (Merton, 1957), (3) various biological conditions (Mednick and Christiansen, 1977), (4) previous reinforcements for similar behavior (Akers, 1977), and (5) interpersonal insecurity. Under various conditions, these factors are postulated to contribute different amounts to motivation. For one condition, intrusive behavior, the theory suggests that interpersonal insecurity will account for 60 percent of the motivation to intrude, past association will account for 25 percent and so on. Continuing, the theorist maintains that another variable in the equation—the degree of *constraint* for any individual contemplating intrusive behavior—is a product of (1) social bonds to conforming other (Hirschi, 1969), (2) perceived chances of being sanctioned by the law (Zimring and Hawkins, 1973), (3) level of moral feelings against particular types of acts (Parsons, 1951), (4) certain biological conditions (Eysenck, 1970), and (5) a particular kind of bodily chemical imbalance (Podolsky, 1955). The theory postulates that these factors contribute variously to constraint under different conditions and that in the case of intrusive behavior, social bonds contribute 50 percent to the level of constraint, perceived chances of being sanctioned by the law, 30 percent and so on. Similarly, the processes and variables affecting the other variables in the equation—*competing motives, opportunity,* and *ability*—are spelled out.

Furthermore, the theory provides an intellectual rationale for all its internal linkages and postulates, continually attempting to answer the question of why at all steps along the way. For instance, in this hypothetical example interpersonal insecurity is theorized to be the primary determinant of motivation to intrude into the private domains of others. The theorist might maintain that this is because interpersonal insecurity causes anxiety about personal autonomy in regulating one's own privacy, making the individual feel relatively disadvantaged in the social arena, where others are perceived as having more complete control of their domains. Since feelings of disadvantage are discomforting, the individual attempts to reduce them by intruding into the privacy of others to equalize automony.

In like manner, and calling often upon other theory fragments, the scheme provides explanatory rationales for every proposed interconnection that will in the aggregate specify the conditions under which each element of the main causal statement takes various values. Moreover, the theory goes on to show how the inputs to that main causal process are themselves influenced by other causal processes. Thus the degrees of interpersonal insecurity, differential association, social bonds, and so on must themselves be explained by designation of the variables or processes influencing them to various degrees under given conditions and by provision of theoretical rationales for these effects.

The result of all this would be a pyramidlike edifice of general theory. The most abstract statement would be at the apex because it applies to all instances. Other abstract statements would be at a lower level in the pyramid because each applies only to specific parts of the more abstract statement at the top and each is expressed in conditional terms. And still less abstract, more conditional, statements will fit at a still lower level toward the base of the pyramid. In this way all supposed causal variables and processes having a systematic influence are part of one theory, linked together in a hierarchical network to feed one causal process at the top. Any degree of complexity and any number of causal factors could thereby be accommodated (see Glaser, 1980), and the explanatory process could extend as far down as anybody wanted to take it.

Failure

Although it is easy to agree that theoretical efforts in criminology have not succeeded in producing a general theory that satisfactorily explains all the phenomena within any given domain, it does not necessarily follow that the theoretical enterprise is a failure or that the task is impossible. In fact, there is room for optimism. Criminology already possesses many powerful theories, the potentials of which have not yet been realized. Their true value is unappreciated because each has been evaluated as itself constituting a general theory rather than as a segment or part of an emerging general theory. This has happened partly because most theoretical work represents some individual's effort to counter a mode of thought prevailing at the time the theory was formulated. As a result, most theories end up polemically limited, although usually conceived as all-encompassing by the author or his or her followers. And critical assessment typically involves attacks by the offended parties directed at the most vulnerable aspect of the theory— its presumed inclusive nature. Consequently, little appreciation of how a particular limited theory might contribute to a larger emanating scheme is generated. Consider two outstanding, but by no means exhaustive, examples.

Sutherland's (1942) differential association theory was formulated in reaction to popular psychological explanations, and he felt compelled to tout it as the final answer to the question of why people commit criminal acts. For the reason, it almost invited attack as a megalith, provoking polarized response. To this day some believe it to be the criminologist's "stone" (Andrews, 1980), while others regard it a total failure (Glueck, 1956). But hardly anybody has viewed it simply as an important brick in an emerging edifice of general theory (although social learning theorists see it as an attenuated form of another general process; Burgess and Akers, 1966; Jeffery, 1965). Although imprecise and ambiguous (Hagen, 1973), Sutherland's scheme does depict a general process through which *ability* and generalized *desire* to commit crimes are presumably acquired. But it totally ignores the possible influence of contending situational motivations, constraints (situational or habitual) that might block the expression of criminal desires and orientations, and opportunities to commit crime. Moreover, it takes its dynamic factor (differential association with criminal definitions) as a given, excluding any explanation as to why it varies from individual to individual (Sutherland, 1944). In view of this, the remarkable thing is not that the theory fails to explain all crime, or that it fails to explain well the ones to which it does apply. The wonder is that as a general theory it enjoys so much empirical support (Glaser, 1979). Were it properly regarded as a small part of a larger general theory, a segment that partially explains variations only in *criminal motivation*, enthusiasm for this scheme might well be widespread.

Similarly, Hirschi's social bond formulation counters an almost obsessive focus by most theories on criminal motivation to the neglect of control or constraint (Hirschi and Gottfredson, 1979; Kornhauser, 1978), but by so doing it becomes narrowly focused. Assessed as a general theory, then, it must necessarily fail because it ignores or discounts possible variations in situational or habitual impulses to deviance, opportunities for criminal behavior, and abilities to carry out criminal plans. And just as Sutherland regards differential association as a given, Hirschi begins with social bonds, neglecting to explain why some have strong bonds that others lack. Yet, in view of its narrow emphasis, the degree of empirical support it enjoys is truly astonishing (Jensen and Rojeck, 1980; Wiatrowski et al., 1981). Were it properly weighed as a contributing part in a larger general theory, a segment designed to help account only for the degree of *inhibition against expressing criminal impulses*, Hirschi's theory might well elicit a uniformly favorable reaction.

The point is that neither the differential association nor the social bond system of thought is by itself a general theory, although both are often assigned the status of failed exemplars. Rather, a general theory that accounts for criminal behavior by spelling out the interconnections among motivations, constraint, opportunities, and abilities will probably include these two formulations, or at least some of their ideas, as segments helping to explain and predict the conditional degrees of motivation in the one instance and constraint in the other. Were various extant theories integrated into a general, hierarchical, conditionally specified scheme along the lines described earlier, the theoretical enterprise of criminology would look a lot more promising than it does now.

Unfortunately, those who have tried to integrate some existing theories have stopped far short of the goal (Conger, 1976; Elliott et al., 1979; Glaser, 1979; Voss, 1969). They have confined their efforts to only a few contenders and have really done little more than identify variables or processes that may be operative. They have not merged the explanatory principles in a way that satisfies the scholarly community with answers to why questions and spells out the conditions under which one or another concept or variable will be felt or one or another outcome occur (but see Colvin and Pauly, 1983, for a more promising effort). Yet observing that a comprehensive integration has not yet been achieved should not provoke despair. Rather, the fact that some attempts are being made to integrate existing explanatory formulations into more general theories suggests a growing awareness of the need and possibility for treating current theories as parts of a whole. Acceleration of that trend may signal a breakthrough—not a rally of new ideas (Meier, 1980), but a creative recombination of old ones.

A sense of theoretical failure has also been fostered by a malfunctioning interplay between theory and research. Theory grows as initial formulations are modified in light of empirical evidence. But criminologists rarely modify their theories through research reciprocation. Like all social scientists (Freese, 1972a), they repeatedly test original statements, conclude they are wrong, and let it go at that. For instance, anomie theory is much the same today as it was when first formulated, despite decades of empirical research, and it is regarded as just one of many failed general theories. Had anomie theory been expanded, altered, conditionalized, refined, and restructured by various scholars as the results of research and logical critique were fed back into it, it would now be quite different, having a cosmopolitan texture, and producing better explanations that would be more congruent with empirical facts. And had this same process been followed for each of the various theories in the criminological repertoire at the same time that they were being merged into one general theory along the lines suggested before, judgments about the failure of general theory would probably now be muted.

The tendency to preserve theories in their original infantile state while condemning them as failures is also the result of misapplied criteria of success. If A causes B, it does so under particular conditions, including specific degrees of A and other variables such as C, D, ... Z, and it produces specific degrees of B. The ultimate job of theory is to detail those conditions, tell why the process works as it does, and portray the circumstances under which A, C, D, ... Z will assume particular values. But this full conditional specification cannot emerge full blown from the minds of individual thinkers. To achieve it, one must continuously pump research information back into the theoretical structure and elaborate the theory to accommodate that information. This means that scholars must treat universal-appearing assertions, such as "A causes B," that might be derived from infantile theories as actually only tentative, incomplete starting points. When such hypotheses are regarded as actual truth claims to be accepted or refuted whole, theories are killed before they can grow. Rigid testing of hypotheses strictly for judging the merits of a theory is appropriate only for the advanced stages of theoretical development, when mature schemes are comprehensively structured and deductively organized. Judging infant theories by adult standards is self-defeating and leads to unwarranted pessimism.

In light of all this, it cannot be said that efforts to construct general theories in criminology have failed or must necessarily fail; it is more appropriate to say that such efforts have never really been put forth. We have no idea what might be accomplished because criminologists have never seriously engaged in a collective movement to *build* general theory.

DISCIPLINARY OBSTRUCTIONS

Characteristics of the subject matter of criminology such as ambiguity, uniqueness, apparent indeterminacy, and complexity do not preclude general theory, nor does the relative weakness of the current product. They do, however, mandate careful attention to strategy. The tactics necessary for building general theory include (1) abstractive categorization and generalization; (2) integrative, hierarchical, conditional structuring of diverse causal processes; and (3) flexible reciprocation between theory and research. Yet it is precisely these strategic tactics that have been suppressed by academic subcultural and organizational norms and processes.

The first of these obstructions is the inability of the criminological community to mobilize enough scientifically oriented scholars to do the job. Theory building is a collective endeavor that requires a lot of people to add their contributions within a similar framework. But, despite ostensible commitment to science, criminology is actually so fragmented in its work philosophy that concerted efforts are difficult. Many criminologists literally have no consistent sense of what they are doing or how to do it. Scientific scholarship oriented from beginning to end toward theory is not a clear enough priority, and even those who claim to appreciate the theoretical task often misunderstand what it is. This is shown by the fact that a modern criminologist can find as much justification to seek (1) to improve the world through political activity as to explain it, (2) to vicariously comprehend human situations as to account for behavior, (3) to prevent crime as to understand it, (4) to work in criminal justice agencies or other client contexts as to engage in scientific scholarship, or (5) to construct plans for effective living, stirring visions of the future, or empirical models as to help build a general theory. Such incoherent goals could not have been expected to lead to theoretical advance (Freese, 1972a: 475).

Second, employment of the necessary tactics for building general theory has been impeded by a collective adversarial approach to theoretical work. It seems that the social scientific community is more united in trying to prove the impossibility of general theory than it is in trying to construct one. New ideas or attempts to advance the theoretical enterprise are typically greeted with a barrage of attacks designed to refute those ideas rather than evaluate and use them. Innovators feel compelled to defend their offerings as if they were the whole truth, resisting modifications; and the collectivity refuses to rest until it has convinced itself of the utter worthlessness of a given theoretical effort. Thus the academic community polarizes itself into opposing camps, with critics bent on making would-be theorists admit they are wrong (as well as naive for ever having thought they might make a contribution to theory), while innovators and their defenders feel forced to prove they are right. The result is little cooperative movement toward achieving a common goal and, in addition, thinkers are made reluctant to introduce bold, clear statements for fear of being mauled. And in the service of adversarial norms, the social scientific community has placed inordinate emphasis on destructive criticism that inhibits integrative theoretical efforts and fruitful theory-research reciprocation. While skepticism and demanding appraisal are valuable hallmarks of careful work, it is easy to forget that demolition is easier than construction or that restorative surgery is more admirable than meat-ax assaults.

Third, scholarly training has failed to convey the crucial difference between empirical variables and theoretical constructs, thereby hampering abstract formulation and research-theory reciprocation. Inability to understand and act on this fundamental duality has caused much grief. Among other things, it allows some to think they can measure aspects of empirical reality without theoretical guidance; that is, that important features inhere in phenomena themselves. And it leads others into despair because empirical observations per se refuse to yield to theoretical expression. Formulating theoretical ideas requires escape from the yoke of empirical minutiae to grasp abstract generalities. But empirical constraints must later be reimposed so that hypotheses drawn from theory can be tested. This two-way street mandates imagination on one hand and empirical discipline on the other. Unfortunately, students are sometimes persuaded that imagination is enough, although this is a rare fault. More often they are misled into believing that empirical discipline will suffice, particularly as this is embodied in routinized methodological procedures. Learning standard methods for data collection and analysis often diverts students from the ultimate goal, encouraging the belief that data contain within themselves knowledge that can be ferreted out mechanically (Coser, 1975). Tools in the hands of a skilled carpenter with a plan can lead to wonderful things, but their use without a plan will rarely produce anything worthwhile. And, of course, tools in the hands of those with neither skills nor plans can be positively dangerous.

Fourth, the criminological community has rendered theoretical progress difficult by promoting status criteria that emphasize individualized achievement rather than collective benefit. Social scientists are taught to be loners, self-possessed and defensive. Theories are assumed to belong to individuals and are not to be tampered with except by the inventors. This means that they cannot easily be adjusted to empirical results or merged into a larger scheme. But it is totally unrealistic to imagine that any one person can invent an adequate general theory. Such a theory must grow through the cooperative efforts of many scholars, as they add their small contributions. Criminology will be on the right track when its practitioners stop talking about so-and-so's theory and begin to speak of the theory of socially disapproved behavior, the theory of law (or social disapproval), or the theory of managerial organization (as it bears on management of socially disapproved behavior), signifying by these designations integrated products with many subparts. Then theory will rightfully be regarded as every scholar's responsibility (Freese, 1972a).

Finally, criminologists have handicapped theoretical work by tolerating confusing, tautological, amphibolic writing. Theories must contain clear, unequivocal ideas, propositions, and implications, so that they can be understood and manipulated, and made to yield genuine predictions for empirical test. Otherwise there can be no meaningful feedback and no progress. There is no gain when journal space, time, and resources are expended in arguments about what was said, what was meant by what was said, or whether a given test is relevant to a theory under consideration (see, for example, Kitsuse, 1975; Schur, 1975; also see discussions by Hagen, 1973; Tittle, 1975). Since communication is never completely successful, even under the best of conditions, it is mandatory that any scholarly endeavor strive for clarity, particularly in its theoretical work. But the criminological community has been so tolerant of meaningless language that many empty, disappointing schemes have provoked serious attention because it took so long to figure out what they were saying.

CONCLUSION

Although general theory is the preeminent goal of scientific criminology, not all agree that it is possible or desirable. Examination of aspects of criminological phenomena that have been alleged to prevent general theory suggests that critics are mistaken. Cultural and organizational features of the community of scholars have, however, thwarted the theoretical enterprise, and will continue to do so unless corrected. Nevertheless, there are hopeful signs that the theoretical enterprise is healthier than many realize.

REFERENCES

AKERS, R. L. (1977) Deviant Behavior: A Social Learning Approach. Belmont, CA: Wadsworth.
ANDREWS, D. A. (1980) "Some experimental investigations of the principles of differential association through deliberate manipulations of the structure of service systems." American Sociological Review 45 (June): 448-462.
BARNES, H. E. and N. K. TEETERS (1959) New Horizons in Criminology. Englewood Cliffs, NJ: Prentice-Hall.
BECKER, H. S. (1963) Outsiders: Studies in the Sociology of Deviance. New York: Free Press.
BRAITHWAITE, R. B . (1960) Scientific Explanation. New York: Harper & Row.
BURGESS, R. L. and R. A. AKERS (1966) "A differential association reinforcement theory of criminal behavior." Social Problems 14 (Fall): 128-147.
COHEN, A. K. (1962) "Multiple factor approaches," pp. 77-80 in M. E. Wolfgang et al. (eds.) The Sociology of Crime and Delinquency. New York: John Wiley.
——— (1955) Delinquent Boys: The Culture of the Gang. New York: Free Press.
COLVIN, M. and J. PAULY (1983) "A critique of criminology: toward an integrated structural-Marxist theory of delinquency production." American Journal of Sociology 89 (November): 513-551.
CONGER, R. D. (1976) "Social control and social learning models of delinquent behavior: a synthesis." Criminology 14 (May): 17-40.
COSER, L. A. (1975) "Presidential address: two methods in search of a substance." American Sociological Review 40 (December): 691-700.
DOUGLAS, J. D. (1967) The Social Meanings of Suicide. Princeton, NJ: Princeton Univ. Press.
ELLIOTT, D. S., S. S. AGETON, and R. J. CANTER (1979) "An integrated theoretical perspective on delinquent behavior." Journal of Research in Crime and Delinquency 16 (January): 3-27.
ERIKSON, K. T. (1966) Wayward Puritans. New York: John Wiley.
EYSENCK, H. J. (1970) Crime and Personality. London: Granada.
FERDINAND, T. N. (1966) Typologies of Delinquency: A Critical Analysis. New York: Random House.
FREESE, L. (1972a) "Cumulative sociological knowledge." American Sociological Review 37 (August): 472-482.
——— (1972b) "Cumulative sociological knowledge: an addendum." American Sociological Review 37 (August): 486-487.
FRIEDMAN, L. M. (1977) Law and Society: An Introduction. Englewood Cliffs, NJ: Prentice-Hall.
GARFINKEL, H. (1967) Studies in Ethnomethodology. Englewood Cliffs, NJ: Prentice-Hall.
GIBBONS, D. C. (1981) Delinquent Behavior. Englewood Cliffs, NJ: Prentice-Hall.
——— (1966) "Problems of causal analysis in criminology: a case illustration." Journal of Research in Crime and Delinquency 3 (January): 47-52.
GLASER, D. (1980) "The interplay of theory, issues, policy, and data," pp. 123-142 in M. W. Klein and K. S. Teilman (eds.) Handbook of Criminal Justice Evaluation. Beverly Hills, CA: Sage.

———(1979) "A review of crime-causation theory and its application," pp. 203-237 in N. Morris and N. Tonry (eds.) Crime and Justice: An Annual Review of Research. Chicago: University of Chicago Press.
GLUECK, S. (1956) "Theory and fact in criminology." British Journal of Delinquency 7 (October): 92-109.
GOODE, E. (1978) Deviant Behavior: An Interactionist Approach. Englewood Cliffs, NJ: Prentice-Hall.
HAGEN, J. L. (1973) "Conceptual deficiencies of an interactionist perspective in deviance." Criminology 11 (November): 383-404.
HARTJEN, C. A. (1981) "Crime as commonsense theory." Criminology 18 (February): 435-452.
HIGGINS, P. C. and R. R. BUTLER (1982) Understanding Deviance. New York: McGraw-Hill.
HIRSCHI, T. (1980) "Postscript," pp. 293-302 in W. R. Gove (ed.) The Labelling of Deviance. Beverly Hills, CA: Sage.
———(1969) Causes of Delinquency. Berkeley: University of California Press.
———and M. GOTTFREDSON (1979) "Introduction: the Sutherland tradition in criminology," pp. 7-19 in T. Hirschi and M. Gottfredson (eds.) Understanding Crime: Current Theory and Research. Beverly Hills, CA: Sage.
HIRSCHI, T. and H. C. SELVIN (1967) Delinquency Research: An Appraisal of Analytic Methods. New York: Free Press.
JACOBS, J. (1972) Getting By: Illustrations of Marginal Living. Boston: Little, Brown.
JEFFREY, C. R. (1965) "Criminal behavior and learning theory." Journal of Criminal Law, Criminology and Police Science 56, 3: 294-300.
———(1956) "The structure of American criminological thinking." Journal of Criminal Law, Criminology and Police Science 46 (January/February): 658-672.
JENSEN, G. F. and D. G. ROJEK (1980) Delinquency: A Sociological View. Lexington, MA: D.C. Heath.
KITSUSE, J. I. (1975) "The 'new conception of deviance' and its critics," pp. 273-284 in W. R. Gove (ed.) The Labelling of Deviance. New York: John Wiley.
KORNHAUSER, R. R. (1978) Social Sources of Delinquency. Chicago: University of Chicago Press.
LISKA, A. E. (1981) Perspectives on Deviance. Englewood Cliffs, NJ: Prentice-Hall.
LOWNEY, J., R. W. WINSLOW, and V. WINSLOW (1981) Deviant Reality: Alternative World Views. Boston: Allyn & Bacon.
MACIVER, R. (1962) "Social causation," pp. 73-76 in M. E. Wolfgang et al. (eds.) The Sociology of Crime and Delinquency. New York: John Wiley.
McNALL, S. G. (1983) "Variations on a theme: social theory." Sociological Quarterly 24 (Autumn): 471-487.
MacNAUGHTON-SMITH, P. (1968) "The second code: toward (or away from) an empirical theory of crime and delinquency." Journal of Research in Crime and Delinquency 5 (July): 189-197.
MATZA, D. (1964) Delinquency and Drift. New York: John Wiley.
MEDNICK, S. and K. CHRISTIANSEN [eds.] (1977) Biosocial Bases of Criminal Behavior. New York: Gardner.
MEGARGEE, E. I. and J. E. HOKANSON [eds.] (1970) The Dynamics of Aggression. New York: Harper & Row.
MEIER, R. F. (1980) "The arrested development of criminological theory." Contemporary Sociology 9 (May): 374-376.

MERTON, R. K. (1957) "Social structure and anomie," pp. 131-194 in R. K. Merton (ed.) Social Theory and Social Structure. New York: Free Press.
PARSONS, T. (1951) The Social System. New York: Macmillan.
PFUHL, E. H., Jr. (1980) The Deviance Process. New York: Van Nostrand.
PHILLIPSON, M. (1974) Understanding Crime and Delinquency: A Sociological Interpretation. Chicago: Aldine.
PODOLSKY, E. (1955) "The chemical brew of criminal behavior." Journal of Criminal Law, Criminology and Police Science 45 (March): 675-678.
POLSKY, N, (1967) Hustlers, Beats, and Others. Chicago: Aldine.
QUINNEY, R. (1974) "A critical theory of criminal law," pp. 1-26 in R. Quinney (ed.) Criminal Justice in America: A Critical Understanding. Boston: Little, Brown.
ROEBUCK, J. B. (1963) "A criticism of Gibbons and Garrity's criminal typology." Journal of Criminal Law, Criminology and Police Science 54 (December): 476-478.
SCHUR, E. M. (1979) Interpreting Deviance: A Sociological Introduction. New York: Harper & Row.
——— (1975) "Comments," pp. 285-294 in W. R. Gove (ed.) The Labelling of Deviance. New York: John Wiley.
——— (1968) Law and Society: A Sociological View. New York: Random House.
SHELEY, J. F. (1983) "Critical elements of criminal behavior explanations." Sociological Quarterly 24 (Autumn): 509-525.
SUDNOW, D. (1965) "Normal crimes: sociological features of the penal code in a public defender office." Social Problems 12 (Winter): 255-276.
SUTHERLAND, E. H. (1944) "Critique of the theory," pp. 30-41 in A. Cohen et al. (eds.) The Sutherland papers. Bloomington: Indiana University Press.
——— (1942) "Development of the theory," pp. 13-29 in A. Cohen et al. (eds.) The Sutherland papers. Bloomington: Indiana University Press.
——— and D. R. CRESSEY (1978) Criminology. New York: J. B. Lippincott.
TITTLE, C. R. (1975) "Labelling and crime: an empirical evaluation," pp. 157-179 in W. R. Gove (ed.) The Labelling of Deviance. New York: John Wiley.
TURK, A. T. (1964) "Prospects for theories of criminal behavior." Journal of Criminal Law, Criminology and Police Science 55 (December): 454-461.
VOSS, H. L. (1969) "Differential association and containment theory: a theoretical convergence." Social Forces 47 (June): 381-391.
WALKER, N. (1977) Behavior and Misbehavior: Explanations and Non-Explanations. New York: Basic Books.
WEINBERG, S. K. (1964) "Juvenile delinquency in Ghana: a comparative analysis of delinquents and non-delinquents." Journal of Criminal Law, Criminology and Police Science 55 (December): 471-481.
WELLFORD, C. (1975) "Labelling theory and criminology." Social Problems 22 (February): 332-345.
WIATROWSKI, M. D., D. B. GRISWOLD, and M. K. ROBERTS (1981) "Social control theory and delinquency." American Sociological Review 46 (October): 525-541.
WILLER, D. and WEBSTER, Jr. (1970) "Theoretical concepts and observables." American Sociological Review 35 (August): 748-757.
WILSON, T. P. (1970) "Conceptions of interaction and forms of sociological explanation." American Sociological Review 35 (August): 697-710.
ZIMRING, F. E. and G. J. HAWKINS (1973) Deterrence: The Legal Threat in Crime Control. Chicago: University of Chicago Press.

6

The Assumption that Theories Can Be Combined with Increased Explanatory Power:
Theoretical Integrations

DELBERT S. ELLIOTT

There is an obvious historical continuity in crime and delinquency theory, with each generation attempting to build upon the views of earlier generations by challenging certain ideas and by extending or modifying others. This theory development process has typically resulted in a particular theoretical perspective dominating the intellectual scene for a time, only to be challenged successfully and replaced by some alternative view until some new modification or extension is proposed that again brings this perspective into prominence. Old theories never die, they just fade away, only to reemerge in slightly modified form at more opportune times.

Typically, this theory development process has been a competitive one, with different theoretical perspectives competing with one another for ideological acceptance and empirical verification. However, theory development over the past half decade has emphasized a different process, focusing more heavily upon a synthesis of theoretical perspectives, a combining of elements of historically divergent theories into more inclusive and powerful theoretical models. This is not to say that some degree of synthesis was not involved in earlier periods of theoretical development or that some comparison of traditional theoretical perspectives is not involved in current integration efforts.[1] However, the

---

Author's Note: I would like to acknowledge the helpful comments and suggestions of David Huizinga on an earlier draft of this chapter.

major emphasis has shifted in recent years from an interest in crucial tests of competing hypotheses and the question of which perspective is "right" to an interest in increasing the overall explanatory power of our theoretical models and the question of how propositions from divergent theoretical traditions can be combined into a coherent and more inclusive explanation for crime and delinquency. My objectives in this chapter are to describe briefly the assumptions and objectives underlying this approach, to review the various approaches to theory integration, to evaluate the success of integrated models to date, and to speculate on the future direction of integration efforts.

THE ASSUMPTIONS AND OBJECTIVES OF INTEGRATION

The interest in integrating theoretical perspectives is a direct response to the growing dissatisfaction with the empirical adequacy of classical theories of crime and delinquency and with respect to the competitive hypothesis approach to theory building and verification. Much of earlier verification work involved single-variable tests of null hypotheses and bivariate measures of association. The introduction and use of multivariate statistical methods in crime and delinquency research led to the discovery that different constructs or variables within a given theoretical perspective were often highly redundant and that the overall explanatory power of theoretical models derived from traditional theories was relatively weak. In particular, the "explained variance" interpretation of multiple regression and causal modeling techniques provided a new yardstick for evaluating the combined predictive power of a set of variables derived from a particular theory. In terms of this measure of predictive power, multivariate tests of the pure forms of our traditional theories with cross-sectional data indicate that these explanatory schemes typically account for only 10 percent to 20 pecent of the variance in illegal behavior and on rare occasions as much as 30 percent to 40 percent (Aultman, 1979; Wiatrowski et al., 1981; Linden, 1978; Paternoster and Anderson, 1981; Krohn and Massey, 1980; Jensen and Eve, 1976; Segrave and Hastad, 1983; Meade and Marsden, 1981; Matsueda, 1982; Cernkovich, 1978). Genuine predictive tests involving longitudinal data yield substantially lower levels of explained variance (Thomas and Hyman, 1978; Conly, 1979; Paternoster and Anderson, 1981; Elliott and Voss, 1974). For example, Conly (1979) reports simultaneous gamma coefficients of .20 to .30 between measures of

Hirschi's (1969) four dimensions of the social bond and self-reported delinquency for a national sample of adolescent males. These values are very similar to those reported by others in cross-sectional studies (Hirschi, 1969; Jensen, 1972; Eve, 1978; Linden, 1978; Thomas and Hyman, 1978; Segrave and Hastad, 1983; Meade and Marsden, 1981; Gottfredson, 1982; Krohn and Massey, 1980; Johnson, 1979). Yet when prior delinquency was controlled in the analysis and subsequent delinquency was the criterion, the partial gamma coefficients ranged from .03 to .10 and none were statistically significant. Elliott and Voss (1974) and Elliott et al. (1985) report a similar loss in predictive power using strain variables. The decline in explained variance when the correct temporal order is imposed and prior delinquency is controlled appears least for traditional social learning or differential association variables, but even here the generalization holds (Elliott and Voss, 1974; Elliott et al., 1985).[2] Stated simply, the level of explained variance attributable to separate theories is embarrassingly low, and, if sociological explanations for crime and delinquency are to have any significant impact upon future planning and policy, they must be able to demonstrate greater predictive power.

Blalock (1984) notes that sociological theory in general has fallen into disrepute, and the same may be said for criminological theory. One of the primary reasons for this declining interest in theory is that our traditional explanations for crime are overly simple and, as such, are inadequate to model the actual processes leading to crime or to account for any major portion of the observed variation in criminal behavior. Each theory accounts for some small amount of variance, just enough to avoid its rejection and total elimination, but not enough to generate any confidence in its utility for prevention or treatment programming or public policy.

Researchers have also been dissatisfied with the competitive hypothesis approach to theory building and verification. The strategy of pitting one theory against another in a series of crucial tests in which clearly different outcomes were predicted proved to have limited utility for theory verification and modification. Classical theories of crime and delinquency rarely provided competing hypotheses that were testable, theories with very different assumptions and causal propositions frequently predicted similar outcomes, and in those instances where such tests were possible the results were seldom definitive. Further, there are logical problems involved in posing two hypotheses as simple alternatives to one another and presuming that the acceptance of one implies the rejection of the other (Blalock, 1984: 40). Researchers came to recognize that these crucial tests rarely provided evidence that justified a conclusion that one hypothesis was correct and the other incorrect. At best these tests provided evidence that one hypothesis was more plausible or more powerful than the other (for example, see Jensen, 1972; Eve, 1978; Segrave and Hasted, 1983; Hepburn, 1976; Thomas and Hyman, 1978; Cernkovich, 1978; Meade and Marsden, 1981; Gottfredson, 1982; Johnstone, 1981; Wiatrowski et al., 1981). The observation that both hypotheses might be correct and might account for independent portions of the variance in crime was typically overlooked by researchers focusing upon crucial tests, because the objective was to prove one theory right and the other wrong (for some examples, see Elliott et al., 1985). Further, crucial tests often exaggerate the importance of small differences by focusing upon statistical significance rather than the magnitude of the association or the level of explained variance (Blalock, 1984). Finally, it is also the case that crucial tests of competing hypotheses nearly always involved a single indicator of a single theoretical variable, and the results of these tests have provided little evidence for the overall predictive power of the combined set of propositions specified by the theories involved (see Hirschi, 1969). In sum, the competitive hypothesis approach has often served to inhibit theory development rather than to enhance it.

At the heart of the integration approach is an assumption that the causes of crime and delinquency are multiple. The causal processes leading to criminal behavior are viewed as more varied and complex than posed by traditional explanations. There are at least two senses in which integrationists assume that the causes of crime are multiple. Several of those proposing integrated models have suggested that there may be a link between a given theory and a particular type of delinquency or crime. They have at least implied that the integration of theories will increase overall explanatory power by capturing a wider range of illegal activity (Fagan et al., 1983; Elliott et al., 1979; Meade and Marsden, 1981; Figueira-McDonough et al., 1981; Aultman, 1979). For example, several researchers have noted that control theory provides a more satisfactory explanation of minor offenses than serious ones, whereas strain and learning theories provide a more powerful explanation for serious than for nonserious offenses (Meade and Marsden, 1981; Johnstone, 1981; Elliott et al., 1979; Aultman, 1979; Burkett and White, 1974; Kelley and Pink, 1973). If this were the case, it could be said that an integration of these social psychological theories might account for a larger portion of the total variance in criminal behavior than either alone. However, to the extent that these separate theories offer explanations for different types of illegal acts, the increase in explanatory power is achieved by broadening the class of behavior identified as criminal acts; that is, by increasing the inclusiveness of the criterion.

While this is one sense in which it may be said that there are multiple causes of crime, this is not the primary sense in which this claim is made (Elliott et al., 1979, 1985). Rather, the claim is that there are multiple variables involved in the etiology of the same type of behavior; that there may be more than one set of causal conditions sufficient for explaining involvement in a given behavior; and that there may be more than one temporal ordering for a given set of predictors. In a developmental sense, it is a claim that there may be more than one causal path or sequence that leads to the same behavioral outcome. Such a claim does not preclude the possibility of some common "necessary" cause(s) in the explanation of crime, but neither does it require a common causal variable.

If we take the multiple-cause assumption seriously, it demands both more complex theoretical statements and new approaches to theory verification, issues that will be considered in more detail later. The significance of this assumption at this point is that the potential gain in explanatory power resulting from an integration of diverse theoretical perspectives is not tied specifically to the inclusiveness of the definition of crime.

The significance of the multiple-cause assumption must also be viewed in the light of the logical structure of classical theories of crime. A careful examination of sociological theories of crime reveals that these explanations involve relatively few theoretical variables. In fact, they might be more appropriately described as classical hypotheses than as theories, given that they typically involve a single explanatory variable. For example, social control theory postulates that variation in crime is a result of variation in restraints; for strain theory it is variation in perceived aspiration-opportunity disjunctions; for culture-conflict theory it is variation in cultural norms; for differential association it is variation in definitions favorable or unfavorable to violations of the law; for anomie theory it is variation in one's location in the social structure.

Empirical tests of these theories often involve multiple indicators of the theoretical variable, but rarely does a test of a "pure" model involve more than a single independent variable and a single theoretical proposition. For example, multivariate tests of control theory typically involve one or more separate measures of Hirschi's (1969) four dimensions of the social bond and tests of differential association often involve separate measures of Sutherland's (1955) four modes of association. But in each case these measures are indicators of a single conceptual variable and involve a single theoretical proposition, for instance, they reflect variation in restraints or degrees of association. There is no set of propositions derivable from these theories that describes the causal relationships between the "elements of the bond" or the "modes of association." It is this fact that accounts in part for the redundancy typically found in these theory tests (Aultman, 1979; Wiatrowski et al., 1981; Linden, 1978; Krohn and Massey, 1980; Meade and Marsden, 1981; Thomas and Hyman, 1978; Voss, 1964; Short, 1957; Glaser, 1960).

The multiple-cause assumption requires either the identification of new causal variables or the utilization of variables from divergent theoretical perspectives in an effort to generate more complex theories of crime. From a practical standpoint, the consideration of variables that appear to have some established predictive validity is a logical first step. In this sense, the multiplicity of criminological theories constitutes a resource for the theory development task, providing a valuable set of potential explanatory variables.

There is little question that the major objective in attempts to integrate divergent theoretical perspectives was to increase the explanatory power of our theories (Eve, 1978; Cernkovich, 1978; Conger, 1976, 1978, 1980; Akers, 1977; Minor, 1977; Elliott et al., 1979; Johnson, 1979; Aultman and Welford, 1979; Hawkins and Weis, 1980; Meade and Marsden, 1981; Segrave and Hastad, 1983; Fagan et al., 1983; Johnstone, 1978; Elliott et al., 1985). While the explanatory power of individual theories was relatively low, there was the logical possibility that these theories were accounting for different parts of the variation in criminal behavior. In this event, if the major variables could be integrated at the theoretical level into a coherent set of assumptions and interrelated propositions, the resulting explanatory scheme held some promise for an increased level of explanatory power. The utility of an integrated model is thus to be judged by whether or not there is an increase in the level of explained variance as compared to that achieved by the separate theories that contribute to it.

It is important to note that the interest in increasing explanatory power is not limited solely to criminal behavior, but includes other endogenous variables (if specified in the model). A theoretical model that demonstrates only a marginal increase in explained variance in criminal behavior over the pure theoretical models it incorporates would be evaluated positively if it extended the explanation of criminal behavior by specifying a series of intervening variables and if empirical tests demonstrated that the theory accounted for a significant portion of the variance in these variables. The increased explanatory power criterion is thus used to evaluate the model as a whole; that is, it applies to all endogenous and outcome variables in the model, not solely to the final outcome variable. The demonstration of causal sequences or conditional relationships is extremely important because it is the intervening variables in the explanatory model that are most frequently the targeted objectives for change in treatment and prevention programs. However, relatively few complex models of delinquency or crime have been tested to date and nearly all of those proposing or testing an integrated model have stated that their objective was to increase the explained variance in delinquency or crime. We are thus forced to focus most heavily upon an increased explanatory power for criminal behavior in evaluating the adequacy of current integration efforts. However, as integrated theoretical perspectives become more complex, a more general evaluation of their explanatory power will be possible.

APPROACHES TO INTEGRATION

A number of generalizations can be made about the current approaches to theory integration. First, recent attempts to integrate different theoretical perspectives have typically involved a single level of explanation (Cohen and Short, 1976; Short, 1979). Most current statements proposing an integrated perspective involve a synthesis of social psychological theories and an individual level of explanation; that is, an explanation for variation in individual rates of criminal behavior (Conger, 1976, 1978, 1980; Hawkins and Weis, 1980; Elliott et al., 1979; Cernkovich, 1978; Johnson, 1979; Minor, 1977; Aultman and Welford, 1979; Segrave and Hastad, 1983; Meade and Marsden, 1981; La Grange and White, 1983; Elliott and Voss, 1974; Braukmann et al., 1980; Elliott et al., 1985). There have been a few recent attempts to integrate theories across levels of explanation (for example, see Mednick et al., 1982; Johnstone, 1978, 1983; Merton and Bursik, 1983; Elliott et al., 1983;

Craven, 1984), but, in general, theories involving macrosociological or microsociological explanations for crime have not been included explicitly in integration efforts. While some theoretical perspectives (such as social control theory) offer explanations at more than one level, it is primarily the individual-level explanations that have been utilized in integration efforts. Short (1979) notes thtat the penultimate integration will bring together all three levels of explanation, but it is clear that integration efforts to date are much more modest and remain primarily at the individual level of explanation.

Second, while many have proposed some combination of variables (or specific measures of variables) from divergent theoretical perspectives in a single path diagram or causal model, the level of theoretical integration achieved varies substantially. An integrated theory is one that combines variables from divergent theoretical perspectives based upon some logical reconciliation of different basic assumptions. It also provides some explanation of how the new combined predictors are related to one another as well as to criminal behavior in a coherent interrelated set of propositional statements. Few attempts at integration have attended fully to these theoretical issues, some have addressed them partially, and the remainder have focused almost exclusively on observed empirical relationships. In this regard it would be well to distinguish between integrated theoretical models and "mixed" causal models. Mixed models are those in which there is little or no attempt to reconcile differences in the basic assumptions or to explain the expected relationships between the combined set of independent variables. Mixed models rely heavily upon known empirical relationships between specific predictor measures and measures of criminal behavior, with relatively little regard for the conceptualization of variables or the conceptual validity of measures. They are in essence multiple-factor models. They have a significant role to play in the theory development process, but they should not be confused with theoretical statements, which involve at least some degree of logical and conceptual integration. While it is possible to obtain some estimate of the explained variance attributable to mixed models, the interpretation of this "explained variance" is problematic.

It is interesting to note that the two social psychological theories most frequently combined are social learning or differential association theory and social control theory (Conger, 1976, 1978, 1980; Simons et al., 1980; Poole and Regoli, 1979; Johnstone, 1981; Johnson, 1979;

Akers and Cochran, 1983; Elliott et al., 1985; Patterson and Dishion, forthcoming; Meade and Marsden, 1981; La Grange and White, 1983; Gottfredson, 1982; Hawkins and Weis, 1980; Braukmann et al., 1980). Yet these theories have very different historical roots and conflicting assumptions. It is not possible to integrate these two perspectives into a single coherent theory without reconciling these assumptions (Kornhauser, 1978; Elliott et al., 1985): The motivation for crime is either a constant (control theory) or it is a variable (social learning theory).

If one deals with this problem by rejecting control theory's natural motivation assumption, which is the resolution adopted by most of those attempting this integration (Elliott et al., 1979, 1985; Conger, 1980; Braukmann et al., 1980; La Grange and White, 1983), then the unique contribution of control theory to the integration must be made explicit. Relatively few of those combining variables central to these two theories have been fully explicit about these underlying theoretical issues.

There have also been a number of attempts to integrate social control and strain theories at the individual level of explanation (Aultman and Welford, 1979; Segrave and Hastad, 1983; Cernkovich, 1978) and a number of attempts to integrate social learning/differential association, social control and strain (Simons et al., 1980; Johnstone, 1981; Meade and Marsden, 1981; Johnson, 1979; Elliott et al., 1979, 1985; Figueira-McDonough et al., 1981). Still other integrations involve labeling theory (Aultman and Welford, 1979; Simons et al., 1980), social disorganization theory (Johnstone, 1978, 1981, 1983), deterrence theory (Minor, 1977), and culture conflict theory (Eve, 1978). Kornhauser (1978) suggests that there may be less theoretical difficulty in integrating strain and social control theories because they have a common historical tradition. Still, the synthesis of any two or more theoretical perspectives requires a careful review of basic assumptions, definitions, and propositions and, in most cases, requires some modification to one or more of these theoretical elements. The integrated models proposed to date vary greatly in the extent to which they have dealth explicitly with the logical and conceptual dimensions of the integration. In many respects, the approach has been more empirical than theoretical.

Third, there is considerable variation in the structural form of the integrations proposed. Hirschi (1979) describes three structural arrangements or strategies used to integrate theories: Theories may be placed end to end, side by side, or up and down (that is, they can be integrated by raising the level of abstraction). While not capturing all of the structural arrangements employed in recent integration efforts, this typology is still useful in describing the various structural approaches employed. The position taken here is that each is a reasonable and valid strategy for arranging variables (or theories) in an integrated model.

Hirschi's position is that each of these structural forms poses critical problems for integrations and, in light of these problems, he predicts the failure of integration efforts. While agreeing with Hirschi that the arrangement of the variables in the integration has implications for the explanatory power of the integrated theory relative to the separate theories being combined, I do not agree with his analysis of the problems associated with these structural forms. In light of his criticism of theoretical integrations, his argument will be reviewed in some detail as it relates to the current use of these strategies in integration efforts.

Hirschi's criticisms of the side-by-side form of integration are (1) that it avoids the need to reconcile the incompatibilities between theories and (2) that the gain in explanatory power is the result of using a more inclusive definition of criminal behavior, capitalizing upon the differential power of the theories to explain specific types of criminal acts. It is true that mixed causal models typically take the side-by-side form (see Simons et al., 1980; Ginsberg and Greenley, 1978; Akers and Cochran, 1983). It is also the case that models that have attempted a theoretical integration rarely assume a simple side-by-side form (Johnson, 1979; Elliott et al., 1979, 1985; Hawkins and Weis, 1980; Johnstone, 1981; Aultman and Welford, 1979; Patterson and Dishion, forthcoming; La Grange and White, 1983). There is thus some basis for Hirschi's criticism. However, there is nothing inherent in this form or approach to integration that precludes the reconciliation of different assumptions and a claim that the effects of variables (or theories) are primarily independent. Further, the claim that any increase in explained variance is necessarily the result of using a more inclusive definition of the criterion measure is logically unwarranted and contradicted by the empirical evidence (Meade and Marsden, 1981; Poole and Regoli, 1979; Elliott et al., 1985; Akers and Cochran, 1983). Hirschi's position appears to reflect the rather limited perspective on multiple causation discussed earlier.

The criticism of end-to-end integration is that the predictor variables of the last theory in the sequence absorb all of the predictive power of those theories located earlier in the sequence and that the integrationist "must argue in effect that all theories but the last one in the sequence are *wrong*" (Hirschi, 1979: 35; emphasis added). This argument reveals a commitment to the competing hypothesis logic and approach to theory development. The argument that a variable (or a theory) in a causal chain is not a cause unless it is the most proximate cause is very curious. It is true that in a pure sequential model, the more distal predictors in the causal sequence add nothing to the predictive power of the most proximate predictor and, in that sense, are "unnecessary" to the prediction. But one could also make the case that for prevention and treatment strategies it may be the more distal causes that are of more practical importance, particularly if the most proximate causes involve characteristics, conditions, or situations that are difficult to influence in a planned intervention.

In any case, it is one thing to claim that the initial variable in a sequential model is unnecessary to the prediction of an outcome given the presence of other more proximate causal variables, and quite another to claim that the initial variable has no causal influence on the outcome and that its causal claim can be rejected. Rosenberg (1968) specifically notes that a sequential ordering does not negate any causal argument about the effect of the initial variable in the causal chain. In most cases, the intervening variables are considered to specify the process through which the initial variable's causal influence is exerted on the final outcome variable. Hirschi's argument would reduce all developmental and sequential theories to a single hypothesis involving the final variable in the causal chain. Even if a variable makes no independent contribution to the prediction, it still contributes to our understanding or explanation of the dependent variable if it can be shown to have a substantial indirect effect. Finally, if the evidence were to support a true sequential ordering and the most proximate variable (theory) were to account for all of the explained variance, we should be willing and prepared to argue this point. Hirschi's concern that this form of integration might discount or diminish the significance of some particular theoretical perspective is both uncharacteristic of his general approach to evaluating theory (Hirshci and Selvin, 1967; Hirschi, 1969; Hirschi and Gottfredson, 1980) and a questionable basis for rejecting this form of integration.

Most of the recent attempts to integrate theories have involved some sequential structuring of variables, but it would be a serious misrepresentation to describe these integration efforts as arranging *theories* end to end. No simple end-to-end integrated theories have been proposed. Those involving some temporal ordering of variables from different historical perspectives typically postulate both direct and indirect effects for the more distal variables (Hawkins and Weis, 1980; Johnson, 1979; Johnstone, 1981; Segrave and Hastad, 1983; Gottfredson, 1982; La

Grange and White, 1983; Aultman and Welford, 1979). The integrated strain, social control, social learning model developed by Elliott et al. (1979, 1985) probably comes closest to being a simple end-to-end model, postulating that the effects of weak social controls and strain are mediated by delinquent peer group reinforcements. However, the theoretical argument is that the relationship between delinquent reinforcements and delinquent behavior is a conditional one, dependent upon the earlier level of bonding to conventional values and groups; that is, delinquency is the result of the combination of weak restraints and reinforcements for delinquency, with reinforcements being the most proximate cause of delinquency. This model is not a simple end-to-end model, because an interaction effect between theories is postulated. Theoretically, the delinquent reinforcement variable by itself does not capture all of the model's explained variance because this relationship is specified by the level of conventional bonding. It is a necessary causal variable but it is not a sufficient cause.

In sum, a simple end-to-end integration strategy has not been employed, although there is a clear tendency to order the effects of specific social contexts according to their location in the life span. To some extent this has ordered the theories on the basis of the social contexts emphasized (for example, family influences precede peer influences). But even if a simple end-to-end strategy were employed as an integration approach, I do not view the empirical verification of such a theory as evidence that the more distal theory was incorrect. Further, although the level of explained variance in the dependent variable could not exceed that of the most proximate theory, the explained variance of the model as a whole might well be increased; that is, the explained variance of the intervening variables in the most proximate theory might be increased.

The final structural approach is the up-and-down strategy, in which the level of abstraction in the integrated theory is raised to the point where separate historical perspectives become specific applications of a general theory of deviance. Hirschi's (1979: 36) criticism of this approach is "a marked tendency on the part of integrationists to accept without question the truth of any partial theory their general theory subsumes." Historically, relatively few initial formulations of a theory simultaneously provided a full empirical test of the theory. It is incumbent upon the person proposing a theory to consider whether the available empirical evidence is consistent or inconsistent with the theory's postulates and, if inconsistent, to offer some possible explanation for this inconsistency. One should not propose a theory that contains postulates that are clearly contrary to established empirical findings.

At the same time, it would be a truly rare event if all of the postulated relationships in a new theoretical integration had already been examined empirically. New theoretical insights, while often building upon available empirical findings, almost always go beyond available evidence and require the examination of new relationships. The modifications to prior theories resulting from the integration often render earlier tests of these relationships marginal or irrelevant to the new set of proposed relationships. In sum, it is to be expected that some of the causal relationships in a new theory are proposed on purely logical grounds, with no direct empirical evidence to support or refute them. They are proposed as hypotheses; they are not accepted without question. There is an obvious distinction between proposing a theory and validating a theory.

In general, those proposing integrations have paid attention to earlier empirical findings. The level of theoretical justification is sometimes weak, but there is nearly always a reasonable empirical justification for the proposed causal paths or relationships. I suspect that we may not all agree with Hirschi's judgment of which perspectives or parts of perspectives are "true" and which are not, and that is the basis of this criticism. But there is little evidence that integrationists have ignored the available evidence pertaining to proposed relationships and incorporated theories or parts of theories that are generally acknowledged to be unfounded.

In fact, the up-and-down strategy is a sound one, but to my knowledge few integrationists working on theories of crime and delinquency have adopted this strategy. It is interesting to note, however, that most recent theoretical statements of an integrated theory are accompanied by at least a preliminary test of the proposed causal model. As a result we are often in a good position to evaluate the adequacy of the proposed integrations and do not need to accept specific propositions on the basis of their logical justification alone.

In summary, most integration efforts involve some side-by-side and end-to-end structural arrangement of variables. To some degree the observed sequential ordering of variables reflects a logical ordering of theories based upon the social contexts they emphasize. I see no inherent logical problems with any of these structural approaches to integration; for example, not all side-by-side arrangements reflect an attempt of the integrationist to avoid the problem of reconciling different theoretical assumptions or definitions. Given the relatively low level of explained variance attributable to traditional theories of crime, the value of simple end-to-end structures can certainly be questioned because they hold no promise for increased explanatory power relative to the dependent variable. However, to my knowledge none of the recent attempts to achieve a genuine theoretical integration proposes such an arrangement. Virtually all such efforts have employed some combination of side-by-side and end-to-end structural arrangements and will thus hold some potential for increasing the level of explained variance.

INTEGRATED THEORIES AND EXPLAINED VARIANCE

With few exceptions, tests of integrated theoretical models have demonstrated an increased level of explained variance over that of the separate theories included in the integration. In some instances the gains are quite modest and in others they are more substantial. Since there is some variation in this generalization by specific theories included in the integration, a brief review of particular theoretical combinations is presented.

When strain and social control perspectives are combined, there is a small (2 percent to 3 percent) additional increment in explained variance over that obtained from control predictors alone (Cernkovich, 1978; Segrave and Hastad, 1983). Although not employing a multiple regression approach, Eve (1978) also found that both strain and control measures had independent effects upon delinquent behavior, supporting the conclusion that their integration would yield a higher level of explained variance. Cernkovich (1978) and Segrave and Hastad (1983) report similar levels of explained variance for strain (6-8 percent) and control (12-13 percent) as separate causal models. Although the increase in explained variance resulting from their integration is small in absolute magnitude, it constitutes a 23 percent to 25 percent increase over that achieved by the set of control predictors alone. The power of the integrated model remains relatively weak, however, with a total explained variance of approximately 15 percent in these two studies.

With few exceptions, tests of integrated models or mixed models involving social control and either social learning or differential association predictors also reveal that a synthesis of these two perspectives produces an increase in overall explanatory power (Patterson and Dishion, forthcoming; Linden, 1978; La Grange and White, 1983; Gottfredson, 1982; Johnson, 1979; Johnstone, 1981). In each of the above-referenced studies, one or more predictors from each theoretical perspective made an independent contribution to the total explained variance and the increase in explained variance over that of the social learning/differential association predictors alone was substantial (a 14-40 percent increase for those studies in which this increase could be calculated). In most cases there was evidence that some of the effects of social control predictors were being mediated by social learning/differential association measures. The overall explanatory power of these tests ranged from 26 percent (Johnson, 1979) to 54 percent (Patterson and Dishion, forthcoming). While not employing a multiple regression analysis, studies by Jensen (1972), Linden and Hackler (1973), and Poole and Regoli (1979) also support the claim that an integrated social control, social learning/differential association model yields a higher level of explained variance than either model separately.

Several additional studies incorporated measures of variables from all three theoretical perspectives (strain, social control, and differential association) in empirical tests of mixed theoretical models (Meade and Marsden, 1981; Figueira-McDonough et al., 1981; Simons et al., 1980). In all three studies, predictors from each theoretical perspective contributed to the overall explanatory power of the model, although the net increases in explained variance over that accounted for by differential association predictors was typically small.

There is one test of an integrated model where social control variables contribute no additional explanatory power to that of differential association variables (Matsueda, 1982).[3] However, the weight of the available evidence suggests that when social control variables are combined with differential association or social learning variables, the result is an increase in overall explanatory power.

When combined with social learning/differential association predictors, strain predictors contribute relatively little or no additional explained variance (Elliott and Voss, 1974; Simons et al., 1980; Meade and Marsden, 1981; Figueira-McDonough et al., 1981). It was also the case that when strain predictors were combined with social control and labeling predictors in a mixed theoretical model, the effects of strain were entirely mediated by labeling predictors (Aultman and Welford, 1979).

In general, then, at an individual level of explanation strain predictors add explanatory power to social control predictors, but not to social learning/differential association or labeling predictors. It also appears that, when combined with social learning/differential association predictors, the influence of social control predictors is at least partly mediated by the social learning/differential association predictors. In most test these predictors also have weak to moderate independent effects as well. Given these findings, it appears that the integration of social control and social learning or differential association perspectives can indeed increase the level of explained variance, and in some cases the increase is substantial.

With the exception of the Elliott and Voss (1974) study, all of the research mentioned above involved cross-sectional data with an ambiguous or incorrect temporal ordering of predictor and criterion measures and no controls for prior levels of delinquency involvement. It is thus possible that the above studies seriously overestimate the explanatory power of the models and of particular sets of predictors in these models. Tests conducted by Elliott et al. (1985) of an integrated strain, social control, and social learning model involve a set of genuine predictive analyses with longitudinal data from a national youth panel. Since the results of these tests might possibly be construed as providing negative evidence for the claim that integrating theories can increase explanatory power, these findings will be reviewed in more detail.

The initial test involved a path analysis in which the temporal order of measures was controlled utilizing the first two waves of the National Youth Survey.[4] The analysis also included an independent replication using waves two and three of the panel. In both the initial analysis and the replication, the only direct effects observed were from prior delinquency and a measure of involvement with delinquent peers (conceptualized as an indicator of peer reinforcements for delinquency). The influence of delinquent peers was slightly stronger than that of prior delinquency in the initial test, but it was slightly weaker in the replication. The effects of strain and conventional bonding (traditional control) predictors were all mediated by the social learning predictors (Elliott et al., 1985). In none of the analyses involving males and females and various types of delinquency and substance use did we observe any significant direct effects for the set of strain or control predictors. Prior delinquency and involvement with delinquent peers accounted for 52 percent of the variance in total delinquency in the initial test and for 58 percent of the variance in the replication.[5]

However, the general path analysis did not take into account the conditional relationship postulated in the integrated theory; that is, that while social reinforcement for delinquency is the most proximate cause of delinquent behavior, this relationship is a conditional one, depending upon preexisting weak controls or restraints. Several additional analyses were undertaken to test for this interaction, which is critical to the logic of the integration and the claim that the integrated model will account for more explained variance. First, partitioning the panel into youth with lower and higher levels of conventional bonding, we replicated the path analysis for each subsample. The zero-order correlation between delinquency and involvement with delinquent peers was .42 for those with high conventional bonding and .65 for those with low conventional bonding; prior delinquency and delinquent peers together accounted for 31 percent of the variance in delinquency in the high conventional bonding group and for 57 percent in the low group (initial test, total delinquency).[6]

Additional support for the postulated interaction was obtained from an analysis in which youth were classified as having high or low conventional bonding (to the family and school) and as having relatively delinquent or prosocial friends. A cross-classification of these two classifications generated four types of youth: (1) those with strong bonds to family and school and conventional friends, (2) those with strong bonds to family and school and delinquent friends, (3) those with weak bonds to family and school and conventional friends, and (4) those with weak bonds to family and school and delinquent friends.

Youth in the two groups with conventional friends reported a substantially lower average number of offenses than would be expected on the basis of their prior delinquency ($\overline{X} = -11.09$ and -12.43). There were no significant differences between these groups. In the face of conventional peers, having weak or strong family and school bonds appears to have little impact on subsequent delinquent behavior. Those in the group with delinquent peers and strong family and school bonds had close to the expected number of offenses given their prior self-report delinquency involvement ($\overline{X} = -2.06$). Finally, those with delinquent friends and weak family and school bonds reported substantially more offenses than expected, given their prior self-report delinquency scores ($\overline{X} = +23.13$). In the replicated analysis and separate analyses for males and females, this same pattern was observed, with approximately the same between-group differences (Elliott et al., 1985). There is clear evidence for the postulated interaction effect here. Among those with delinquent reinforcements from friends, having weak or strong bonds to the family and school clearly influenced the likelihood of an increase in subsequent delinquency. Strong family and school bonds do serve to insulate one

TABLE 6.1
Explained Variance Attributable to Sets of Individual Theoretical Predictors and Combined Sets of Predictors: National Youth Survey, 1976-1980

Theoretical Predictor Sets[a]	Number of Predictors	R^2	Cumulative R^2	Percentage Increase[b] R^2
Initial Test (1976-1977)				
(1) strain	3	2.1	2.1	—
(2) social control	5	11.7	12.9	10.3
(3) social disorganization	2	1.3	14.0	19.7
(4) social learning	2	32.4	34.0	4.9
(5) integrated theory	13	36.4	36.4	12.3
Replication (1979-1980)				
(1) strain	3	3.4	3.4	—
(2) social control	5	9.3	11.2	20.4
(3) social disorganization	2	3.5	13.9	49.5
(4) social learning	2	29.5	31.5	6.8
(5) integrated theory	13	33.0	33.0	11.9

a. Measures: strain = family strain, occupation strain, educational strain (goal-expectation discrepancies); social control = attitudes toward deviance, involvement in conventional activities (family and school), perceived family sanctions for deviance, importance of family and school, conventional aspirations; social disorganization = perceived crime in neighborhood, family crises (divorce, unemployment, illness, etc.); social learning = normative orientation of peers (normlessness), involvement with peers, weighted by delinquent peer activities.
b. The percentage increase in R^2 over that of the strongest individual theory set included in the regression.

from the delinquent influences of friends. These findings are clearly supportive of the interaction postulated in the integration and the claim that the integration leads to an increased predictive efficiency.

Finally, in a separate lagged multiple regression analysis not reported in Elliott et al. (1985), a conventional bonding by delinquent friends interactive term was included in the multiple regression equation along with a slightly expanded set of predictors from each theoretical domain (compared to those used in the initial path analysis).[7] Three measures accounted for the vast majority of the explained variance: a measure of the perceived importance of family and school (beta = .29); a measure of involvement with friends that was weighted by the amount of delinquent activity engaged in by friends (beta = .26); and the interaction term (involvement in family and school activities × the above involvement with delinquent friends measure, beta = .46). The interaction term was clearly the strongest predictor of delinquency in this analysis.

The increase in explained variance over a simple additive model involving strain, social control, and social learning predictors is indicated in Table 6.1. Based upon a series of lagged multiple regression analyses, the explained variance in self-reported delinquency attributable to each individual set of theoretical preditors and cumulative combinations of theoretical sets is presented along with that for the integrated model. The initial test involves data from waves one and two of the panel (median age 14-15) and the replication involves waves four and five data (median age 17-18). Prior delinquency was not included as a predictor in any of these analyses. The predictors included in each theoretical set were the strongest predictors from the total set available and capture the vast majority of explained variance attributable to the total set. The "percentage increase in explained variance" column in the table refers to the gain in predictive power over the strongest predictor set included in the model to that point.

These results are consistent with those reported earlier. Both strain and social disorganization sets account for relatively little variation in delinquency as individual models (1-3 percent); social control predictors account for modest levels of explained variance (9-12 percent), and social learning predictors account for the highest level of explained variance (approximately 30 percent). Combining strain and social control predictors does increase the level of explained variance. The absolute gain is small (1-2 percent), but the relative gain is more substantial (10-20 percent). Including both strain and social disorganization predictors increases the level of explained variance by 20 percent to 50 percent over that of the social control predictors alone. While strain and disorganization predictors are clearly weak predictors, they appear to be largely independent of social control predictors.

Combining strain, disorganization, and control predictors with social learning predictors results in a relatively small increase in explained variance (5-7 percent) over that of the social learning set alone. The two social learning predictors capture nearly all of the explained variance accounted for by the other predictors. The small gain is primarily the result of social control predictors, with little or none of it attributable to strain or disorganization predictors. The integrated model that includes the interaction effect does result in a substantial increase in explained variance over that of the social learning predictors alone. The net increase is approximately 4 percent and the relative increase approximately 12 percent in both the initial test and the replication.

The above review of the empirical evidence supports the claims that at the individual level of explanation, traditional theories are best viewed as partial theories, and that integrated theoretical models can increase the level of explanatory power. It is also clear that the gains realized to date are modest rather than dramatic when compared to the most powerful traditional theory (social learning theory) in a genuine predictive test. The gains are typically larger in cross-sectional tests.

It must be acknowledged that I have not addressed conceptual or theoretical issues in the above review. For example, I have accepted uncritically the conceptualizations of measures as reported by particular investigators. The strongest predictor in the work of Elliott et al. (1985) (involvement with friends weighted by friends' involvement in delinquency) is conceptualized as a measure of peer reinforcements for delinquent behavior; that is, a social learning variable. However, it is likely that a pure control theorist would view this measure as a control variable; that is, a measure of weak peer restraints on delinquency (Hirschi, 1969; Hirschi and Gottfredson, 1980). While the National Youth Survey analysis of peer involvements and delinquency supports the social learning as opposed to the social control interpretation,[8] the resolution of these types of conceptual issues is beyond the scope of this chapter. Still, the empirical evidence is quite supportive of the claim that theoretical integrations can increase explanatory power, at least to the extent that the measures frequently used in the research literature as indicators of key theoretical variables are valid indicators of these variables.

DIRECTION OF FUTURE INTEGRATION EFFORTS

It appears that the gains in explanatory power resulting from theoretical integrations, while substantial with reference to earlier levels, are not large in an absolute sense. A net increase of 4 percent and a relative increase of 12 percent are, after all, rather modest levels of increase. In part, these low net gains are a result of the low levels of explanatory power associated with traditional strain and social control perspectives. The gains in cross-sectional studies were generally greater. In any case, even a modest improvement is important, for it indicates that the predictive power of these individual theories is at least partially additive, lending credibility to this general approach to theory development.

It is also the case that an increase in explained variance for the final outcome variable—that is, delinquency and crime—is only one of several criteria by which the value and utility of integrated theories should be judged. The specification of major intervening variables and developmental sequences also increases the usefulness of a theory and increased explanatory power relative to these intervening variables also enhances the general predictive efficiency of a theory. Future integration efforts may well focus more heavily upon improving overall predictive efficiency—that is, in accounting for variation in the more proximate causal variables identified in traditional theories—thereby increasing our understanding of the important intervening variables in causal sequences.

It should also be acknowledged that none of the empirical tests reviewed above involved a definitive test. Analyses that more adequately represent the full set of variables and relationships specified by these theories (traditional and integrated) may well result in higher levels of explained variance. In particular, improved conceptualization, measurement, and analysis techniques may well increase our estimates of the predictive efficiency of our theories. Future integration efforts and theory tests will clearly have to attend to some serious conceptualization and measurement problems (Blalock, 1984).

The integrationist approach to theory development has also highlighted the need to consider reciprocal causal relationships. One clear example of this involves the classic argument over the causal direction of the delinquent companions-delinquent behavior relationship, with alternative causal orderings suggested by control and learning theorists. Rather than asking which hypothesis is correct (the competing hypothesis approach), integrationists are more interested in examining the possibility that both are correct. This involves postulating a reciprocal relationship between delinquent friends and delinquent behavior. This could result in an escalating causal influence of delinquent friends on delinquent behavior over time as the result of the feedback effect of delinquency upon subsequent peer association patterns. The recent work of Thornberry and Christenson (1984) involving a nonrecursive causal modeling of the relationship between unemployment and crime is another example. One thing seems clear: Traditional unidirectional causal theories are overly simple and do not adequately reflect the actual causal processes leading to criminal behavior (Blalock, 1984; Thornberry and Christensen, 1984). The development of theories with more complex causal relationships will almost certainly necessitate the development of new methods for evaluating them.

We have already noted some preliminary attempts to integrate criminological theories across levels of explanation (for example, Elliott et al., 1983; Mednick et al., 1982; Merton and Bursik, 1983; Craven, 1984; Wolfgang et al., 1983) and there is some evidence that these efforts will further increase explanatory power. The work of Johnstone (1978, 1983), Clark and Winninger (1962), and Craven (1984) indicates that general features of the larger social environment have direct effects upon individual offending rates, that is, effects that are not mediated by the perceptions of individuals in these social contexts. There is thus some potential for increased explanatory power with integrations across levels of explanation, particularly with integrations involving macro-level, social system variables.[9] These studies also highlight the importance of social organizational variables in accounting for variation in social psychological variables such as personal bonding to the family, school, and community organizations; exposure to delinquent peers and gangs; and perceptions of risk associated with criminal behavior. These effects have an indirect relationship to crime, but can improve the general explanatory power of our theoretical formulations and increase our understanding of criminogenic environments and processes. It appears likely that future integration efforts will move beyond the single level of explanation that has characterized efforts to date.

The interest in theoretical synthesis and integration is likely to continue, given the generally positive results of recent integration efforts. The explanatory power of these theories appears to be greater than traditional theories, and frequently these theoretical statements specify conditional relationships and intervening variables that are not found in the traditional perspectives. As a result, the interest in criminological theory has been rekindled and the potential for significant advances in our ability to explain and predict criminal behavior has been increased.

NOTES

1. For example, Cohen (1966) notes that his theoretical perspective in *Delinquent Boys* (1955) was a step toward the convergence of diverse theoretical traditions, and Cloward and Ohlin acknowledge in their forward to *Delinquency and Opportunity* (1960) their intellectual indebtedness to Robert Merton (anomie theory) and Edwin Sutherland (differential association theory).

2. The fact that traditional strain and social control variables lose virtually all of their predictive power when prior delinquency is controlled suggests that the causal relationship

is very weak or that the causal ordering implied by this theory is incorrect. The data are much more consistent with the hypothesis that delinquency leads to weak social controls or strain than vice versa. Indeed, the temporal ordering of theoretical predictors and criterion measures in most cross-sectional tests is not just simultaneous or ambiguous, but the reverse of that hypothesized. Delinquency is always measured retrospectively and the social control and strain variables are nearly always instantaneous measures, such as attitudes, beliefs, and perceptions at the point of data collection.

3. This review is limited to studies employing self-reported measures of delinquency as the dependent variable. There are also a number of empirical tests of integrated or mixed models in which drug use is the dependent variable (for example, see Kandel et al., 1978; Akers and Cochran, 1983; Winfree et al., 1981; Meier and Johnson, 1977; Ginsberg and Greenley, 1978). The Akers and Cochran (1983) study found no increase in explained variance when adding either strain or social control predictors to social learning predictors. The other studies report some increase in overall explanatory power resulting from the combination of predictors derived from different theoretical perspectives. The conclusion that integration does increase explanatory power thus holds for drug use as well as for delinquency.

4. For a description of the National Youth Survey, see Elliott and Ageton (1980) or Elliott and Huizinga (1983).

5. Excluding the influence of prior delinquency, the level of explained variance was less, but still substantial; for example, 42 percent, initial test, total delinquency, total sample (Elliott et al., 1985).

6. It should be noted that some of the assumptions of linear modeling are violated in this analysis (for example, homoscedasticity). While this method is quite robust, some caution is necessary. We do not rely exclusively on this analysis in concluding that there is support for the postulated interactive relationship (see Elliott et al., 1985).

7. A measure of prior self-reported delinquency was not included as a predictor in this analysis and the measure of delinquency was a slightly more restricted measure (SRD C) than employed in the initial path analysis (for instance, all status offenses were excluded). All predictor measures were wave one (initial test) or wave four (replication test) measures, except for involvement measures, which were simultaneous with the delinquency measure (that is, both covered the same time interval).

8. In the NYS analysis, youth with *no* friends reported close to the expected number of delinquent acts when prior levels of delinquency were controlled. If the effect of delinquent peers was limited to an absence of peer restraints, there should be no differences in levels of reported delinquency for those with no friends and those with predominantly delinquent friends. Given that those with delinquent friends reported dramatically higher than expected levels of delinquency and those with no friends reported close to expected levels, the influence of peers must be more than one of weak restraints on delinquent behavior.

9. These are in fact only partial integrations, because social system/environment variables are employed in the theory as causes of individual rates of crime. The dependent variables from macrosociological theories (for example, area or subsystem crime rates and patterns) are not included as dependent variables in these theoretical statements.

REFERENCES

AKERS, R. L. (1977) A Social Learning Perspective. Belmont, CA: Wadsworth.
——— and J. K. COCHRAN (1983) "Adolescent marijuana use: a test of three theories of deviant behavior." University of Florida, Gainesville. (unpublished)
AKERS, R. L., M. K. KROHN, L. LONZA-KADUCE, and M. RADOSEVICH (1979) "Social learning and deviant behavior: a specific test of a general theory." American Sociological Review 44: 636- 655.
AULTMAN, M. G. (1979) "Delinquency causation: a typological comparison of path models." Journal of Criminal Law and Criminology 70: 152-163.
——— and C. F. WELFORD (1979) "Towards an integrated model of delinquency causation: an empirical analysis." Sociology and Social Research 63: 316-327.
BLALOCK, H. M., Jr. (1984) Basic Dilemmas in the Social Sciences. Beverly Hills, CA: Sage.
BRAUKMANN, C. J., K. A. KIRIGIN, and M. M. WOLF (1980) "Group home treatment research: social learning and social control perspectives," pp. 117-130 in T. Hirschi and M. Gottfredson (eds.) Understanding Crime. Beverly Hills, CA: Sage.
BURKETT, S. R. and M. WHITE (1974) "Hellfire and delinquency: another look." Journal for the Scientific Study of Religion 13: 455-462.
CERNKOVICH, S. A. (1978) "Value orientations and delinquency involvement." Criminology 15, 4: 443-458.
CLARK, J. P. and E. P. WINNINGER (1962) "Socioeconomic class and area correlates of illegal behavior among juveniles." American Sociological Review 27: 826-834.
CLOWARD, R. A. and L. E. OHLIN (1960) Delinquency and Opportunity. New York: Free Press.
COHEN, A. K. (1966) Deviance and Control. Englewood Cliffs, NJ: Prentice-Hall.
———(1955) Delinquent Boys: The Culture of the Gang. New York: Free Press.
——— and J. F. SHORT, Jr. (1976) "Crime and juvenile delinquency," pp. 47-100 in R. K. Merton and R. Nisbet (eds.) Contemporary Social Problems. New York: Harcourt Brace Jovanovich.
CONGER, R. D. (1980) "Juvenile delinquency: behavior restraint or behavior facilitation," pp. 131-142 in T. Hirschi and M. Gottfredson (eds.) Understanding Crime. Beverly Hills, CA: Sage.
———(1978) "From social learning to criminal behavior," pp. 91-104 in M. D. Krohn and R. L. Akers (eds.) Crime, Law, and Sanctions. Beverly Hills, CA: Sage.
———(1976) "Social control and social learning models of delinquent behavior: a synthesis." Criminology 14, 1: 17-40.
CONLY, C. H. (1979) "An empirical analysis of control theories of delinquency: drift or the bond to conformity." Presented at the meetings of the American Society of Criminology, Philadelphia.
CRAVEN, D. (1984) "Social disorganization and delinquency." University of Colorado, Boulder. (unpublished)
ELLIOTT, D. S. and S. S. AGETON (1980) "Reconciling race and class differences in self-reported and official estimates of delinquency." American Sociological Review 45: 95-110.
ELLIOTT, D. S. and D. HUIZINGA (1983) "Social class and delinquent behavior in a national youth panel: 1976-1980." Criminology 21: 149-177.

ELLIOT, D. S. and H. VOSS (1974) Delinquency and Dropout. Lexington, MA: D. C. Heath.

ELLIOTT, D. S., S. A. AGETON, and R. J. CANTER (1979) "An integrated theoretical perspective on delinquent behavior." Journal of Research in Crime and Delinquency 16: 3-27.

ELLIOTT, D. S., D. HUIZINGA, and S. S. AGETON (1985) Explaining Delinquency and Drug Use. Beverly Hills, CA: Sage.

ELLIOTT D. S., D. HUIZINGA, and F. W. DUNFORD (1983) "Understanding delinquency and crime: a longitudinal multidisciplinary study of developmental patterns and conditions leading to criminal behavior." Grant application submitted to the Justice Program Study Group of the John D. and Catherine T. MacArthur Foundation. Behavioral Research Institute, Boulder, Colorado.

EVE, R. (1978) "A study of the efficacy and interactions of several theories for explaining rebelliousness among high school students." Journal of Criminal Law and Criminology 69: 115-125.

FAGAN, J., K. V. HANSEN, and M. JANG (1983) "Profiles of chronically violent juvenile offenders: an empirical test of an integrated theory of violent delinquency," pp. 91-120 in J. R. Kluegel (ed.) Evaluating Juvenile Justice. Beverly Hills, CA: Sage.

FIGUEIRA-McDONOUGH, J. B. BARTON, and R. SARRI (1981) "Normative deviance: gender similarities in adolescent subcultures," pp. 17-45 in M. Q. Warren (ed.) Comparing Female and Male Offenders. Beverly Hills, CA: Sage.

GINSBERG, I. J. and J. R. GREENLEY (1978) "Competing theories of marijuana use: a longitudinal study." Journal of Health and Social Behavior 19: 22-34.

GLASER, D. (1960) "Differential association and criminological prediction." Social Problems 8: 6-14.

GOTTFREDSON, G. D. (1982) "Role models, bonding, and delinquency: an examination of competing perspectives." Report 331, Center for Social Organization of Schools, Johns Hopkins University.

HAWKINS, D. J. and J. G. WEIS (1980) "The social development model: an integrated approach to delinquency prevention." Center for Law and Justice, University of Washington.

HEPBURN, J. R. (1976) "Testing alternative models of delinquency causation." Journal of Criminal Law and Criminology 67: 450-460.

HIRSCHI, T. (1979) "Separate and equal is better." Journal of Research in Crime and Delinquency 16: 34-38.

——— (1969) Causes of Delinquency. Berkeley: University of California Press.

——— and M. GOTTFREDSON (1980) "Introduction: the Sutherland tradition in criminology," pp. 7-19 in T. Hirschi and M. Gottfredson (eds.) Understanding Crime: Current Theory and Research. Beverly Hills, CA: Sage.

HIRSCHI, T. and H. C. SELVIN (1967) Delinquency Research: An Appraisal of Analytic Methods. New York: Free Press.

JENSEN, G. F. (1972) "Parents, peers and delinquent action: a test of the differential association perspective." American Journal of Sociology 78: 562-575.

——— and R. EVE (1976) "Sex differences in delinquency." Criminology 13: 427-448.

JOHNSON, R. E. (1979) Juvenile Delinquency and Its Origins. Cambridge: Cambridge University Press.

JOHNSTONE, J.W.C. (1983) "Recruitment to a youth gang." Youth and Society 14: 281-300.

——— (1981) "The family and delinquency: a reappraisal," in A. C. Meade (ed.) Youth and Society: Studies of Adolescent Deviance. Chicago: Institute for Juvenile Research.

——— (1978) "Social class, social areas and delinquency." Sociology and Social Research 63: 49-72.

KANDEL, D. B., R. C. KESSLER, and R. Z. MARGULIES (1978) "Antecedents of adolescent initiation into stages of drug use: a developmental analysis," in D. B. Kandel (ed.) Longitudinal Research in Drug Use. New York: John Wiley.

KELLY, D. H. and W. T. PINK (1973) "School commitment, youth rebellion and delinquency." Criminology 10: 473-485.

KORNHAUSER, R. R. (1978) Social Sources of Delinquency. Chicago: University of Chicago Press.

KROHN, M. E. and J. L. MASSEY (1980) "Social control and delinquent behavior: an examination of the elements of the social bond." Sociological Quarterly 21: 529-543.

LA GRANGE, R. L. and H. R. WHITE (1983) "Age differences in delinquency: a test of theory." Presented at the meetings of the American Society of Criminology, Denver, Colorado.

LINDEN, R. (1978) "Myths of middle-class delinquency: a test of the generalizability of social control theory." Youth and Society 9: 407-432.

——— and J. C. HACKLER (1973) "Affective ties and delinquency." Pacific Sociological Review 16: 27-46.

MATSUEDA, R. L. (1982) "Testing control theory and differential association." American Sociological Review 47: 489-504.

MEADE, A. C. and M. E. MARSDEN (1981) "An integration of classic theories of delinquency," in A. C. Meade (ed.) Youth and Society: Studies of Adolescent Deviance. Chicago: Institute for Juvenile Research.

MEDNICK, S. A., B. POLLOCK, J. VOLAUKA, and W. F. GABRIELLI (1982) "Biology and violence," pp. 85-158 in M. E. Wolfgang and N. H. Weiner (eds.) Criminal Violence. Beverly Hills, CA: Sage.

MEIER, R. F. and W. T. JOHNSON (1977) "Deterrence as social control: the legal and extralegal production of conformity." American Sociological Review 42: 292-304.

MERTON, D. E. and R. J. BURSIK (1983) "Dynamics of early adolescent development and delinquency." Grant application submitted to NIMH. Center for Urban Affairs and Policy Research, Northwestern University, Evanston, Illinois.

MICHALOWSKI, R. J. (1977) "Perspective and paradigm: structuring criminological thought," pp. 17-40 in R. F. Meier (ed.) Theory in Criminology: Contemporary Views. Beverly Hills, CA: Sage.

MINOR, W. W. (1977) "A deterrence-control theory of crime," pp. 117-138 in R. F. Meier (ed.) Theory in Criminology: Contemporary Views. Beverly Hills, CA: Sage.

PATERNOSTER, R. and L. S. ANDERSON (1981) "Testing social control theory: a longitudinal analysis." Presented at the meetings of the American Society of Criminology, Washington, D.C.

PATTERSON, G. R. and T. J. DISHION (forthcoming) "Contributions of families and peers to delinquency." Research in Criminology.

POOLE, E. D. and R. M. REGOLI (1979) "Parental support, delinquent friends, and delinquency: a test of interaction effects." Journal of Criminal Law and Criminology 70: 188-193.

ROSENBERG, M. (1968) The Logic of Survey Analysis. New York: Basic Books.

SEGRAVE, J. O. and D. N. HASTAD (1983) "Evaluating structural and control models

of delinquency causation: a replication and extention." Youth and Society 14: 437-456.
SHORT, J. R., Jr. (1979) "On the etiology of delinquent behavior." Journal of Research in Crime and Delinquency 16: 28-33.
——— (1957) "Differential association as a hypothesis." Social Problems 8: 14-25.
SIMONS, R. L., M. G. MILLER, and S. M. AIGNER (1980) "Contemporary theories of deviance and female delinquency." Journal of Research in Crime and Delinquency 17: 42-57.
SUTHERLAND, E. H. (1955) Principles of Criminology. Philadelphia: J. B. Lippincott.
THOMAS, C. W. and J. M. HYMAN (1978) "Compliance theory, control theory and juvenile delinquency," pp. 73-90 in M. D. Krohn and R. L. Akers (eds.) Crime, Law and Sanctions. Beverly Hills, CA: Sage.
THORNBERRY, T. P. and R. L. CHRISTENSEN (1984) "Unemployment and criminal involvement: an investigation of reciprocal causal structures." American Sociological Review 49: 398-411.
VOSS, H. L. (1964) "Differential association and delinquent behavior." Social Problems 12: 78-85.
WIATROWSKI, M. D., D. B. GRISWOLD, and M. K. ROBERTS (1981) "Social control theory and delinquency." American Sociological Review 46: 525-541.
WINFREE, L. T., H. E. THEIS, and C. T. GRIFFITHS (1981) "Drug use in rural America: a cross-cultural examination of complementary social deviance theories." Youth and Society 12: 465-489.
WOLFGANG, M. E., D. J. DENNO, R. M. FIGLIO, P. E. TRACY, and N. A. WEINER (1983) "A longitudinal study of the theoretical and empirical bases of high risk delinquent and criminal behavior: a multi-cohort multi-wave design." Proposal submitted to the Justice Program Study Group of the John D. and Catherine T. MacArthur Foundation. Center for Studies in Criminology and Criminal Law, University of Pennsylvania, Philadelphia.

7

The Assumption of the Efficacy of Middle-Range Explanation:
Typologies

DON C. GIBBONS

A large part of the professional socialization of the sociologist-criminologist involves learning to "talk funny," that is, acquiring and becoming comfortable with a large body of concepts and perspectives dealing with crime and criminality that are alien to the way of thinking of most laypersons. Criminologists are persons who employ such arcane notions as "definitions favorable to the violation of law," "anomie," "illegitimate opportunity structures," "social bond," and "relative deprivation."

However, the typological approach in criminology is another matter, for it has much in common with the citizen's perception that rape and rapists seem unlike burglars and burglary, which in turn are different from corporate crimes and white-collar criminals, murder and murderers, and various and sundry other crimes and criminals. Of course, the layperson's typological approach is often only an intuitive one, for he or she may well be only dimly aware of the way or ways in which one type of offender or offense presumably differs from another. By contrast, the typological arguments of criminologists have usually been a good bit more explicit and theoretically sophisticated. At the same time, it would be well to refrain, at least in this case, from invidious comparisons between the naive criminological "theories" of laypersons and the high-powered viewpoints of criminologists, for, as we shall see, the typological arguments of sociologist-criminologists have often failed to rise much above a commonsense level.

What is the typological approach? The core assumption of this perspective is that crimes and criminals are neither all alike nor unique events or persons; instead, a number of distinct "types" or groups of offenses and/or offenders exist and can be identified and studied. This view has been in existence, at least in rudimentary form, for nearly as long as persons have paid serious attention to the study of lawbreaking and lawbreakers. For example, Italian positivist physician and criminologist Cesare Lombroso (1836-1909), who has often been identified as the father of modern criminology, is most commonly remembered for his claims about atavism and born criminals. However, in his last book, published after his death, he contended that there were three types of lawbreakers: *born* criminals, *insane* criminals, and *criminaloids*. This last group, involving over half of the population of offenders, was said to be made up of persons of normal physical and psychological makeup who have committed crimes because of unusually stressful life circumstances.

Reports on the existence of a large number of criminal types surfaced a number of times in nineteenth-century England, at a time when lawbreaking was on the rise and many English citizens had become convinced that they had much to fear from members of "the dangerous class." For example, Low (1982: 25-27) has reported that Patrick Colquhoun, a Scottish businessman, social philosopher, and police reformer, estimated that there were at least 115,000 members of "the dangerous and criminal class" in London, engaged in full-time criminal pursuits of one kind or another. Moreover, Colquhoun identified 24 separate groups of offenders, including such types as "professed and known receivers of stolen goods" and "a class of suspicious characters, who live partly by pilfering and passing base money—ostensibly costard mongers, ass drivers, dustmen, chimney sweepers, rabbit sellers, fish and fruit sellers, flash coachmen, bear baiters, dog keepers (but in fact dog stealers), etc., etc."

Colquhoun's classificatory efforts were exceeded a few decades later by social reformer Henry Mayhew, who produced a listing of more than 100 types of criminals who were said to constitute "the criminal class" in late nineteenth-century England (Tobias, 1967: 62-65). Mayhew's list included such types as "'stook buzzers', those who steal handkerchiefs," and "'snow gatherers,' or those who steal clean clothes off the hedges."

Typological thinking in criminology has not been cumulative, hence there is no straight line of development from the costard mongers, ass drivers, stook buzzers, and snow gatherers of Colquhoun and Mayhew and the offender typologies now in existence in criminology. Even so, these premodern arguments are not wholly unrelated to contemporary ones. In particular, it will be shown in a later section of this chapter that one central problem that has plagued the typological approach from the time of Colquhoun and Mayhew to the present is the rather large number of categories that seem to be required in order to capture the variability among lawbreakers.

The underlying rationale for the development of typological schemes in criminology is self-apparent. First, if distinct groupings or types of lawbreakers or crime forms exist, explanation or causal analysis probably requires that we develop separate etiological accounts for each of the forms of lawbreaking or kinds of lawbreakers. Perhaps some offenders are the product of psychological pressures of one kind or another, while others become engaged in lawbreaking because of social learning experiences, situational pressures, or other causes. A second, closely related, argument in support of typologies has centered about treatment or rehabilitation goals. If it is the case that a number of distinct types of criminals or delinquents exist, each produced by a different causal process, it would clearly be a mistake to apply a single form of correctional intervention to these persons. Instead, what appears to be called for is "different strokes for different folks," in which a variety of different treatment strategems would be fitted to those offender types to which they are relevant—group therapy for some, psychiatric treatment for others, and cosmetic surgery for still another group.

Although these contentions about the usefulness of typologies have a ring of plausibility, they may nonetheless be flawed. These arguments may be overly clinical, thus the medical metaphor on which they are based may be misleading. Criminality may consist of myriad forms of activity that defy classification, while involvement in lawbreaking may arise out of circumstances that are so numerous and varied that clear-cut etiological processes cannot easily be identified. These are issues to be probed further in the pages to follow.

A few more prefatory remarks about the typological approach are in order. Criminological analysis, particularly in the United States, has been monopolized by sociologists (Gibbons, 1979). As a consequence of the domination of criminological work by sociologists, most of the typologies addressed in this chapter have been produced by sociological criminologists. However, it is also true that a considerable number of psychologists and psychiatrists have devoted attention to lawbreaking and lawbreakers, with the result that psychologically oriented classifications also exist in some number.

One early example of psychological categorizations of lawbreakers is found in the writings of psychologist Raymond Corsini (1949), who sorted offenders into seven groupings, including irresponsible, neurotic, psychoid, and psychopathic criminals. Similarly, psychiatrist Manfred Guttmacher (1960: 13-106) claims that there are normal, sociopathic, alcoholic, and avenging murderers, as well as those who are schizophrenic or temporarily psychotic. Neustatter (1957) offers a parallel psychiatric typology of murderers. Finally, the research efforts of Jenkins and Hewitt (1944), which resulted in the identification of two basic types of delinquency, unsocialized aggressive youths and "pseudo-social delinquents," have exerted a good deal of influence upon a number of students of delinquency.

Two more recent lines of typological work by psychologists have received a good deal of attention. Megargee and his associates (1979) have used test scores derived from the MMPI (Minnesota Multiphasic Personality Inventory) to sort offenders into a number of psychological groupings that they claim provide a useful basis for intervention efforts. Warren (1976: 176-204) and a number of collaborating researchers and correctional administrators in California have evolved an elaborate classificatory scheme that assigns officially identified juvenile offenders to one of three levels of interpersonal maturity and to one of nine subtypes within these levels, including such groupings as *asocial, passive; cultural conformist*; and *neurotic, acting out*. Further, the I-Levels (interpersonal maturity levels) system includes a collection of different intervention tactics thought to be appropriate to these various offender types, along with recommendations that treatment workers with particular kinds of work skills be assigned to the separate types of offenders, hence it is a complex program for providing "different strokes to different folks by different strokers." The closeness of all of this to the medical model of treatment should be obvious.

Although the I-Levels scheme has received much favorable attention, others have noted a number of problems with it, including its ambiguity on the issue of whether it is intended as a causal theory of delinquency, its unreliability in practice as a diagnostic system, and other flaws (Gibbons, 1981: 115-118).

Returning to typological endeavors within the field of sociological criminology, three relatively distinct lines of work make up the typological tradition. First, a number of researchers have gone about singling out one or another form of crime or presumed "type" of offender for study. These empirical investigations concerning particular variants of lawbreaking or lawbreakers represent the empirical building blocks of the typological perspective. Limitations of space do not allow an enumeration of all of the specific studies of offender patterns or types of criminality, for this is the stuff of which full-length criminology texts are composed, in large part (see Gibbons, 1982). However, mention might be made of a representative sampling of this research. Studies of specific kinds of criminality have included Wolfgang's (1958) inquiry on homicide and research on burglary patterns by Scarr et al. (1973). Edwin Lemert's investigations of naive check forgers (1953) and systematic check forgers (1958) are cases in point of research on offender types, as is Roebuck's (1966) typological classification deriving out of his study of inmates in a District of Columbia prison.

Advocates of typologies in criminology have also made much of those reports about the colorful social roles or "argot roles" played by inmates, in both men's and women's prisons. On this point, Sykes (1958) and Schrag (1961: 11-16) have both described the inmate social system and social roles in maximum security prisons, noting that prisoners refer to each other and relate to their peers in terms of labels such as "right guy," "outlaw," "ding," or "ball buster." These apparently represent an inmate form of verbal shorthand for individuals who differ from each other in criminal attitudes, preprison experiences, and the like. Parallel accounts of a rich system of social type labels employed by prisoners in women's institutions have been provided by Giallombardo (1966) and Heffernan (1972). Those who favor the typological approach have sometimes argued that prison social types are a within-prison manifestation of the existence of patterns or modalities among lawbreakers that exist outside the prison walls as well. But, as we will see, that argument may be a shaky one, in that these accounts of inmate social roles have oversimplified the richness of social life and social roles within penal institutions.

The third line of activity, which most often comes to mind when criminologists speak of the typological approach, consists of those efforts made by some criminologists to explicate a comprehensive listing of types of offenders or crime patterns. Three of the most well-known of these schemes are represented by the work of Clinard and Quinney (1973) and Glaser (1972, 1975), and by my efforts (Gibbons, 1965). Much of the remainder of this chapter revolves around the strengths and weaknesses of these typological statements.

ON CLASSIFICATION AND TYPOLOGIES

To this point, little has been said about various technical aspects of classification schemes, typologies, techniques of typology construction, and the like. These are complex matters, discussion of which could take us too far afield in this brief chapter, but a few remarks about them are required at this point.

To begin with, as many have pointed out, typification and naming behavior—that is, sorting of sense impressions into categories and types to which labels are then assigned—is a basic social process of everyday life. For example, high school youths often identify their peers as "hoods" or "soshes," industrial laborers speak of some of their fellow workers as "rate busters," and police officers sometimes speak of "hubcap thieves," "hot prowlers," or other presumed types of lawbreakers. And, as we have already seen, prison inmates often organize their responses to their peers in terms of designations such as "right guys," "wolves," "center men," or other prison argot labels.

Typifications arising out of social interaction are often called "existential types" and are contrasted to the "constructed types" that are deliberately invented by sociologists and other theorists as conceptual aids. Typologies of offenders or of offense patterns developed by criminologists are examples of constructed types.

The underlying dimensions or variables on which types are based are usually only implicit in existential classifications, but are a good bit more explicit in many constructed type schemes. Even so, social theorists, including criminologists, have often put forth typological schemes, the identifying dimensions of which have been unclear. Property-space analysis and the methodology of substruction of property-space have been developed as procedures for making the underlying conceptual structure of constructed types explicit (Barton, 1955: 40-53).

Although the terms "classification," "taxonomy," and "typology" have not always been used consistently, a "classification system" or "taxonomy" usually refers to the full range of categories within a variable or set of variables in which instances of some phenomenon can be placed. The Stanford-Binet intelligence test provides an example of a single-dimension classification, for it allows the placement of individuals into intelligence score groupings along an intelligence scale. A multivariate classification would be illustrated by a scheme for sorting out individuals according to sex, educational attainment, and income, in which the classification system would include all of the logically possible combinations of assignments along these dimensions. Some of the classes within the scheme might actually be "unpopulated," that is, no actual cases would be found to fall within them.

Typologies differ from classification schemes in that they make truth claims, that is, they assert that only a certain number of the logically possible classes of phenomena to which the typology is directed exist in the real world. For example, in an offender typology based upon offense behavior, intelligence, and socioeconomic status of lawbreakers, one logically possible pattern might be that of an embezzler of low intelligence from a lower-income background, but that type might be excluded from the typology because it is assumed to occur rarely if ever among actual offenders.

In the sociological literature, a distinction between "ideal types" and "extracted types" or "empirical types" has often been made, in order to draw attention to the point that some typological descriptions are presumed to describe real-world phenomena more closely than do others (McKinney, 1970: 249-250). One well-known example of an "ideal type" is Max Weber's description of modern bureaucratic social organizations, which was put forth as a benchmark portrait that deliberately exaggerated the features of this social form. By contrast, a typological sketch of the naive check forger, drawn from Lemert's research (1953), is more directly tied to empirical observations. Although John McKinney and others pointed out that the ontological contention that so-called extracted or empirical types are more "real" than are ideal ones is highly dubious, it is true that most criminological typologies have been offered as empirical ones that fairly accurately describe real-life lawbreakers. And, as we will see in the pages to follow, the accuracy of this claim is *the* central issue concerning criminological typologies.

What are the criteria for evaluating criminological typologies? First, they must be relatively *clear* and *explicit* so that actual offenders can be assigned to categories of the typology. The defining attributes of particular offender or offense types must be specified in detail so that persons or events can be assigned to them in a consistent, reliable fashion. Second, typologies should be made up of *mutually exclusive* types or categories so that actual offenders or crime events fall into only one of the types of the system. Additionally, the criterion of *parsimony* means that the number of types in the scheme should be relatively limited. In all likelihood, an offender or offense pattern categorization that includes a hundred or more "types" would be too unwieldy to be of much use to criminologists.

The final criterion of *empirical congruence* requires that a typology exhibit a reasonable degree of "isomorphism with reality." In turn, one aspect of empirical congruence is concerned with the "closeness of fit" between typological categories and actual offenders or offenses. For example, offenders may be encountered who are similar to but not identical to the profile contained in a typology. A second facet of empirical congruence concerns the extent to which lawbreakers fall outside the typology, being assigned to a residual category of unclassified cases.

As we will soon see, many of the specific typological schemes that have been put forth by criminologists have been seriously deficient in terms of one or another of these criteria.

TYPOLOGIES IN MODERN CRIMINOLOGY

Looking Backward

We have already noted that observations on prisoner social types, empirical studies of specific offenders or offense patterns, and comprehensive arguments about lawbreakers and lawbreaking make up the contemporary version of the typological perspective. A few additional remarks are in order about typological efforts, before we begin an examination of the details of this approach.

First, some criminological investigators have employed a *crime-centered* approach focused upon types of crime and have endeavored to identify offense regularities or recurrent crime forms such as residential burglary, "car clouting," organizational crime, or political crime. A crime-centered analysis examines differences among various form of criminality, including information on the correlates of these patterns such as the social areas in which they are committed, temporal variations in their occurrence, and kindred facts. As one simple example of this line of thought, I have recently organized a criminology textbook around a relatively crude taxonomy of crime forms, including such types as organizational crime, mundane crime, and "garden variety" predatory crime (Gibbons, 1982).

However, the largest share of typological work has been *person-centered* or *criminal-centered*, in which efforts have been made to identify varieties of criminal or delinquent persons. These latter efforts have been couched in such terms as "offender types," "syndromes," "criminal careers," or "criminal roles" exhibited by lawbreakers.

There is abundant empirical evidence that demonstrates that there are observable regularities among collections of crimes or that lawbreaking is patterned (see Gibbons, 1982). However, it is less clear that offenders can be easily sorted out into homogeneous types of groupings of lawbreakers. For example, even though residential burglaries often show many similarities and thus can be said to be patterned, it does not follow that these offenses are committed by "burglars," that is, individuals who specialize in burglaries to the exclusion of other offenses. And it may be even more difficult to sort real-life offenders into types based on such variables as attitudes, self-concepts, and the like.

A second observation is that typological efforts have been much more common among those sociologists who center their attention on adult offenders than they have been among specialists on juvenile delinquency. Moreover, although a few delinquent typologies have appeared in the literature, including my own claims (Gibbons, 1965: 74-79) about nine juvenile offender types and Cohen and Short's (1958) contentions concerning varieties of "delinquent subcultures," subsequent empirical studies have failed to support those arguments (see Gibbons, 1981). Accordingly, the remainder of this chapter is concerned with allegations about adult offenders and crime patterns, rather than with delinquency or delinquents.

Looking Forward

Having come this far, where do we go now in this probing of the typological approach? The plan for the remainder of this chapter is as follows. First, let us take up in more detail the three relatively comprehensive typologies that have been drawn up by Clinard and Quinney, Glaser, and me, with particular emphasis upon the extent to which these schemes meet the requirements of clarity and the like. That discussion will then be followed by an examination of a portion of the empirical evidence that can be marshaled in order to evaluate the accuracy of typological characterizations.

THREE COMPREHENSIVE TYPOLOGIES

Clinard and Quinney:
Criminal Behavior Systems

Let us begin with the typological formulation of Clinard and Quinney (1973: 1-23), which appears to be a somewhat ambiguous blend of offense-centered and person-centered arguments. Although Clinard and Quinney (1973: 13) speak of "criminal behavior systems" and "types of crimes," using the former as the title of their book, they also argue that their behavior system typology is intended to "suggest how persons with certain characteristics and behaviors develop patterns that have a certain probability of becoming defined as criminal and receive a particular reaction from society." On this same point, the Clinard and Quinney typology is based on five dimensions: legal aspects of selected offenses, group support of criminal behavior, correspondence between criminal and legitimate behavior, societal reaction and legal processing, and criminal career of the offender. The last of these dimensions implies a concern with kinds of criminal actors rather than with different forms of criminal activity.

Clinard and Quinney enumerate nine criminal behavior systems, identified in terms of these five dimensions:

- violent personal criminal behavior
- occasional property criminal behavior
- public order criminal behavior
- conventional criminal behavior
- political criminal behavior
- occupational criminal behavior
- corporate criminal behavior
- organized criminal behavior
- professional criminal behavior

In the specific chapters in which Clinard and Quinney collate a body of evidence regarding these criminal behavior systems, their comments move back and forth between remarks about offenders and offenses, so that part of the time they speak of murder, assault, or rape, while at other times they comment about murderers, assaultists, or forcible rapists. Obviously, observations about the "criminal careers" of offenders who fall into these behavior system groupings imply that individuals specialize in these crime forms, which may well be a faulty assumption on the part of Clinard and Quinney.

There is another problem with the Clinard and Quinney scheme, namely, that these typological rubrics are overly broad, lumping unlike offenses and offenders together. For example, public order criminal behavior brings together such diverse activities as prostitution, homosexual behavior, drunkenness, and drug use. Similarly, political criminality is a label for a diverse grab bag of unlike activities (Turk, 1982). As a result, it is difficult to avoid the conclusion that their typological argument is more heuristic than it is precise.

Glaser's Adult Crime Careers

Next, consider the typological description of adult offenders that has been put forth by Glaser (1972: 27-66; 1975). He describes ten offender patterns, identified in terms of the underlying dimensions of offense descriptive variables and career commitment variables:

- adolescent recapitulators
- subcultural assaulters
- addiction-supporting predators
- vocational predators
- organized illegal sellers
- avocational predators
- crisis-vacillation predators
- quasi-insane assaulters
- addicted performers
- private illegal consumers

According to Glaser (1972: 28), adolescent recapitulators are "persons who periodically repeat the pattern of delinquency begun in adolescence," while subcultural assaulters are "persons who live in a subculture emphasizing violence as a value" (p. 32) and vocational predators are defined as "persons who support themselves for many years primarily by unlawfully taking money or property from others" (p. 44).

There are several things to be said about this typology. First, as Glaser (1972: 14) himself acknowledges, these categorizations gloss over the rich mixture and gradations of characteristics of persons in the real world; in short, these are ideal types. Also, some forms of criminal conduct are missing from the typology, such as political criminality, along with various low-visibility offenses that some have termed "folk crime" or "mundane crime" (Gibbons, 1983). Then, too, some of the descriptions, such as of adolescent recapitulators or crisis-vacillation predators, have to do with offense patterns and criminal careers of individuals and others with the etiology of their behavior, thus they involve dimensions additional to those on which the typology is alleged to be based. On the positive side, Glaser's narrative comments about these types provide a good deal of detail about them and also are based upon a large criminological literature dealing with offender behavior, so that they seem to ring true in a number of cases; that is, they are plausibly connected to the evidence on lawbreakers. But on a different note, the identifying characteristics of the types in Glaser's typology are somewhat vague. A good deal of difficulty would probably be encountered if one were to try to sort out a collection of actual offenders into these ten types, with different observers disagreeing in their assignments of specific persons to these categories.

Gibbons's Role-Career Typologies

I have developed one of the most detailed and comprehensive typological formulations in criminology (Gibbons, 1965: 75-125; 1979: 85-92). Those role-career typologies of adult offenders and of juvenile delinquents describe offender roles in terms of the dimensions of current offense behavior, the interactional setting within which the offense occurred, and the criminal career or prior criminal record of the offender, as well as the self-concept patterns and role-related attitudes presumably exhibited by lawbreakers. The characteristics of particular offender types, identified in terms of these five dimensions, are specified in detail in the role-career typologies. It is also the case that these typologies involve claims about the causal backgrounds out of which putative types are thought to be produced, arranged within the rubrics or dimensions of social class, family background, peer group associations, and contacts with defining agencies (the police, courts, prisons, and so on). The reader will doubtless note a good deal of similarity between this scheme and the Clinard and Quinney formulation.

Mention has already been made of my typology of juvenile delinquents. The adult offender typology involves the following types:

- professional thief
- professional "heavy" criminal
- semiprofessional property criminal
- property offender, "one-time loser"
- automobile thief—"joyrider"
- naive check forger
- white-collar criminal
- professional "fringe" violator
- embezzler
- personal offender—"one-time loser"
- "psychopathic" assaultist
- violent sex offender
- nonviolent sex offender, "rapo"
- nonviolent sex offender, statutory rape
- narcotic addict—heroin

Like the typologies of Clinard and Quinney and Glaser, this one was constructed in part upon a substructure of evidence from research studies on lawbreaking and lawbreakers, hence it has *some* degree of empirical accuracy. Offender typologies are not bizarre, wholly erroneous ravings produced by criminologists gone mad. However, the central question remains: How close to comprehending the nature of the real world of crime and criminals do these schemes come? Regarding my typological argument, one early critic of this formulation (Lemert, 1965) concluded that it was overly clinical, medical, and individualistic in form—a judgment that I have come to share. Let us turn our attention at this point to some of the direct and tangential evidence bearing upon offender typologies.

CRIMINAL CAREERS AND RESEARCH FINDINGS

Inmate Social Roles

We saw at the beginning of this chapter that a number of criminologists have reported the existence of typification systems among male and female prisoners in penal institutions and that they have sometimes been invoked as support for typological arguments about offenders at large, on the assumption that they indicate the existence of behavior patterns among offenders.

In one of these accounts, Schrag (1961: 346-56) asserts that male prisoners exhibit patterns of social role behavior and are identified in inmate argot as "square Johns," "right guys," "outlaws," "dings," and "politicians." These roles center on loyalty to other convicts, hence the "right guy" is a dependable member of the inmate subculture, involved in resistance to the authorities, while the "square John" is an alien in the convict subculture. Schrag also argues that the criminal histories, prison adjustments, and other characteristics of inmates can be predicted in terms of their positions in this system of inmate roles.

However, there is only a relatively loose fit between this inmate typology and the real world. For example, Garabedian (1964: 338-347) conducted research in the same prison in which Schrag's informal observations were made. He identified inmate role incumbents through a series of attitude questionnaire items, but found that about one-third of the prisoner sample was unclassifiable through this procedure. He also discovered that the linkages between background characteristics and social roles were relatively weak.

Further negative evidence was found in a study by Leger (1979: 346-365), who used Garabedian's attitudinal items to identify inmate roles and also employed self-nominations by inmates, guards' judgments as to which prisoners fit particular role types, and social background information on convicts as independent measures of these social roles. Little agreement was found among these four techniques, either in terms of the total number of prisoners who were identified as incumbents of social types or in terms of the consistency with which individuals were assigned to a single type.

Still another serious challenge to inmate social role arguments came from an investigation conducted by Poole et al. (1980: 317-324) in a Virginia maximum security prison. These investigators applied a set of attitudinal items similar to those used by Garabedian and Leger to an inmate sample. They found that these attitudinal items, each of which was supposed to provoke a certain response from inmates of one type and a different response from the rest of the prisoners, actually had low internal consistency. Stated another way, the individual items that made up the scales through which role incumbents were identified failed to discriminate among these alleged role incumbents. Also, Poole et al. found that the salient criminal career variables that are supposed to differentiate among role incumbents were almost invariant across the identified role types. Finally, the role type categorizations were not related to institutional misconduct and/or official sanctions against prisoners, contrary to claims that have been made about inmate social types.

What are we to make of these data on inmate social roles? The most reasonable conclusion would appear to be that the accounts of inmate roles stand as useful conceptual caricatures that highlight some behavior patterns and attitudes that are observable in relatively clearcut fashion among a relatively few inmates. At the same time, many convicts do not behave consistently in the manner that is described by these inmate typologies. A good many prisoners apparently manage to maintain a low profile in the institution, such that neither they nor anyone else is able to single them out as "right guys" or "square Johns," or to apply any other of these labels to them.

Comprehensive Typologies and Research Evidence

What about the empirical status of the typologies of Clinard and Quinney, Glaser, or myself? There are no research investigations that have directly examined the first two typologies, probably in part because of the fuzziness of parts of these arguments. However, two investigations have been conducted specifically on the role-career typology. In one of these, a group of probation officers in a California county probation department attempted to sort probationers into the role-career categories (Hartjen and Gibbons, 1969: 56-62). They employed abridged typological profiles of offenders, with groups of three officers acting as independent judges who read case files on probationers in order to decide whether they could be assigned to types. Slightly less than half of the probationers were placed in a type, even using these relatively loose sorting procedures. Subsequently, Hartjen sifted through the records of the unassigned cases and, using offense records, placed most of them into seven ad hoc types such as nonsupport offenders or petty property criminals. However, these types did not differ markedly from each other in terms of commitment to deviance, social backgrounds, or other characteristics.

McKenna (1972) also conducted research on the role-career typology, in which he classified prisoners in a state correctional institution into offender types through examination of their arrest records, with about 90 percent of them being placed in twelve offender types. He then examined whether the other combinations of characteristics said to differentiate role-career incumbents actually occurred as predicted. Only in one of the twelve offense-based types did the hypothesized pattern of behavior and social psychological characteristics emerge. In the remainder, prisoners who had been assigned to one or another type in terms of offense patterns showed a good deal of similarity to members of other offense types in terms of attitudes, self-image patterns, and interactional setting of the offense. Thus these findings indicate that many real-life offenders cannot be assigned with much precision to the role-career typology.

There are some other, tangential studies that reinforce this conclusion about the marked variability among lawbreakers. In one of these, conducted in a federal probation office, the investigators sorted probationers into types, based upon their current offense, age, prior criminal record, and score on a personality test (Adams et al., 1971). This empirically generated scheme resulted in 54 possible combinations or types (such as Dyer Act violators who were under 25 years of age, had no prior record, and scored in the midrange on the personality inventory). Furthermore, there were probationers found in each of the 54 categories!

Somewhat similar results have been reported by McCaghy (1967), who found in a study on child molesters that these persons were sufficiently varied that six subtypes of molesters could be identified. Also, Conklin (1972: 59-78) has indicated that there are at least four subtypes of robbers: professionals, opportunists, drug-addicted, and alcoholics.

The Rand Criminal Career Studies

There is another set of research investigations bearing upon the typological perspective that should be singled out for special attention, namely, a series of studies funded by the federal Law Enforcement Assistance Administration and conducted by the Rand Corporation. Taken together, these inquiries have provided a large body of evidence dealing with behavioral regularities among offenders.

The initial Rand study was conducted among 49 "armed robbers" in a California prison (Petersilia et al., 1977), that is, persons who had been singled out as robbers because their current prison sentences were for that crime. The average age of the prisoners was 39, thus most of them had been criminally active for some time. When these offenders were asked to report the number of times they had committed any of 9 specific crimes since becoming involved in lawbreaking, they confessed to over 10,000 offenses, or an average of 214 per offender! Even more striking, they admitted collectively to 3,620 drug sales, 2,331 burglaries, 1,492 automobile thefts, 995 forgeries, 993 grand thefts, and 855 instances of robbery. Obviously, these lawbreakers were not specialists in armed robbery—instead, they might better be described as "jack-of-all-trades" offenders.

The second Rand study, conducted in 1976, involved over 600 inmates from 5 California prisons (Peterson et al., 1980). These prisoners were asked to indicate the number and kinds of crimes they had committed during the three-year period prior to their current incarceration, as well as to answer questions dealing with such things as drug use, economic circumstances, reasons for committing crimes, and their perceptions of the risks and payoffs from lawbreaking.

Briefly summarized, nearly half of the prisoners reported committing four or more different types of offenses during the recent past. For each type of crime studied, most of those who reported engaging in it said they did so relatively infrequently, but a minority of prisoners confessed to committing the crime with regularity. The authors conclude that the inmate sample included two broad kinds of offenders, occasional criminals and broadly active ones. Still another finding was that there were few prisoners who claimed to have committed a single kind of crime at a high rate, hence *there appeared to be few career specialists in these prisons*. Crime switching was commonplace among the felons. Not surprising, the most highly active lawbreakers were the ones who were most likely to think of themselves as criminals. Finally, about half of the respondents claimed that economic pressures were the main causes of their misbehavior, while about a third of them reported the desire for high living to be central to their criminal deviance.

The third and most ambitious of these Rand studies was conducted among approximately 2,200 jail and prison inmates in institutions in Texas, Michigan, and California (Chaiken and Chaiken, 1982). The respondents were administered a lengthy questionnaire that included self-report crime items and a variety of other questions as well. The prisoners were asked to report the number of times that they had committed robberies, assaults, burglaries, forgeries, frauds or thefts, and drug deals during the preceding 24 months.

About 13 percent of the prisoners asserted that they had not committed any of the offenses studied during the previous two years. The remainder, who reported involvement in one or more of the crimes, most commonly claimed to have done those offenses at relatively low rates. Put differently, most of the respondents were apparently persons who dabbled in crime, were not "career criminals," and had been in the civilian labor force prior to incarceration. On the other hand, the crime rate distributions were skewed, in that a sizable minority of offenders reported having committed one or more crimes extremely frequently prior to incarceration.

One of the major findings of this study had to do with the offense versatility or crime switching reported by large numbers of prisoners. Criminal specialization was *not* characteristic of very many of these persons. But, even though the researchers discovered a good many instances in which offenders reported engaging in a mixed bag of crimes, they nonetheless did attempt to create a typological scheme from these data. The results of those efforts are shown in Table 7.1 (Chaiken and Chaiken, 1982: 27).

Examination of Table 7.1 reveals that the Rand investigators categorized 15 percent of the prisoners as "violent predators," who had committed robbery, assault, and drug deals in the past year or so, and who often had also engaged in burglary and/or theft. "Burglar-dealers" were prisoners who confessed to burglary and drug deals, but who also frequently were involved in thefts, frauds, or forgeries. The offense patterns of the other "types" can be determined from a study of Table 7.1.

Several remarks are in order concerning the table and the other findings of this Rand study. Although it is clear that there was some patterning of offenses exhibited by the prisoners studied, so that they did not usually engage in completely random and unpredictable collections of crimes, and even though some "types" of offenders were uncovered by the researchers, the categorization in Table 7.1 differs considerably from most of the typological systems or arguments that have been advanced by criminologists in the past. For one thing, criminologists have often assumed that lawbreakers are frequently crime specialists such as "robbers," "burglars," "drug dealers," and the like. But relatively few of the offenders in Table 7.1 appear to have concentrated their misdeeds upon a single kind of criminality. Also, a fact not revealed in the table is that many of the "low-level robbers" actually engaged in robberies *less frequently* than did "violent

TABLE 7.1
Definition of Hierarchical Varieties of Criminal Behavior

Group	Robbery	Assault[a]	Burglary	Theft,[b] Fraud, Forgery, Credit Card Crimes	Drug Deals	Number of Respondents	Percentage
Violent predators (robber-assaulter-dealers)	+	+	?	?	+	306	15.0
Robber-assaulters	+	+	?	?	0	160	7.8
Robber-dealers	+	0	?	?	+	188	9.2
Low-level robbers	+	0	?	?	0	240	11.8
Mere assaulters	0	+	0	0	0	105	5.1
Burglar-dealers	0	??	+	?	+	199	9.8
Low-level burglars	0	??	+	?	0	171	8.4
Property and drug offenders	0	0	0	+	+	128	6.3
Low-level property offenders	0	0	0	+	0	168	8.2
Drug dealers	0	0	0	0	+	112	5.5
Total[c]						1777	87.1

NOTE: + = group member commits this crime, by definition; 0 = group member does not commit this crime, by definition; ? = group member may or may not commit this crime; analysis shows that nearly all members of the group do; ?? = group member may or may not commit this crime; most don't.
a. Includes homicide arising out of assault or robbery.
b. Includes auto theft.
c. The remaining 12.9 percent did not report committing any of the crimes studied. Respondents with missing data (150 out of 2190) were excluded in calculation of percentages.

predators" and, similarly, "drug dealers" often conducted fewer drug sales per person per year than did some of the other "types" shown in the table. Indeed, the Rand researchers reported some difficulty in settling upon appropriate labels or names for these empirical types (Chaiken and Chaiken, 1982: 26).

There are other problems with these Rand data that make them less than perfect. One of these is that the research was confined to incarcerated offenders and did not deal with lawbreakers at large, hence it may have concentrated upon a biased sampling of "losers" in crime. There are no white-collar offenders, swindlers, or organized crime figures represented in these data. Also, a large number of inmates were nonrespondents, so that the inmate samples may have been biased as well. Then, too, the accuracy of self-report data is open to question. Perhaps some respondents inflated their criminal records, confessing to more crimes than they had actually committed, while others may have concealed some of their offenses and still others of them may have simply failed to recall crimes that they had actually carried out. Finally, if crime switching is as common as indicated by these data, these typological assignments are probably unstable in many cases, such that an individual who is classed as a "drug dealer" in a study this year may turn out to be a "burglar-dealer" or a "violent predator" when next encountered by prison officials or a researcher. However, the import of all of these reservations about the Rand studies is that they provide even further reason for skepticism about the long-term value of traditional typological approaches and perspectives in criminology.

TYPOLOGIES:
WHERE DO WE GO FROM HERE?

The central message of this chapter is a negative one: The typological idea is a fairly simple and straightforward one that has superficial plausibility, but it is also an idea whose time has probably gone. Many of the typological systems that have been suggested by criminologists, particularly those that assign criminal or delinquent persons to a relatively small number of distinct types, are fuzzy and ambiguous, making it difficult if not impossible to scrutinize them through research efforts. It is one thing to cast about among real-life offenders with whom one has contact for individual cases that in some vague, intuitive sense seem to be similar to a description of "adolescent recapitulators," for example, and quite another thing to conduct a precise count of the number of such persons in a large sample of offenders.

In my own case, I have devoted about a quarter of a century to work of one kind or another on offender typologies (Gibbons and Garrity, 1959: 51-58). The role-career typology of adult lawbreakers that I developed is relatively clear and explicit in spelling out the identifying characteristics of various putative types of criminals. But the research evidence we have examined here indicates that I have been engaged in a relatively fruitless endeavor, as have other architects of comprehensive typologies. The degree of patterning of offense behavior and other dimensions assumed in existing typologies is much greater than that which exists in the real world of lawbreaking. There are some violators who resemble the descriptions in typologies, but they are mixed in with a much larger number of offenders who do not fit into any type category. Behavioral diversity rather than offense specialization characterizes many offenders, with the result that it is difficult to place them in a typology.

Some criminologists will probably continue to employ typological accounts of crime patterns and/or types of offenders. In particular, the relatively crude taxonomies of crime forms or types of offenders noted at the beginning of this chapter will probably continue to show up in the pages of undergraduate textbooks. These typologies do have some heuristic value in that they alert students to broad groupings of crime forms or of lawbreakers, providing benchmarks against which actual offenders or criminal incidents can be compared. However, it is also to be hoped that criminologists will be more careful than they have been in the past to emphasize the "ideal type" nature of typological accounts. We ought to refrain from encouraging students into supposing that actual offenders go about with real or figurative tags attached to them, announcing that they are "naive check forgers," "subcultural assaulters," or some other kind of obvious behavioral type.

Classifications and typologies of offenders will probably also continue to show up in correctional settings, particularly now that modern computer technology provides researchers and administrators with techniques by which large masses of information on offenders can be processed, resulting in the sorting of these individuals into ad hoc "types" that are useful for various administrative purposes, such as sentence setting, custodial assignments, and kindred decisions.

In my view and that of a number of other criminologists, too much attention has probably been paid in the past to person-centered efforts to discover answers to the question, "Why do they do it?" The typological perspective has played a part in this search for answers as to why specific individuals engage in acts of lawbreaking. However, it would be difficult to argue that those who have mined this criminological vein have produced a large number of nuggets of insight. Moreover, criminologists have been unduly concerned about the etiology of individual acts of lawbreaking and have not given sufficient attention to queries about crime patterns, crime rates, and the social-structural conditions that are predictive of crime in the aggregate.

I do not have space in this chapter to present a detailed argument about the study of crime patterns, but an illustration or two may be helpful. In my view, there is much to recommend in the "routine activities" approach found in the work of Cohen and Felson (1979). These investigators have argued that changes in the rates and extent of certain property crimes, such as residential burglaries, in recent decades are to be explained by changes in three general sets of factors: the supply of potential offenders, the supply of suitable targets, and the absence of capable guardians. In their research probing of this argument, they assume a relatively constant supply of potential offenders and conclude that crime changes are to be explained principally in terms of shifts in the household activity ratio, that is, the proportion of married females employed outside the home and the like. Alterations in the employment patterns of men and women and related structural changes have resulted in increased crime opportunities and a decline of deterrents to crime in the form of neighborhood surveillance and other impediments to lawbreaking.

Although their argument may not be entirely correct, the work of Cohen and Felson is illustrative of directions that ought to be pursued by criminologists. Carroll and Jackson (1983: 178-94) have recently taken issue with Cohen and Felson, arguing that it is variations in income inequality across urban communities, rather than variations in the household activity ratio, that account for varying levels of predatory criminality. On this same general point, a recent investigation by Ellis and Beattie (1983: 74-93) examining the feminist argument that rape is a reflection of sexual inequality is also a clear departure from the person-centered tradition of queries about the personal background characteristics of rapists. In my opinion, it is this kind of theorizing and research that is called for, rather than more typologizing and typologies.

It is time for emphasis upon sociological accounts of crime, rather than the social psychological and, often, overly clinical directions that have been associated with the typological perspective.

REFERENCES

ADAMS, W. P., P. M. CHANDLER, and M. G. NEITHERCUTT (1971) "The San Francisco Project: a critique." Federal Probation 35: 45-53.
BARTON, A. H. (1955) "The concept of property-space in social research," pp. 40-53 in P. F. Lazarsfeld and M. Rosenberg (eds.) The Language of Social Research. New York: Free Press.
CARROLL, L. and P. I. JACKSON (1983) "Inequality, opportunity, and crime rates in central cities." Criminology 21: 178-194.
CHAIKEN, J. M. and M. R. CHAIKEN (1982) Varieties of Criminal Behavior. Santa Monica, CA: Rand Corporation.
CLINARD, M. B. and R. QUINNEY (1973) Criminal Behavior Systems. New York: Holt, Rinehart and Winston.
COHEN, A. K. and J. F. SHORT, Jr. (1958) "Research on delinquent subcultures." Journal of Social Issues 3: 20-37.
COHEN, L. E. and M. FELSON (1979) "Social change and crime rate trends: a routine activities approach." American Sociological Review 44: 588-607.
CONKLIN, J. F. (1972) Robbery and the Criminal Justice System. Philadelphia: J. B. Lippincott.
CORSINI, R. J. (1949) "Criminal psychology," pp. 108-115 in V. C. Branham and S. B. Kutash (eds.) Encyclopedia of Criminology. New York: Philosophical Library.
ELLIS, L. and C. BEATTIE (1983) "The feminist explanation for rape: an empirical test." Journal of Sex Research 19: 74-93.
GARABEDIAN, P. (1964) "Social roles in a correctional community." Journal of Criminal Law, Criminology and Police Science 55: 338-347.
GIALLOMBARDO, R. (1966) Society of Women. New York: John Wiley.
GIBBONS, D. C. (1983) "Mundane crime." Crime & Delinquency 29: 213-227.
——— (1982) Society, Crime, and Criminal Behavior. Englewood Cliffs, NJ: Prentice-Hall.
——— (1981) Delinquent Behavior. Englewood Cliffs, NJ: Prentice-Hall.
——— (1979) The Criminological Enterprise. Englewood Cliffs, NJ: Prentice-Hall.
——— (1965) Changing the Lawbreaker. Englewood Cliffs, NJ: Prentice-Hall.
——— and D. L. GARRITY (1959) "Some suggestions for the development of etiological and treatment theory in criminology." Social Forces 38: 51-58.
GLASER, D. (1975) Strategic Criminal Justice Planning. Rockville, MD: National Institute of Mental Health.
——— (1972) Adult Crime and Social Policy. Englewood Cliffs, NJ: Prentice-Hall.
GUTTMACHER, M. S. (1960) The Mind of the Murderer. New York: Farrar, Straus & Giroux.
HARTJEN, C. A. and D. C. GIBBONS (1969) "An empirical investigation of a criminal typology." Sociology and Social Research 54: 56-62.

HEFFERNAN, E. (1972) Making It in Prison. New York: John Wiley.
JENKINS, R. L. and L. E. HEWITT (1944) "Types of personality structure encountered in child guidance clinics." American Journal of Orthopsychiatry 14: 84-94.
LEGER, R. G. (1979) "Research findings and theory as a function of operationalization of variables: a comparison of four identification techniques for the construct, 'inmate type.' " Sociology and Social Research 63: 346-374.
LEMERT, E. M. (1965) "Review." American Sociological Review 30: 965.
——(1958) "The behavior of the systematic check forger." Social Problems 6: 141-149.
——(1953) "An isolation and closure theory of naive check forgery." Journal of Criminal Law, Criminology and Police Science 44: 296-307.
LOW, D. A. (1982) Thieves' Kitchen. London: J. M. Dent and Sons.
McCAGHY, C. H. (1967) "Child molesters," pp. 75-88 in M. B. Clinard and R. Quinney (eds.) Criminal Behavior Systems. New York: Holt, Rinehart & Winston.
McKENNA, J. (1972) "An empirical testing of a typology of adult criminal behavior." Ph.D. dissertation, University of Notre Dame.
McKINNEY, J. C. (1970) "Sociological theory and the process of typification," pp. 235-269 in J. C. McKinney and E. A. Tiryakian (eds.) Theoretical Sociology. New York: Appleton-Century-Crofts.
MEGARGEE, E. I., M. J. BOHN, Jr., J. E. MEYER, Jr., and F. SINK (1979) Classifying Criminal Offenders. Beverly Hills, CA: Sage.
NEUSTATTER, W. L. (1957) The Mind of the Murderer. New York: Philosophical Library.
PETERSILIA, J., P. W. GREENWOOD, and M. LAVIN (1977) Criminal Careers of Habitual Felons. Santa Monica, CA: Rand Corporation.
PETERSON, M. A., H. B. BRAIKER, and S. M. POLICH (1980) Doing Crime. Santa Monica, CA: Rand Corporation.
POOLE, E. D., R. M. REGOLI, and C. W. THOMAS (1980) "The measurement of inmate social role types: an assessment." Journal of Criminal Law and Criminology 71: 317-324.
ROEBUCK, J. B. (1966) Criminal Typology. Springfield, IL: Charles C Thomas.
SCARR, H. A., J. L. PINSKY, and D. S. WYATT (1973) Patterns of Burglary. Washington, DC: Law Enforcement Assistance Administration.
SCHRAG, C. C. (1961) "A preliminary criminal typology." Pacific Sociological Review 4: 11-16.
SYKES, G. M. (1958) The Society of Captives. Princeton, NJ: Princeton University Press.
TOBIAS, J. J. (1967) Crime and Industrial Society in the 19th Century. London: B. T. Batsford Ltd.
TURK, A. T. (1982) Political Criminality. Beverly Hills, CA: Sage.
WARREN, M. Q. (1976) "Intervention with juvenile delinquents," pp. 176-204 in M. K. Rosenheim (ed.) Pursuing Justice for the Child. Chicago: University of Chicago Press.
WOLFGANG, M. E. (1958) Patterns of Criminal Homicide. Philadelphia: University of Pennsylvania Press.

PART IV

ASSUMPTIONS ABOUT THE NATURE OF EXPLANATIONS

8

The Neoclassical Theory of Crime Control

ERNEST van den HAAG

THE UNIVERSAL NEED FOR PUNISHMENT

The social order, including the legal system, is not designed. Like language, it accumulates spontaneously, and social rules usually originate as spontaneous customs, later to develop into laws. Yet all societies must impose certain rules on their members on pain of not surviving. A rule restraining everybody from killing anybody is indispensable to secure life and to remove fear, so that individuals are able to associate with one another. Other rules are indispensable too and therefore universal.[1] Further rules articulate and protect the social system of each particular society.

In the past, persons who disregarded customary prohibitions were felt not to be entitled to the advantages yielded by their disruptive acts, nor to the advantages yielded by the tissue of customary prohibitions that they had rent. Such persons became outlaws, bereft of customary protections. Originally left to those harmed by violations, who were authorized to retribute or to negotiate compensation in lieu of retribution, enforcement of the laws, which replaced customs, ultimately was delegated to criminal justice authorities. Lawbreakers thus became not just outlaws exposed to approved private vengeance, but criminals exposed to public retribution. They were to be apprehended, judged, and punished by public authorities.

The desire for vengeance, legitimized through custom and social approval in prelegal times, persists in all societies and convinces us that crimes "deserve" legal punishment. Vengeance, socialized and qualified by safeguards and limitations, becomes "retribution," distributing "just deserts" to lawbreakers. Those actually harmed by crime and motivated to seek vengeance do so now through legal retribution. But others, not themselves victimized, also fear criminals: They may be the next victims, so they, too, want to "see justice done." Further, all law-abiding persons feel that they are restrained by the accepted moral standards of society and the threats of the law from reaping the advantages available through lawbreaking. Law-abiding citizens thus resent those who reap illicit advantages and want them taken away. If crimes are profitable, refraining from them is not; those who refrain end up feeling cheated and foolish, unless criminals are deprived of the advantages achieved by breaking the law and are punished as deserved. In all societies, justice is felt to require no less.

THE JUSTIFICATION OF PUNISHMENT

Explanations of the functions and origins of the criminal law, such as the one just sketched, often are confused with what they are not: justifications. However, justifications not only must tell why some acts are, but also why they should be prohibited and punished by law; further, they must tell how severe a legal punishment is justified for each crime. Most important, justifications must tell what we mean to achieve by the punishments to be inflicted for each crime and why we are entitled to achieve our ends by imposing punishments.

In the main there are but two normative justifications of punishment: Punishment is justified either by the sense of justice (by the feeling of resentment of crimes and by the socialized desire for vengeance expressed by retribution), or by the need for social control and protection. Satisfaction of that need in turn must be normatively justified. However, theories that stress control tend to deal mostly with the means used, and postulate the end, control, and its justification, or follow implicitly some utilitarian justification. In contrast, retributive theories often are more concerned with ends than with the size of the actual punishments used to achieve them. Theories differ in relating justice and social control, in their emphasis on either, and in the inferences drawn from them.

Justice means that every crime deserves punishment (retribution) proportionate to its gravity and to the culpability of the criminal.² To punish accordingly is to do justice. In its pure form justice deals exclusively with the blameworthiness of crimes committed in the past and the punishment deserved, disregarding all future consequences of punishment, such as rehabilitation or deterrence, disregarding even the future effects on the social order of doing justice, such as the effect of retribution on the continued willingness to obey the law. Justice, as a deontological concept, is an end in itself, independent of any usefulness, and indeed of any consequences: *fiat justitia pereat mundus*. Further, punishment, rather than being an evil, becomes a good by being necessary to justice.

In contrast, when justified by the need for social control, punishment is regarded as a means and an evil justified teleologically by the expected good effects. Punishment is threatened by law as a disincentive, to deter persons, in the future, from prohibited acts; it is imposed for past acts because threatened. Acts are prohibited because they are thought harmful (it does not matter whether the harm is material or moral). The degree to which a social need, or desire, to deter from crime is felt and the size of the threat required to deter from it to that degree determine the size of the threatened punishment, unless the required threat is thought to be disproportionate to the reduction of crime it is likely to produce. The costs of the credible threat, moral and material, are balanced against the benefits of crime reduction. (Classical deterrence doctrine proposes punishments that minimize the crimes they punish. Here I have added the realistic provision that the punishment is to reduce the rate at which the crime is committed by as much as the community wishes to reduce it in view of the moral and material cost of additional reductions.)

In its pure form the deterrence justification of punishment postulates the moral desirability of crime reduction, but disregards what may be morally deserved by past acts and focuses exclusively on consequences, specifically on the disincentives needed to deter future crimes. Unavoidably, if uneasily, the penal provisions of the laws and the sentences of courts combine the desert and consequentialist justifications of punishment. As will be seen, they complement eact other, although at times they lead to different sentences.

Retributive and deterrence justifications of punishment, contrary to widespread impressions, are not inconsistent with one another for the simple reason that they respond to quite different questions. The retributionist answers the question: What is justly deserved for past crimes? Deterrence theory responds to the question: What threat of punishment will best reduce future crimes? The questions deal with different subjects. If they lead to different punishment prescriptions, one has to choose whether to give more weight to justice or to deterrence. (They seldom diverge much.) Nonidentical punishment prescriptions are not logically inconsistent, nor are the theories mutually exclusive. Believing in one, one can believe in the other: It is quite possible to say, This punishment is deterrent but unjust, or vice versa, or, it is deterrent as well as just.

THE IRRELEVANCE OF REHABILITATION AND INCAPACITATION TO THE CRIME RATE

Customarily, incapacitation and rehabilitation are mentioned as additional purposes of punishment. They will be neglected here. Incapacitation, although usually temporary, does, at any time, keep a proportion of criminals out of action.[3] Yet (with few exceptions), incapacitation is unlikely to reduce the rate at which most crimes are committed. As for rehabilitation, it does not succeed often enough to warrant considering it among the purposes of punishment.[4] Further, even if it did deactivate a major number of criminals, rehabilitation would have little effect on the crime rate.

Neither incapacitation nor rehabilitation reduces the number of active offenders engaged in market-dependent crimes (crimes the proceeds of which are sold). Offenders are likely to be replaced when incapacitated or rehabilitated. The rate at which market-dependent crimes are committed is determined by factors independent of the number of persons who cease to engage in them because they are rehabilitated or incapacitated. When the expected net gain from crime suffices to attract others, incapacitated or rehabilitated offenders are readily replaced. The number of potential new entrants is practically unlimited.

Persons incapacitated because of non-market-dependent crimes are not necessarily replaced.[5] However, many of these crimes are committed by nonprofessionals, who may not engage in other crimes, or by first offenders, who cannot be rehabilitated or incapacitated before their first offense. Therefore, the rate at which both non-market-dependent and market-dependent crimes are committed is not much affected by incapacitation or rehabilitation of those caught (see van den Haag, 1982, 1983a).

If there were a finite number of persons likely to commit crimes— whether that number were the actual criminal population or exceeded it to a given extent—incapacitation or successful rehabilitation could indeed reduce crime rates. But this is the case at best for a few highly idiosyncratic crimes, and not for such crimes as burglary, auto theft, rape, or assault. There are far more persons capable of committing these crimes than do commit them and far more opportunities than are utilized. The rate at which these crimes are committed, then, is unlikely to be affected—except for short periods—by the elimination of any number of practitioners, whether through incapacitation or rehabilitation. The crime rate will respond only to increases or reductions in the comparative net benefit produced by crimes. Such changes are achieved mainly by changing the cost of crimes to offenders, that is, the probability and severity of punishment.

Not least, both incapacitation and rehabilitation are obviously irrelevant to justice: They are meant to protect society, or to improve the future conduct of criminals, not to punish them according to what their past crimes deserve.[6] We may neglect incapacitation and rehabilitation as justificatory purposes of punishment, then, since, even when achieved, neither can do justice or contribute significantly to controlling the crime rate.

DETERRENCE

I shall be concerned here with the function of punishment as a deterrent and with deterrence as a justification of punishment. I shall consider retribution only because the idea of desert may modify deterrent punishments and because retribution, although by definition not intended for deterrent effects nor justified by them, necessarily deters. Conceivably, retribution was spawned by observed deterrent effects, which, in the course of history, were separated from and contrasted with it. Obviously, when it can be so anticipated as to function as a threat, retribution or the threat of retributive punishment is no less deterrent than the threat of deterrent punishment. However, retributive punishment, by definition, can be inflicted only on culpable offenders, whereas deterrence might also work if innocent persons, perceived as guilty, are "punished."

Deterrence theory assumes that people respond to incentives (gains, advantages) and to disincentives (costs, disadvantages). This assumption seems quite safe, but tells us little about who will respond, how, to what incentives or disincentives. Cesare Bonesana, Marchese di Beccaria, originally popularized the latent notion of deterrence, in very sketchy form, in his *Dei Delitti e Delle Pene*. A little later, Jeremy Bentham articulated and applied it carefully.

DETERRENCE AND UTILITARIANISM

Bentham also was one of the fathers of the philosophical doctrine of utilitarianism. Because he based his version of deterrence theory on the philosophical and psychological doctrines of utilitarianism, deterrence theory has remained associated with utilitarianism in folklore and in the minds of scholars.

Benthamian utilitarianism sees the legitimate purpose of social institutions in maximizing the happiness and minimizing the suffering of individuals. Bentham's moral doctrine prescribes as much. Questions about distribution, indeed, potential conflicts between maximal and equally distributed happiness were not fully recognized. Bentham also believed that people individually do act in the pursuit of their happiness. This belief was part of his psychological doctrine, although he arrived at it deductively. It was complemented by his view that happiness was fungible, homogenous, divisible, and quantifiable both ordinally and cardinally. Bentham also believed that people are rational enough in their behavior to engage in the "felific calculus"; that is, to calculate what course of action would maximize their happiness and by and large to follow it.

These views led Bentham to propose that punishments should deter people from crime, by threatening enough pain to decrease the happiness of the offender by more than the prospective crime would have increased it. The threatened pain should not exceed the amount necessary to deter from the crime, for any excess would unnecessarily decrease the total amount of happiness in society.[7]

Thus it would be morally wrong to impose the maximum punishment for all crimes—even if it were the most deterrent—for to do so would reduce aggregate happiness. Bentham was aware as well of another reason for grading punishments. He realized that a burglar threatened with the same punishment as a murderer would have no reason for not committing murder in addition to burglary, since the additional crime would not result in additional punishment.[8]

CRITIQUE OF BENTHAMIAN VIEWS

Bentham's moral (prescriptive) hedonism—which postulates happiness as our ultimate moral end—has been shown to be more questionable than he thought. His empirical doctrine, that people do have happiness as their goal, is either definitional—whatever people do or strive for, by definition, becomes the pursuit of happiness, however detrimental it may be to their perceived happiness—or it is simply wrong: People do many things detrimental to their happiness, either for the sake of other things they value more, or because they are not as rational as Bentham believed.

Happiness is not homogenous, fungible, divisible, and quantifiable, and cannot be cardinally measured. This makes the "felific calculus" impossible.[9] Equally important, people are not rational calculators most of the time. They are unable to anticipate what will make them happy much of the time, and unwilling or unable to do it; human action is controlled by emotion far more than Bentham believed, and by reason less. Finally, from a normative viewpoint, what makes for happiness may not coincide with what is right, although Bentham thought so, being misled by his own definitions. It has not bee shown, then, either that happiness is, or that it ought to be, the ultimate goal of all human action. To illustrate just one counterintuitive result of Benthamian morality: Consider an unhappy person whose happiness (five units) is increased by ten units when he rapes a happy woman (she has twenty units) whose happiness is decreased by five units as a result. The rape would (a) increase total happiness by five units (b) increase the happiness of the worse-off individual, the rapist, at the expense of the better-off person, the victim, which would please such "maximin" egalitarians as John Rawls, particularly since rapist and victim become equally happy (they have fifteen units each) in the end. Rape would become a civic duty. So would, *mutatis mutandis*, other crimes. I am not suggesting that Bentham would approve this result. However, his theory would. The theory is improved by such Kantian "side constraints" (as Robert Nozick calls them) as John Rawls would suggest, but not enough to save utilitarians even in the Rawlsian (that is, Kantian) version.[10]

Utilitarianism in the classic Benthamian form must be abandoned, although more sophisticated and realistic versions certainly are alive and kicking among philosophers, and most people accept some utilitarian doctrines, to some degree, as common sense. They certainly believe that they want to be happy.

DETERRENCE INDEPENDENT OF UTILITARIANISM

To what extent is the theory of deterrence affected by the demise of classical utilitarianism and its notion of happiness? To what extent does deterrence theory depend upon philosophical doctrine more than, say, chemical theories do, and to what extent does the theory of deterrence depend upon Bentham's rationalistic psychological doctrines about human behavior?

Despite the historical association, I believe that the theory of deterrence can stand quite independently of classical utilitarian notions. Many psychological or moral objections to the theory of deterrence fall away once that independence is recognized and the theory restated without its philosophical integument, and without rationalistic psychology. It depends upon neither.

Like economic theory, with which it has much in common, including attacks directed against alleged axioms, the theory of deterrence rests on common, easily verified observations.

Animals as well as persons are drawn to opportunities perceived as rewarding. Both try to avoid whatever is perceived as painful or dangerous, unless the rewards appear to exceed the perceived disadvantages. Animals act in this manner on the basis of instinct and of their own direct experience; they learn and can be trained through ad hoc incentives and disincentives. Animals also imitate others, and may benefit from the experiences of those they imitate.

Unlike animals, people are able to learn directly from the experiences of others and from verbal communication of future experiences. Thus (general) deterrence can be observed in people, but has not been demonstrated in animals.[11]

It would be hard to understand how the human race could have survived if we had not learned to avoid danger (the risk of pain and deprivation) and to seek out rewarding occasions. There is nothing normative about such an observation, which may be rephrased: People tend to minimize whatever they see as costs and to maximize whatever they see as advantages. Costs and advantages may consist of anything people perceive as such. Individuals within the same culture may have somewhat different perceptions of costs and advantages, and differences are greater among individuals who belong to different cultures or subcultures. Further, individuals differ greatly in their perception of risk and their willingness to bear it. Still, death, deprivation, confinement, and the infliction of pain are seen as punishments (disincentives) everywhere, throughout history, and power, prestige, income, or wealth as rewards (incentives).

As was noted above, societies will find it advantageous to prohibit some actions, such as stealing, robbing, or murdering, although individuals may find them advantageous on occasion.[12] To make the prohibition effective and because the prohibited act may be perceived as advantageous by some individuals, societies must make prohibited actions costly—so costly that most people, most of the time, will be deterred from violating the prohibitions of the law. Societies do this by threatening punishments. This is the basic proposition of deterrence theory.

DETERRENCE AND CALCULATION

Deterrence theory has often been thought to presume that people, including prospective offenders, calculate their actions and are deterred from lawbreaking by a conscious cost-benefit calculation. This may well have been Bentham's belief, but deterrence theory does not require it. The theory merely observes that most people respond to incentives and disincentives *as though* calculating. Whether they do calculate is irrelevant. That the responses occur can be shown by observation.

Rats running a maze do not calculate, although calculations and even mathematical models may be helpful in predicting their paths as they respond to incentives and disincentives. To calculate the incentives needed to attract to one path, or the disincentives to deter from another, is not to assume that the rats calculate.

Businesspeople often try to calculate the responses of customers to price and product changes. Economists consider various elasticities. Such calculations, based on data generated by experience, do not assume that the customers whose demands are being calculated themselves calculate. They follow habit, or form it; they learn, imitate, and respond according to new incentives and disincentives. Similarly, legislators interested in deterrence should calculate (actually they tend to follow tradition, occasionally adding disincentives when the crime rate seems excessive) and vaguely do so. Legislators do realize that the threat of three years in prison will deter from rape more than will the threat of a $5.00 fine—even though they may be unsure whether five years may deter still more, or two years less. They calculate the probable response of prospective criminals—the public at large—to disincentives. In doing so they need not assume that the respondents themselves calculate. They merely adapt.

Criminologists may or may not be rational. However, observation suggests they they tend to seek employment where conditions, including pay, are optimal, given their qualifications and preferences. Criminologists respond to incentives. So do criminals. Both also respond to disincentives. They do not have caviar with a bottle of Montrachet 1979 for lunch, but rather a hamburger and a beer. The cost of the alternative is the disincentive. Were hamburgers and beer more expensive than caviar and Montrachet, they might lunch on the latter. But there is no daily calculation and perhaps no calculation whatever. Behavior, criminal or lawful, is shaped by habit, which, given tastes, is adapted to the realities of costs.

Deterrence theory thus does not depend upon any rationalist psychological theory, but merely upon the quotidian observation that most people, most of the time, are responsive to incentives and disincentives, including anticipated pleasures and pains. Although the nature and quantity of effective incentives and disincentives differ from person to person, imprisonment almost always is a disincentive and income, or wealth, an incentive.

SEVERITY AND PROBABILITY

Since neither expected rewards nor expected punishments are ever quite certain, we implicitly multiply rewards and punishments by the probability of achieving or suffering them. This has led some theorists to stress the probability of punishment more than its severity.

Reaction to these two factors differs according to life situations and personality. For a committed career offender it should make little material difference whether probability is high and severity low, or vice versa. If he commits, say, fifty burglaries a year, whether he is imprisoned once every five years for two years (high severity, low probability), or imprisoned twice for one year each time, he still spends two of the five years in prison. For him severity and probability might be fungible. Still, even if there is no material difference, there may be a psychological difference. Further, many offenders are not so professional.

Among these nonprofessionals some may be more impressed by probability, some by severity. It is clear, however, that highly probable but trivial punishments (trivial compared with the gain from crimes, or in terms of the offender's life situation) are not likely to deter. The deterrent effect of very severe but improbable punishments is less clear. They may have a strong disincentive effect on persons less impressed by the improbability of suffering the punishment than by its severity. After all, all purchasers of lottery tickets are more impressed by the size of the prize than by the improbability of winning it. (However, their stakes usually are small.) Other persons may respond more to the probability of punishment. So far, research has not given many indications of what combination of probability and severity is most deterrent for those most inclined to commit particular types of crimes, such as car theft, robbery, or burglary.[13] Note further that increases in probability cost the taxpayer far more than increases in severity.

CELERITY

It is often pointed out that celerity—the time span between crime and punishment—also may play a role in determining the effectiveness of threats: Long delays may reduce the deterrent effect of punishment.

Delays, anyway, are undesirable for many reasons. Nonetheless, delays are, most of the time, more likely to affect special deterrence—the effect of punishment on the person punished—than general deterrence, the effect of punishment on others, the intensification of the threat. The burglar whose punishment is delayed may commit other burglaries during the delay, and may discount the future and its punishments. He or she also may be less discouraged by punishment when it occurs after long delays.[14] The effect of delayed punishment on general deterrence has never been probed in a satisfactory manner;[15] it is likely that delays reduce deterrent effects both because they are not readily separated from uncertainties and because the future is discounted.

PERCEPTION

So far I have not distinguished threats of punishment from the perception of such threats. Obviously, unknown threats cannot have deterrent effects. On the other hand, it seems unlikely that such effects depend upon specific knowledge of the exact size of the threats.

Law-abiding persons remain law-abiding because they perceive crime as wrong and because they believe that there are legal dangers that outweigh the perceived advantages of crime. Law-abiding conduct does not depend upon specific knowledge of legal threats any more than it depends upon specific knowledge of the advantages of crime. A general perception—"crime does not pay"—is important, however, in the formation of law-abiding habits. It involves a perception only of the general magnitude of legal dangers to offenders. This notion is based on tradition: ultimately, the magnitude and probability of actual punishments will influence this tradition and therewith the formation of law-abiding or criminal habits.

For those already inclined to utilize criminal opportunities, perception of the actual legal threats may play a greater role. However, it is unlikely that, whether accurate or not, their perception will lead to major modifications of the conduct they intend to follow. Wishful thinking about risk factors will discount legal threats once the inclination to crime or the criminal habit has been formed—unless there is a major discontinuity in punishment threats. Thus if burglary previously punished with an average of three years were punished with an average of five, it would affect habit formation (the general magnitude of threats has increased) but probably not habits already formed. However, if the penalty suddenly became actual life imprisonment, and the change became generally known, it may affect the conduct even of some habitual burglars.

THE FORMATION OF CRIMINAL AND LAW-ABIDING HABITS

Classical deterrence doctrine assumed a person disposed to commit an offense for the sake of some gain (it is not clear whether this person was a representative of the general public or of a distinct group, a criminal class), who is to be deterred from it by threats of punishment severe enough to outweigh the potential gain. In a sense, in classical deterrence theory everybody is disposed to—that is, capable of—committing crimes, unless deterred. Realistically, it is probably true to say that nearly everybody is capable of committing crimes under some conditions; more important, many more persons are disposed to commit offenses under fairly ordinary conditions than actually do commit them. Some persons are disposed to crime under most conditions; but the great majority of persons have formed law-abiding habits aided by the belief that "crime does not pay."

The formation of law-abiding or criminal habits certainly does not depend upon the deterrent threats of the law alone. These habits are the product of a multiplicity of exogenous and endogenous factors, affecting groups and individuals; legal threats directed at lawbreakers are only one factor. However, these threats constitute the one factor the government can readily manipulate; and the risk of punishment is the major cost of crime, influencing the prospective net benefit. Other possibly criminogenic factors such as family, religion, ethnic tradition, economic status, employment status, and the many things that constitute Walter Bagehot's "cake of custom" are notoriously resistant not only to change, but specifically to change planned by governments.[16]

Given the punishment, and given the material benefit from crime, the net benefit from it differs among classes of the population—it is usually greater for the poor than for the rich—and among the individual members of these classes, according to life situations and personalities, including the learned inhibitions against lawbreaking or committing particular crimes. Hence different groups of the population and different individuals are attracted to, and seek out, criminal opportunities, or are deterred from utilizing them, to very different degrees.

Deterrent threats and punishments influence habit formation (which is hard to observe) far more than habits once they are formed (which are more readily observed). This is as true for law-abiding as it is for lawbreaking habits. In the words of James Fitzjames Stephen, "Some men, probably, abstain from murder because they fear that if they committed murder they would be hanged. Hundreds of thousands abstain from it because they regard it with horror. One great reason why they regard it with horror is that murderers are hanged." The effect of punishment threats and of incentives, producing a negative or positive net benefit of crimes, is similar, in this respect, to the effects of the net benefit from an occupation on the number of persons pursuing it. A decline in the anticipated comparative net benefit will affect the number of new entrants. But it will have rather minor effects on those who have been pursuing the occupation for some time. So with crime. Higher costs (effective cost, that is, punishment × probability of suffering it, not the list price, the listed punishment), are likely to affect the number of those who may form a criminal habit more than the number of those who have already formed it; the latter are unlikely to change their habits even when these habits are no longer advantageous.

This is of major importance for those who attempt to measure the effects of changes in punishment on the crime rate. Most of the time the effect on criminal habits already formed is measured. To measure the effect on habit formation would require far longer observation periods than are now used. Since habit formation is rarely observed and captured by statistical methods, deterrence theory, which relies upon it far more than upon the habits formed, is sometimes discounted, when it is found that added punishments have not reduced the criminal conduct of those habituated to it.

DETERRABILITY

Given these circumstances, in any society we may distinguish three groups:

(1) Those who, at least in the short run, hardly need deterrent threats to be law-abiding. In the short run at least, even promising criminal

opportunities are habitually ignored by this group; attention is not focused on them. Internalized restraints suffice before external threats fully enter consciousness. However, we do not know how this group would act in the long run in the absence of legal threats. Would they continue to pay for purchases if there were no credible penalty for not doing so? Would they use their power to assault and subjugate weaker persons if there were no legal restraints and threats?

(2) Those who may be restrained by deterrent threats. These include those who actually were deterred because the threats were sufficient in their circumstances, and those who might have been, if the threats had been more severe or probable. This group is responsive to internalized restraints supported by external threats. Increases in external threats reduce the rate of crimes.

(3) Those who are not deterrable, some not by actual, some not by feasible, some not by any conceivable threats. Those not restrained by actual or feasible threats may be quite rational. In their situation crime may lead to net gains. It would be a mistake to believe that even those not deterrable by any conceivable threat mainly are psychotics or defective persons (although such persons are part of the group). Just as a religious believer or a patriotic martyr may not be deterred by any threat, just as mountain-climbing enthusiasts are not deterred by nature's most dire dangers, so some persons attracted to particular crimes may not be deterrable. This group, fortunately, is small. Willing martyrs for any cause are few, but they exist. Persons in this group, though not deterrable by threats of punishment, must nonetheless be punished when they commit crimes. The threats of the law must be carried out. Otherwise the law becomes a bluff. Offenders must be punished to keep the law credible; every actual punishment functions as a threat to future lawbreakers and thus helps deter them. Most lawbreakers are likely to be recruited from the second (responsive) group, the size of which far exceeds the size of the group actually engaged in criminal conduct.[17]

Enough has been said to suggest that the basic doctrine of deterrence remains relevant to punishment, to law, indeed, to social life. However, the doctrine has not been developed much beyond Bentham. The market research that helps a firm to decide what to produce, at what price, so as to provoke the desired response, has not been done for crime. We have learned very little about what threats and punishments are apt to reduce what crime rates, by how much, under what conditions. Very little serious research is being done. Thus optimal punishments and combinations of severity and probability elude us.[18]

DETERRENCE AND MORALITY

**Instrumental Use
of Convicted Criminals**

One reason among many for our failure to do the needed research goes back to the utilitarian origin of deterrence theory that led to moral opposition to it. Bentham thought that crime control by deterrence would increase total happiness, and since utilitarian morality saw this as the end of social action, he had no problems in justifying deterrence. Further, Bentham thought guilty rather than innocent persons should be punished to deter them from future crimes and to deter others from becoming guilty of them. The threats of the law would not deter from crime if the law "punished" guilty and innocent alike, since it would not "pay" to refrain from crime.

Still, utilitarian beliefs might justify the punishment of innocent persons falsely perceived to be guilty. Bentham opposed such a policy, reasonably enough, for he thought that the innocence of the person punished would become known in time, and weaken the deterrent effect of the law by making it less certain that one can avoid punishment by avoiding crime. However, this prudential reasoning does not fully address the moral problem, which Bentham could not see because, according to utilitarian belief, the "punishment" of an innocent person—whether or not the person is publicly perceived as guilty— could be justified if, by saving lives or by averting suffering, it sufficiently increases total happiness.[19] Indeed, Bentham was not averse to using individuals as a means for the common good. This has led to opposition. It has been alleged that deterrence theory controvenes the Kantian injunction (implicit also in other deontological doctrines) never to use a person as a mere means for the ends of others: Everybody must be regarded as an end in himself. Kant objected to rehabilitation and deterrence as justifications of legal sanctions because offenders would be used as mere means for ends they do not share. He favored retribution, which, he thought, alone respects the offender's dignity as an autonomous and rational being.[20] Are offenders used as mere means for ends to which they have not consented when their punishment is used to deter others?

In social life we all use each other as means to our ends; the persons we so use consent to this use, which to them is a means to achieve their own ends; that is, they in turn use us as means. They are not used as *mere* means to other persons' ends, nor are we: We both consent because this is the best way to achieve our own ends. The taxi driver may not share my goal to arrive at my destination. He consents to be used as a means, for the sake of his goal of earning an income (for which I am used). Because of his consent (and mine) and the fact that we both can achieve our goals by serving as a means for one another, we are not used as *mere* means.

Offenders certainly do not consent to being punished and used to deter others. But they do, by their actions, knowingly take the risk of being punished and used to deter others. They consent to that risk as one consents to the risk of death when mountain climbing. They do so because by taking the risk of punishment—which they could avoid by avoiding crimes—they hope to achieve their end, to gain from committing crimes. Thus offenders are used, by being punished, against their wishes, but they consented to take that risk for the sake of their own ends. Their punishment includes the deterrent effect the law wishes to achieve.[21] They volunteered, as a soldier or a police officer may volunteer. Neither volunteers to die for the sake of protecting the public or the country (for the ends of others), but both volunteer to take the risk of dying. Because of his consent, the police officer is not a *mere* means for the protection of others.[22] So offenders take the risk of being caught, and, as part of their punishment, to be used to deter others, without becoming *mere* means, for they consented to take the risk of being so used.

Punishment of Innocents

Utilitarian notions have been strongly opposed also by all those who believe in prelegal individual rights (in the past called "natural" and now more often call "moral" or "human" rights), which Bentham thought "nonsense" or, when imprescriptible, "nonsense on stilts." This is not the place to address the conflict between deontological and utilitarian views of morality. However, it is important and appropriate to ask: Does deterrence theory depend upon the utilitarian views of morality from which it is historically descended? Specifically, does deterrence theory, as distinguished from utilitarianism, require, or permit, the "punishment" of innocents when it is more deterrent than nonpunishment would be? In my view, it does not. Deterrence theory neither justifies nor condemns the "punishment" of innocents. Deterrence theory asserts that, given appropriate circumstances, the "punishment" of persons perceived as guilty may have deterrent effects—just as biological theory may assert that beheading, or certain poisons, will have a lethal effect. Biology does not, nor is meant to, encourage or discourage beheading or poisoning. It deals with the causes that produce effects, the means that achieve ends. The ends themselves must be derived from moral norms, which accordingly encourage or discourage utilization of the means specified by biological or deterrence theory. The theory is not concerned with the desirability of ends or means, only with the suitability of the latter.

Utilitarians may believe that by pretending that an innocent person is guilty and by "punishing" him or her we deter crime and increase total happiness by more than we decrease it, so as to produce a net gain. For a utilitarian the net gain justifies the "punishment," for, given appropriate circumstances, the deception (after all the law provides only for the punishment of the actually guilty) and the decrease of the happiness of the person punished do not matter in view of the gain in net happiness.[23] But nonutilitarians need not believe in the overriding importance of aggregate happiness. They may believe instead that justice and individual rights are primary. They may well accept deterrence theory—the belief that crime can and should be controlled by deterrent punishments—while rejecting the belief that the aim of crime control morally justifies superseding individual rights or individual justice, let alone deception (and crimes) by legal authorities. In short, nonutilitarian advocates of deterrence may subordinate it to all the moral constraints of nonutilitarian morality.

There is nothing in deterrence theory that requires happiness to be the primary and overriding goal of crime control, or crime control to be pursued regardless of the requirements of whatever deontological moral norms are accepted. The view that innocents should be sacrificed to utilitarian goals is a utilitarian view, not inherent in deterrence theory, which merely offers a means of crime control independent of normative ends and adaptable to any. Deterrence theory is quite independent of its original Benthamian integument.

NOTES

1. These indispensable rules are what may be meant by "natural law," when that term is shorn of metaphysical connotations; however, dispensable but advantageous rules may be so labeled as well, and finally even disadvantageous rules that became traditional by some historical accident.

2. The Hegelian justification of punishment, vindicating the equality of crime victim and victimizer, and the Kantian one, vindicating the rationality of both, merely disguise a *lex talionis* that rests on vindictive feeling and is vaguely proportionalized and transmuted.

3. When the death penalty, or actual life imprisonment, is imposed, incapacitation is permanent. But neither sanction is usually justified by the incapacitative effect.

4. "Rehabilitation" is defined here as an effect not of punishment per se, or of age, or of endogenous factors, but of a deliberate program aimed at changing the behavior of convicts after release so as to make them law abiding. Factors other than the effect of rehabilitation programs account for most of the law-abiding behavior of ex-convicts.

5. Burglary (or car theft) is a market-dependent crime. Rape is not: The rapist himself consumes the proceeds in his noninstrumental crime. Mugging, a largely instrumental crime, also does not depend on markets to the extent that the loot consists of money.

6. Incapacitation may be used either to protect society from the incapacitated person independently of punitive intent (as for the insane) or as a punishment. Conceptually, the punitive function, whether meant to be deterrent or retributive, must be distinguished from the incapacitation used to achieve it—although empirically the two functions may lead to an identical sanction.

7. In the historical context Bentham in effect favored decreasing the punishments then threatened.

8. Grading punishments avoids this problem only up to a point. If the death penalty is threatened for a single murder there is, theoretically, nothing to restrain multiple murders, since the range of punishments ends with the death penalty. However, the (nonmandatory) imposition of capital punishment becomes more likely if multiple murders are committed.

9. It is, however, possible, as economists have shown, to rank peoples' actual preferences.

10. It is not contended that John Rawls would deal in units of happiness as Bentham would. Still, I doubt that side constraints and refinement can save the theory.

11. I shall use "deterrence" to refer to "general deterrence" (the restraining effect of credible threats of punishment on any population), sometimes contrasted with "special deterrence" (the restraining effects of punishment on those punished). Special deterrence does not differ from rehabilitation in any respect relevant here; rehabilitation is not relevant for the reasons discussed above.

12. The notion of stealing requires an antecedent notion of property, present in all but the most primitive societies and, *mutatis mutandis*, among many species of animals. Proudhon's "*la proprieté c'est le vol*" is, for this reason, incoherent.

13. Statistics on the matter are far from conclusive, for reasons noted in van den Haag (1983a).

14. However, it has already been pointed out that special deterrence, incapacitation, or rehabilitation are unlikely to affect the rate of crime greatly.

15. "Delays" here are defined as punishment still occurring in time to relate clearly to the crime. Delays so great as to verge on impunity obviously reduce general deterrence.

16. I neglect individual differences despite their great importance because I am interested here only in the average effect of incentives and disincentives.

17. Unfortunately, the three groups are more easily distinguished conceptually than identified empirically.

18. Note that the deterrence doctrine is not incompatible with the belief that changes in social conditions affect the crime rate. The doctrine postulates social conditions as part

of the *ceteris* assumed to be *paribus*. But the doctrine also postulates that some crime will occur, and require deterrent punishment, in many social conditions.

19. These views need not rest on utilitarian beliefs; see van den Haag (1983b).

20. Kant (1963: 55-56) does not seem always to object to deterrence as at least an incidental aim of retribution. He writes (with approval): "Ruling authorities do not punish because a crime has been committed, but in order that crimes should not be committed."

21. This effect is actually achieved by the threat. But if the threat were not carried out, it would not be a credible threat. Actual punishment needs no justification other than that it carries out a threat that was justified.

22. To be sure, the police officer or the soldier may also share the end for which he or she is used as a means, protecting the public. But criminals also share the ends of law enforcement. Not even murderers are in favor of murder. They wish to secure life as do others, even though they make some exceptions, usually not justified by their own reasoning.

23. "Punishment" is in quotation marks here because, by definition, only the guilty can be "punished"—to inflict *scienter* "punishment" on an innocent person is itself a crime as well as a deception.

REFERENCES

KANT, I. (1963) Lectures on Ethics. New York: Harper Torch.
van den HAAG, E. (1983a) "Thinking about crime again." Commentary (December).
——(1983b) "Against natural rights." Policy Review (Winter).
——(1982) "Could successful rehabilitation reduce the crime rate?" Journal of Criminal Law and Criminology 73 (Fall).

9

The Assumption that Crime Is a Product of Individual Characteristics:
A Prime Example from Psychiatry

MICHAEL HAKEEM

Criminology, usually taught in departments of sociology and criminal justice, has traditionally emphasized social explanations of criminality. Though individualistic explanations have never been absent, they have been given a minor place. Recently, some sociologists have begun to show increasing interest in the possible role of such explanations—biological and/or psychological—in the behavior of criminals.

A recent bibliography (LEAA, 1979) of 324 works "representative of a biological approach to the study of criminality" was issued by the National Criminal Justice Reference Service. In Glaser's (1974) edited tome of almost 1200 pages on criminology, the longest chapter by far in the part headed "Explanations for Crime and Delinquency" is allocated to biological and psychophysiological factors. To cite only one more example from among many, a recent work on criminal violence edited by two sociologists devotes 170 out of 350 pages to biological and psychological factors (Wolfgang and Weiner, 1982). Excluding the editors, who contribute only a brief introduction, only 1 of the 11 authors is a sociologist.

Individualistic theories of crime all share the assumption that the cause of crime is found within specific persons—their biology, psychology, or moral character. Because of the variety of individualistic theories of crime, it is impossible to examine all such theories. The assumption that crime comes from within can be illustrated within an influential discipline (psychiatry) and using one of the most famous "types" of criminal (the psychopath).

THE MOST IMPORTANT SOURCE OF INDIVIDUALISTIC THEORY

Of all the disciplines that proffer individualistic theories of the causes of crime and delinquency, the one with towering influence is psychiatry. Its theories dominate in the professional literature, in the public media, in the popular mind, and, particularly, in the practical domain.

In decision making and as formal and informal advisers to decision makers, the influence and power of psychiatrists and their theories are enormous. In actual or proposed policies, they reach their zenith in this regard in criminal justice. Psychiatrists influence whether an individual is declared fit to stand trial; whether he or she is considered criminally responsible; whether, on the basis of a judgment of the individual's psyche, it is likely that he or she would have committed a crime of the type charged; whether or not the death penalty is imposed; whether the individual goes to prison or a mental hospital; whether he or she is imprisoned or put on probation; whether he or she goes to one or another correctional facility; whether he or she is sentenced to prison or ordered to get outpatient psychiatric treatment; whether he or she is paroled, and when; whether, as a sex offender, the individual is dealt with under the regular sentencing procedures or under the sex psychopath laws that allow for indefinite (even lifelong) custody; whether he or she is fit to be released from a hospital for the criminally insane; and whether, as a witness in a criminal trial, he or she is credible. These are only some of the issues upon which the conclusion can depend heavily or entirely on the judgment of psychiatrists.

A THEORY AND DIAGNOSIS REVISITED

When it comes to the psychiatric explanation of crime, the oldest and most widely subscribed to theory is in the form of a diagnosis. It is more than a diagnosis, however. At least, it must be viewed as both diagnosis and theory. As a theory it serves as an umbrella for a multitude of various symptoms and behaviors, posits causal links, claims predictive powers, and points the way to prevention and control. As diagnosis it is used to sift offenders, classify them into categories, and make dispositions of them accordingly. On the basis of this diagnosis/theory (henceforth referred to here as "diagnosis"), psychiatrists have decided the fate—including life or death—of countless accused persons and convicted offenders.

The diagnosis goes under a number of names: "psychopathic personality," "sociopathic personality," "antisocial personality disorder," and quite a number of others. Over 25 years ago, I reviewed this diagnosis, and concluded that it was wholly without merit, and that every aspect of it was chaotic. It was heavily documented that "without exception, on every point regarding psychopathic personality, psychiatrists present varying or contradictory views" (Hakeem, 1958: 669). I further concluded that "to diagnose psychopathic personality, the psychiatrist needs to examine only the subject's FBI record. Numerous psychiatrists have explicitly stated that they can make this diagnosis if they have access to only the social history of the 'patient,' particularly a record of his crimes." Finally, I felt that there was overwhelming evidence to assert that "there is no such thing as a medical (psychiatric) 'disease' called psychopathic or sociopathic personality. . . . Psychopathy is nothing but a synonym for crime and delinquency" (Hakeem, 1958: 674-675).

The diagnosis of psychopathic personality is here revisited. The conclusions reached are the same as those reached 25 years ago. In fact, as will be seen, in 1980 the American Psychiatric Association, through its latest revision of the *Diagnostic and Statistical Manual of Mental Disorders* (DSM-III), provided confirmation for the contention made in the 1958 paper that psychopathic personality is just another term for crime, delinquency, and other antisocial traits and behaviors objectionable to the psychiatrist and others.

As related to the diagnosis itself, no source published before 1970 is cited in this chapter. Most of the current textbooks on psychiatry, numerous treatises dealing with the diagnosis, and all journal articles in *Index Medicus* for the years 1980-1983 have been surveyed. With one or two exceptions, only works by psychiatrists and closely affiliated specialists (particularly neurologists) or in which psychiatrists collaborated have been cited. The neurologists are cited only in connection with the electroencephalography of psychopaths. Almost all the psychiatrists teach in medical schools. Now, as in 1958, no matter what the issue, there is hardly a point made by some authorities on psychopathic personality that is not differed from, contradicted, or brought into doubt by other authorities. It should be pointed out that in every instance where one or two citations are given in support of a position, they are illustrative only, and many more could be given.

THE CONFUSION IN
NOMENCLATURE AND NOSOLOGY

One who embarks on a searching study of the diagnosis of psychopathic personality is in for some troublesome surprises. So chaotic are the nomenclature and nosology used that one's researches are often thrown off track. Terminology is shifting, variable, loose, ambiguous, and often incoherent. Until 1952, the commonly used terms for the syndrome under discussion were "psychopathic personality," "psychopathy," and "psychopath." Those are the terms that I will use here to avoid confusion. In 1952, in an attempt to bring some order into the picture, the American Psychiatric Association adopted the term "sociopathic personality disturbance" in its compendium of psychiatric diagnoses. In 1968, the term was changed to "antisocial personality disorder," which is the current official term. Psychiatrists, however, continue to use all the terms, probably most often the original term, "psychopathic personality." But that is only the beginning of the muddle. Modlin (1983: 133) refuses to relinquish any of the officially superseded terms and combines them with the currently prescribed one when he writes of "the psychopathic-sociopathic-antisocial personality disorder." He is using all these terms as equivalents, but others are said to "regard sociopathy as only one form of psychopathy" (Woodruff et al., 1974: 145). One among many of these others is Willis (1976: 279), who, in his textbook, refers to a "type of psychopathic personality, often referred to as sociopathic." Sometimes it gets even more complicated, however. Rather than making sociopathy merely a type of psychopathy, as in the foregoing example, Smythies and Corbett (1976: 38), in their psychiatric text designed for medical students, make "psychopaths and sociopaths" two subtypes of "personality disorders." But a different psychiatrist classifies "sociopathic personality" alone—he does not mention "psychopathic personality"—under "personality disorders" (MacDonald, 1981: 700). Treating psychopathy and sociopathy neither as two names for the same disorder nor as two different disorders, Planansky (1972: 152) says, "The term *psychopathic* has a connotation of sociopathy." Does he mean to suggest that there are not two names for the disorder or that there are? Pushing the confusion still further, Planansky categorizes psychopathy under the rubric "schizoid personality." This is strange because, in the official diagnostic manual, "schizoid personality" is a distinct and separate diagnostic entry, as is "antisocial personality," both listed under the broad category of "personality disorders." Marmor (1978: 12) makes reference to "certain specific forms of psychopathology . . . sociopathic and psychopathic personalities." Yet, ten years before Marmor wrote this, it should be remembered, the American Psychiatric Association adopted the term "sociopathic personality disturbance" precisely to replace "psychopathic personality." Given all this, it is often not possible to determine whether a writer means to say that psychopathy and sociopathy are just different names for the same diagnosis or are two different diagnoses. For example: "What are often designated as behavioral disorders in children and early adolescents become categorized as psychopathic *or* sociopathic behavior in late adolescence or adulthood" (Monroe, 1970: 160; emphasis added). Does this mean the disorders can be allocated to either one of two diagnoses, or under one or the other of two different names for the same diagnosis? This is not picayune because, as has been shown, psychiatrists can be found expressing either view.

A frequent puzzle is the index entry under which the diagnosis will be found, for there is much inconsistency. For example, if one were to look in the index of Hodge's (1975) text, one would not find "psychopathy," "sociopathy," or "personality disorders." In the chapter titled "Psychiatric Diagnosis," there is a brief discussion under "Personality Disorders" (not indexed) where it is stated: "These are also called behavior disorders or personality problems"—terms neither of which is indexed (Hodge, 1975: 25). Of course they can be called that, but the problem is that some psychiatrists call them that and some do not. Furthermore, one is left in a quandary as to whether "personality problems" and "behavior disorders" refer to antisocial personality and whether "personality problems" is the same as "personality disorders." Hire's (1983) index does list "Sociopathic personality," but it directs the reader to "see Impulse disorders," which again throws one off the track.

This switching in terminology is common enough to create a Tower of Babel. Some psychiatrists refer to "character disorders (such as antisocial personality)" (Imboden and Urbaitis, 1978: 161). Are "character disorders" the same as "personality disorders" or are they "impulse disorders"? And is "impulse neuroses," which Goldberg (1973: 97) says is one of the alternative terms for "personality disorders," the same as "impulse disorders"? Writing some seven years after the term "sociopathic" was replaced by "antisocial personality disorder," two experts on this diagnosis call it "sociopathic character disorders," thus replacing the approved term "antisocial" with the outmoded "sociopathic," and, to throw the reader off further, changing, without explanation, the term "personality" to "character" (Vaillant, 1975: 178). Are personality disorders the same as character disorders, or could one occur without the other? Again, other authors induce puzzlement: "Personality disorders are included in DSM-III as mental disorders and are distinguished from personality traits" (Spitzer et al., 1977: 4). But are not "personality disorders" disorders of "personality traits"? Further, are not *personality* disorders also *mental* disorders? Can there be personality disorders that are not mental? As a matter of fact, Roth (1980: 701) has indicated that "whether psychopathy is a mental disorder" is an unresolved issue, again deepening the mystery. Roth himself deepens it even more when in the same breath he uses the terms "personality disorders," "behaviorally disordered people," and "conduct disorders" to express what presumably is the same concept (U.S. Congress, House, 1982: 66). Halleck (1981: 169) only confounds the confusion when he reports that some view "sociopathy as a tendency or trait rather than a disorder," without even a hint at what this means.

It must not be supposed that this is anything more than a mere sampling of the chaos that surrounds the nomenclature of this alleged disorder. The recitation could be greatly extended with any number of additional examples.

THE SYMPTOMS OF PSYCHOPATHY

What are the symptoms of psychopathy? Though a number of psychiatrists have claimed that psychopaths can be found among highly talented and successful people, the predominant view is that the psychopath is a wholly unsocialized, incompetent, and vile creature. Hitler is often cited by psychiatrists as the personification of the psychopath—the "Prince of Psychopaths," as one put it.

The literature, including the textbooks, is entirely haphazard in citing the symptoms of psychopathy. Some sources may give three or four symptoms; others three or four dozens. Though there is a common core of meaning—namely, that the psychopath is very criminalistic, often violent, and a grave misfit in each and every facet of life—variability in usage far outweighs consensus, descriptions are extraordinarily loose, ambiguity abounds, disagreement is rife, and incoherence is often manifested.

One example of a source that leans toward amplitude of symptomatology is a widely used textbook in psychiatry, now in its tenth edition, the senior author of which, Lawrence C. Kolb, is one of the most eminent professors of psychiatry in the nation and long a leader in the profession (Kolb and Brodie, 1982: 605-608). All the traits and behaviors (symptoms), including repetitiousness, of the psychopath culled from this textbook will be set forth here verbatim or, to rescue them from the gross grammatical infelicities in which they are snarled, paraphrased. Psychopaths, according to this textbook, are chronically antisocial; incapable of forming significant attachments or loyalties to others, to groups, or to codes of living; callous; given to immediate pleasure; devoid of a sense of responsibility; unresponsive to repeated humiliations and punishments resulting in a failure to change their behavior; lacking in social judgment; without a socialized superego or ego ideals, or if these are present they are directed toward self-aggrandizement; emotionally deficient; lacking in keenness and delicacy of sentiment; affectionless; selfish; ungrateful; narcissistic; exhibitionistic; excessively demanding but giving little; devoid of critical awareness of their motives; unable to judge their own behavior from another's standpoint; satisfied with their behavior; expressive of few feelings of anxiety, guilt, or remorse; lacking definite objectives; in a usual state of restlessness resulting from a search of the unattainable; characterized by faulty occupational application and efficiency; intolerably irked by routine; demanding of immediate and instant gratification of desires; devoid of concern for the feelings and interests of others; not possessed of a sense of values; absolutely unreliable, though plausible and talkative; able to adjust only to environments that they can dominate; constantly demonstrating surprising irregularities of ability and inconsistencies of behavior; prone, in some cases, to escape from difficult situations by way of psychotic episodes, while others at the slightest stress resort to alcohol or drugs; poor in their tolerance of alcohol; given to projecting their insecurity by blaming others; morally and ethically blunted; lacking in sympathy for their fellow human beings; characterized by behavior destructive to the welfare of the social order; superficial and affectively cold in their emotional lives; inaccessible; boorish; without a sense of responsibility; seemingly incapable of mature emotional relationships; not able to organize an acceptable, constructive expression of their aggressions; lacking in ambition, application, seriousness of purpose, and foresight; irritable; arrogant; unyielding; brutally egotistical; rarely remorseful for their most serious offenses; frequently rebellious in attitude toward society and authority; subject to sudden changes in mood, often without apparent cause; cynical; devoid of a sense of honor or of shame; lacking in sympathy, affection, gratitude, and other social and aesthetic sentiments; of possible danger to others when frustrated; capable of any crime; prideful of their crimes and find their struggles with the law pleasurable; unable to identify with society and its laws; and not deterred by punishment. Other texts mention symptoms not found in Kolb and Brodie's discussion and fail to duplicate some of their symptoms. Different sets of symptoms are given different emphasis by different writers. Kolb and Brodie give less emphasis to the utter rapaciousness and vicious criminality of the psychopath than do many other authorities, who regard these as the most distinguishing marks of psychopathy. It would be possible to demonstrate that on many of the symptoms there is disagreement, sometimes radical disagreement, some claiming that a symptom is present and some denying it.

DIAGNOSIS OF PSYCHOPATHY

Kolb and Brodie's horrendous catalogue of symptoms cannot be taken seriously. The authors give no indication of how these symptoms are worked into a diagnosis of psychopathy. Do they mean to say that every psychopath shows all the multitudinous symptoms mentioned? If not, then which ones must be present in a given individual to warrant such a diagnosis? In what degree must the symptoms appear? And how often do they have to be manifested over how long a span of time? How were the presence and degree of some of these traits deduced? Many of them are of a highly slippery and subjective nature, about the existence, verification, and measurement of which there swirls endless theoretical disputation and conflicting and contradictory research, none of which is mentioned by Kolb and Brodie. Many, if not most, of the behaviors involved could be defined and explained in different ways by different behavior scientists. Most important, it is not made known on what basis it was decided that if some or all of these behaviors (symptoms) were manifested they perforce had to be attributed to a personality or mental disorder rather than to one or another of the competing theoretical explanations. In fact, the existence and significance of these behaviors in the individual could not be determined for scientific purposes except by lengthy (months and even years) study of carefully designed, highly skilled, controlled, and replicated observations of large samples of persons in real-life situations. That was not the foundation for selection of Kolb and Brodie's symptomatology.

Kolb and Brodie, like most of their colleagues, typically present the symptoms in their extremity, giving them more a flavor of angry pejoratives than scientifically derived descriptions. They say, for example, that psychopaths are "without the capacity to form significant attachments or loyalties to others, to groups, or to codes of living." None whatsoever? Not a shred? Surely unless a human being is a totally deteriorated and vegetating idiot, cut off entirely from contact with reality, he or she has *some*, no matter how slight, such capacity. They "lack social judgment." Entirely? Could one survive long devoid of all semblance of social judgment? Besides, is not the propriety of social judgment often a value question? They "are lacking in sympathy, affection, gratitude, and other social and esthetic sentiments." If they were observed, would they not be found to demonstrate at least a modicum of one or another of these behaviors at one time or another? Surely the characterization is a grotesque overgeneralization.

Examples of the totality with which the symptoms are said to appear abound. The following symptoms, quoted from a wide sampling of psychiatric literature, though often duplicative of Kolb and Brodie, will serve to demonstrate the pervasiveness of the practice: "lacks foresight"; "has really no ethical or moral sense"; "basically immature in his whole emotional life and life style"; "he lives emotionally in the present and completely disregards tomorrow"; "do not have a conscience or personal sense of right or wrong"; "basically unsocialized"; "lack any sense of responsibility"; "entire absence of self-restraint"; "immediate satisfaction of desires imperative"; "unbelievable social irresponsibility and stupidity"; "cannot resist temptation"; "totally unreliable"; "uninhibited acting out of selfish impulses"; "acts without regard for the consequences"; "devoid of any sense of responsibility"; "always very demanding"; "unable to postpone immediate pleasure or gratification of an impulse"; "shows no response to being caught or incarcerated"; "lack the potential to withstand normal human frustrations"; "lack of motivation"; "lacks capacity to feel guilt or experience shame"; "exclusive concern about own needs, wants, desires"; "inability to conform to the prevailing values of society"; "inability . . . to inhibit aggressive impulses"; "failing to engage in 'moral' behavior."

Given all that has been shown, the diagnosis of psychopathy can be little more than an arbitrary and capricious exercise. More than this, psychiatrists can pin the label on anyone who shows any sort of objectionable, deviant, offensive, or criminal behavior. "Some colleagues incline to label 'psychopathic personality' all patients who admit having broken the law" (Menninger, 1973: 92). "The range of antisocial activity displayed by the sociopath is wide and can encompass any type of criminality or social deviancy" (Willis, 1976: 280). "Psychopaths range from those considered queer to criminals, with a large intermediate group made up of cranks, extremists, eccentrics, habitual delinquents, and other social misfits" (Kolb and Brodie, 1982: 607). "Not all criminals, of course, are psychopaths, but an appreciable proportion are, and number among their ranks seducers, bigamists, confidence men, prostitutes, common adventurers, and *pathological liars*" (Curran et al., 1980: 225).

The task of the critic of the diagnosis is made easier by the availability of the frank assertions of a number of psychiatrists that the diagnosis of psychopathy is affixed to persons whose behavior the psychiatrist finds objectionable or whom the psychiatrist does not like. In short, it is a pejorative. Of course, the overwhelming bulk of psychiatrists use the term unquestioningly in the earnest belief that they are making a defensible medical diagnosis, but the tiny minority who are insightful enough to see that the diagnosis is little more than name calling raise profoundly disturbing issues. Tucker and Pincus (1980: 281), two of the minority, say that the diagnostic manual in effect for twelve years "defined [psychopathy] in an almost pejorative manner." A leading forensic psychiatrist does not think it is "almost": "The term is objectionable and pejorative" (Roth, 1980: 703). Nor is there qualification in the letter sent by three psychiatrists to the *New England Journal of Medicine* objecting to an article that contained "the pejorative suggestion that narcotic addicts are sociopathic" (McLeilan et al., 1980: 870). Another psychiatrist admits that until the reformulation promulgated in 1980 (a topic to be discussed shortly), "it was recognized that this term could be misused to include most persons in prison as well as anyone a psychiatrist did not like, who came from a bad background and had been arrested once" (Lion, 1978: 375). MacKinnon and Michels (1971: 299-300) agree that "the diagnosis retains its pejorative quality and this accurately reflects the attitudes of most psychiatrists." Robitscher (1980: 207) affirms the view: "Sociopathy is a catchall or wastebasket diagnosis, often used against a person disapproved of or disliked by the evaluator." Vaillant and Perry (1980: 1563), to cite a final example, observe: "Patients with personality disorders [psychopathy is a personality disorder] are more scorned than studied. Professional training and interest in those patients often lead to little else than scapegoating or, at best, pejorative labeling."

TAUTOLOGY AS DIAGNOSIS

A convincing case can be made that the diagnosis of psychopathic personality is at bottom nothing more than a tautology. The impressive sounding name of a mental disorder or illness is substituted for "criminality," or "social deviance," or "obnoxious personal behavior," or "antisocial conduct," especially when often repeated. The psychiatrist seeking to determine if a "patient" is afflicted with psychopathic personality gets no help from examining his or her body, brain, nervous system, or mind. The psychiatrist examines the patient's social history, especially his or her criminal record. This is not to say that there is agreement on what specific types or amounts of deviance and crime this history has to show to warrant making the diagnosis. Arbitrariness and capriciousness have full play.

In the following statement, the psychiatrist refers to children who commit delinquency as a result of observing the parents' antisocial conduct, which is easy enough to understand. But the psychiatrist, using the newer term for psychopathy, ipso facto has diagnosed a mental disorder in such children, which is hard to understand. "All too often, children identify with their parents' antisocial characteristics and engage in serious delinquency. Such a child is described as suffering from sociopathy" (Berman, 1979: 13). Vaillant and Perry (1980: 1569, 1580) note that to make a diagnosis of psychopathy one does not examine the patient's mental condition but his or her social history secured from courts, schools, employers, and the like, clearly in order to enable the examining psychiatrists to label the patient psychopathic if he or she has been misbehaving. Woodruff et al. (1974: 147) state: "Sooner or later most sociopaths have trouble with the police. Some investigators, in fact, have required police trouble for the diagnosis of sociopathy." Again, in a similar vein, Tucker and Pincus (1980: 2821) say: "To make the diagnosis of antisocial behavior [there is no doubt the authors are referring to psychopathy], the clinician must be able to delineate a pattern of behavior of antisocial acts that began early in childhood and that has persisted into adolescence and adult life." To give one more example from among scores, if not hundreds, that could be given, Eaton and his coauthors (1981: 130-131) join the charade: "The Antisocial Personality is a disorder in which the major manifestations include persistent violations of the laws, mores and customs of the community."

How arbitrary and capricious is the imposition of this diagnosis, which can have portentous consequences for an individual, is graphically demonstrated in a remarkable research (Pfohl, 1978). Under a court order, all the patients in Ohio's hospital for the criminally insane were required to be evaluated psychiatrically. One of the objects was to determine which patients were "psychopathic offenders." Important decisions were to be reached—whether the patient would continue to be incarcerated in a maximum security facility, for example—on the basis of the diagnosis arrived at. Twelve multidisciplinary teams, each made up of a psychiatrist, a clinical psychologist, and a psychiatric social worker, were appointed. Pfohl and his associates undertook to observe and record the actual operations of these teams to determine how they arrived at their diagnoses. Observers were present at the clinical sessions at which the team members arrived at their diagnoses, tape recordings of the sessions were made, transcripts were produced, interviews of the clinicians were conducted, and a mass of other data were collected. Based on this extensive research—it should be remembered that the context was one in which coercive decisions are made—Pfohl concludes that "psychiatric opinions are essentially political judgments." He notes the research staff's "consistent discovery of inconsistency, disguised uncertainty, and negotiated objectivity" (Pfohl, 1978: 229). The data suggest that "expert psychiatric knowledge is a well-managed 'appearance of objectivity' rather than a set of objective facts" (Pfohl, 1978: 230). In fact, Pfohl (1978: 217) regards it as the most significant finding of his research that *"diagnostic decisions are inherently bound to and thus dependent upon a variety of ongoing social or social psychological processes that may have little to do with the psychiatric troubles or emotional disturbances of patients."*

It was revealed in this study that once the psychiatric staff members decided that the person was a psychopath they would latch on to anything as proof of their diagnosis. Traits that ordinarily would be regarded by anyone as positive assets were seized upon as proof of psychopathy.

> We have observed numerous inconsistencies in members' criteria-in-use both within and between teams. Within teams it was suggested that criteria are not applied uniformly from patient to patient. For one patient the "fact" that she or he was attractive, young, intelligent, desirous of college, eager to get married, or committed to getting a good job on the "outside" could be taken as positive indicators of relatively few psychiatric troubles. For the next patient these same "facts" may be taken as evidence of manipulative tendencies and the individual may be seen as a dangerous psychopath. Moreover, the reason that these differences in diagnostic interpretations occur may have little to do with a patient's actual behavior, but a lot to do with what I have referred to as the "essential" and "contingent" features of team members' interaction.
>
> Numerous differences among teams in assumptions and diagnostic practices have also been noted [Pfohl, 1978: 225].

In an attempt to bring some order into the picture, the American Psychiatric Association, in its 1980 revision of its diagnostic manual, set forth a number of criteria for the diagnosis. So far as the diagnosis under review is concerned, these criteria do not refer to anything whatsoever having to do with the patient's body, brain, nervous system, or mental functioning. Rather, they are exclusively related to violations of law or institutional regulations and deviations from the norms and values of what is regarded by many sociologists as the law-abiding, orderly, future-oriented, and decent lifestyle of middle- and upper-class persons. A goodly proportion, perhaps the great majority, of the criteria represent little more than the psychiatrists' condemnatory value judgments of behavior endemic in the lower classes. As Dr. Stone, representing the American Psychiatric Association before a congressional committee, put it: "I suspect that most middle class psychiatrists would diagnose almost everybody in prison as a sociopath" (U.S. Congress, House, 1982: 67). In the main, the behaviors are not operationalized to specify their exact nature and the duration, frequency, and intensity with which they must occur. Further, psychiatrists are given a large number of criteria from which they are free to choose whichever ones they want as a basis for the diagnosis. In one category of criteria, for example, the psychiatrist need not choose more than any three out of twelve items; in another, no more than four out of nine, the nine encompassing a large number of subitems. There is no mention of any of the psychological processes, disturbances, and aberrations commonly looked for in mental illnesses. Nothing in the diagnostic formula would require the psychiatrist to see the "patient," nor would anything relevant to the diagnosis be learned thereby. All the psychiatrist need do is find out if the patient has shown the behaviors designated—which ones, how frequently, and in what degree being left to each psychiatrist to decide as he or she wishes.

CAUSES OF PSYCHOPATHY

Eclecticism

When it comes to the cause of psychopathy, one encounters so weirdly tangled a skein in the psychiatric literature that, no matter how earnestly one strives for accuracy, one can get trapped into misquotation or quoting out of context. Often the same writer will shift uncritically and haphazardly from social to psychological to psychoanalytic to biological factors, often confusedly mixing them up without rhyme or reason, superficially mentioning this and that unsystematically and often incoherently. Typically, a mishmash of causative factors is recounted. There is rarely any attempt made to show how the factors in these drastically different orders of phenomena are interrelated. There is often an aimless recitation of a multiplicity of factors without any hint of exactly how they are related to the generation of psychopathy.

Sometimes the discussion is virtually incoherent. Conditions in the home (lack of mother love, inadequate parental discipline, or presence of antisocial models, for example) and conditions in the body (brain lesion, endocrine dysfunction, and so on) are posited willy-nilly as equally plausible causes of this devastating affliction. Studies are cited thoughtlessly and uncritically, typically no reference is made to opposed or contradictory studies, and much of the time a large number of causative factors are reeled off without documentation at all. Contradictions, disagreements, and controversies surround all causative factors posited.

The most common formulation is an homage to eclecticism. Most often this is put in an entirely noninformative way—a sweeping generalization that imparts no useful knowledge. Modlin's (1983: 133) freewheeling welcome to all factors and disciplines differs from scores of such statements only in its redundancy: "Genetic, constitutional, familial, sociological, cultural, biological, neurological, and psychodynamic factors have been implicated in the causation and development of the syndrome." The most common etiological formulation states that it is not one or another category of factors alone that generates psychopathy but the interaction among them. A typical statement is Rees's (1976: 225): "It is the interaction of both [inherited and environmental factors] rather than either one or the other which is important." It does not occur to those who enunciate the interactional doctrine that it is a simplistic statement, that it is not clear what is meant by it, and that exactly how heredity and environment interact has to be spelled out. Nor, in an extensive survey of the literature, has any psychiatrist been found to give expression to the fact that if psychopathy can be explained by the interaction of heredity and environment, so can saintliness and all other behavior. Therefore, is anything more than a platitude being propounded?

Environment

Psychopathy is said to start in childhood or to have its roots there. Psychiatrists commonly have reference to the socialization of children when they refer to the "environment." The key word here is "superego," a psychiatric term for conscience. If there is faulty socialization because the child either lacks proper behavior models or is presented with antisocial behavior models, his or her conscience (superego)—a sense of right or wrong, of moral values—will not develop properly, and the child will become a psychopath and act in immoral or antisocial ways. "The psychic lesion is primarily in the superego" (Keyes and Hofling, 1974: 315). Mezer's (1970: 114-115) statement of the general principle can stand for all others, whether in popular or technical presentations: "The etiology of the antisocial personality derives from the fact that the superego is either underdeveloped or malformed.... The superego may be malformed if the individual has identified with an unsatisfactory and socially unacceptable object; antisocial personalities are frequently found to come from home environments where there has been obvious antisocial activity by the father and/or mother." Again, psychiatrists have produced a circular theory: If a child does not learn good behavior, he or she will not behave well. But they go on and label this a mental disorder or illness.

The foregoing is the usual formulation, but it is quite common to find all sorts of variations, ambiguities, disagreements, and contradictions. In Gregory and Smeltzer's (1977: 223) view, the superego of psychopaths is "defective or absent." Sim (1981: 265) cites Fenichel, who holds that the superego "is not absent but rudimentary or even pathological." But Goldberg (1973: 103) insists that it is absent. Allen and Allen (1978: 197) teach not that the superego is absent in the psychopath but that it is not "effective" or is too "strong." Leaff (1978: 94) does not find strength in the superego but "weakness," only to be countered by Vaillant and Perry (1980: 1581), who aver that it is "too rigid, not too lenient [weak?]." Rappeport (1974: 297) agrees with Greenacre that the psychopath's superego is "overwhelming," but others do not use the word. Awad (1983: 198) comments on the "strictness" of the superego in such patients but does not indicate if that is the same as being "overwhelming." Kolb and Brodie (1982: 605) think the psychopath fails to develop "a socialized superego and ego ideals," thereby multiplying confusion by pointing to a particular type of superego that is not mentioned by the foregoing psychiatrists and joining it to another concept.

Biological Factors

Despite the incredible morass in which the diagnosis of psychopathy is embedded, and despite the fact that what can be understood of it boils down to a mere tautology, psychiatrists and others have been assiduously at work to find its biological roots. Often the pertinent researches use jumbled samples of psychopaths, with no distinction made between psychopathic criminals, psychopathic noncriminals, and nonpsychopathic criminals, thus yielding dubious and noncomparable findings at best. Despite the fact that the writers and researchers are medically trained, biological and medical terms are used crudely. "Constitutional," "biological," "genetic," "organic," "neurological," "neural," "neurophysiological," "neuropsychological," "hereditary," "psychophysiological," "psychogenic," "psychogenetic" (psychological origin or genetic aspects of psychology?), and other terms are used with such extraordinary looseness, inconsistency, and ambiguity that it is often difficult or impossible to pin down the referents. The psychiatrists have cast a wide net and have left few of the psychopath's anatomical and physiological systems unprobed. Among the factors that have been examined are genes; chromosomes; hormones; neocortex; limbic system; brain stem; temporal lobe; skin conductance; hypothalamus; heart rate; autonomic nervous system; dietary and nutritional status; serum cholesterol levels; glucose metabolism; testosterone, progesterone, and estrogen levels; and food allergies.

It would be possible to cite an extensive series of psychiatrists representing every conceivable position on the contribution made by biological factors to the causation of psychopathy. Only a limited number of examples can be given here. Rockwell (1978: 142) has decided that "the sociopath is neuropsychologically deviant." He also has it that "there is evidence for genetic influence." Vaillant and Perry (1980: 1580) have a different view: "At the present time ... no clear organic basis for antisocial personality disorder is known." The problem is that one cannot tell whether Vaillant and Perry's "organic" has the same referents as Rockwell's "neuropsychologically" and "genetic." Zerbin-Rüdin (1980: 66) is emphatic: " 'True' psychopathy is a genetically determined personality variation." Ludwig (1980: 213), on one page, does not share that definitiveness: "Genetic studies have yielded inconclusive but suggestive results regarding biological predisposition." But on another page, "suggestive" results are elevated to "substantial" results (Ludwig, 1980: 211). To Sim (1981: 264), results are neither suggestive nor substantial, if by "constitutional," the word he uses, he has the same thing in mind that Ludwig has, for he says that "reliable evidence in the vast majority of instances is still lacking." In Cleckley's (1976: 412) opinion, "No neurologic lesion has been regularly demonstrated in the typical psychopath," but one does not know whether by "neurologic" he is referring to something genetic, as in Zerbin-Rüdin's usage, and whether his "typical" psychopath is her "pure" psychopath.

Kolb and Brodie's (1982: 594, 605) textbook is confusing within itself. They claim that constitutional factors have "failed to yield any understanding of the behavior of such persons" (they are referring to personality disorders in general, including psychopaths). However, a few pages later, they cite a study that concludes that "a constitutional difference is present" in psychopaths. This study, in turn, would be countered by Mersky and Tonge's (1974: 217) observation that "so far as their physical characteristics are concerned, psychopaths do not differ from the general population except in one respect"—a brain wave abnormality. But other writings do not refer to that as a physical characteristic. Nor did the study cited by Kolb and Brodie showing the presence of "constitutional" difference. Be that as it may, Mersky and Tonge's notion is badly battered by Curran and his collaborators (1980: 227), whose contradictory finding shows that physicians dealing with psychopaths cannot agree even on whether such patients show easily observable anatomical and physiological differences from the norm: "Physical anomalies are frequent in psychopathic personalities; such are an asthenic build, disproportion in physique, underdevelopment of secondary sex characteristics, vasomotor instability, and an allergic disposition. Many psychopaths, on the other hand, have excellent physiques." These authorities forgot to say whether these anomalies are more frequent among psychopaths than among nonpsychopaths, and, of course, both of their statements can apply to the population in general. In fact, Curran et al. do not indicate whether they are referring to male and female psychopaths or, if only one, which one.

Some psychiatrists have no question at all that psychopathy can develop as a result of encephalitis (Elliott, 1978: 147-149); some deny it (Willis, 1976: 277). "Temporal lobe epilepsy" can cause psychopathy, to cite one source from among many that concur (Vaillant and Perry, 1980: 1566), but "there is no real connection between the aggressive psychopath and epilepsy," another source, one of many, indicates (Sim, 1981: 264), leaving it unclear whether the same types of epilepsy and psychopath indicated in the first source are meant and, if not "real," then what kind of connection there is. In any event, a third source neither affirms nor denies the connection, but says that "the evidence remains conflicting" (Willis, 1976: 271). From a teaching manual on psychiatry, it is learned that "there is some evidence that sociopathic behavior is more common in persons having an extra Y chromosome (XYY males) than in the general population" (Eaton et al., 1981: 132). Another treatise, however, teaches that no study has yet established a relationship so consistent that would make the foregoing flat assertion credible (Lion, 1978: 146). A third source inserts a puzzle into the discussion. It reports that no difference in "XXY genotype" was found among prisoners and the general population (Tucker and Pincus, 1980: 2819), but it is silent about the "XYY" chromosome. Many clinicians, according to one authority who cites only one clinician in support of his observation, are convinced that psychopaths suffer from brain "damage" (Rappeport, 1974: 262). A different expert, who cites no clinicians at all, says that most psychiatrists now feel that "brain disease" is the cause of psychopathy in less than 1 percent of cases (Chapman, 1976: 223), but he does not explain whether brain "disease" and brain "damage" are the same. A third psychiatrist quotes a colleague who attributes psychopathy to "an organic control disorder of frontal lobe-hypothalamic connections," again not explaining whether a "disorder" is synonymous with "damage" or "disease" (Oppenheimer, 1971: 124).

Many psychiatrists have made much of the presence of abnormal electroencephalographic (EEG) findings in psychopaths. They jump to the conclusion, and they seem to be eager to espouse it, that this proves, or at least tends to prove, that there are some biological roots underlying the disorder. They do not cite—and, in fact, they appear to be unaware of—the frequency with which such reservations and cautions as the following occur in the neurological and electroencephalographic literature: "The EEG is not a precise diagnostic instrument.... The report of a 'normal' EEG does not rule out organicity.... Equally significant, even the abnormal EEG is rarely pathognomic of a specific organic process.... Furthermore, abnormal records are described in some 15 to 20 percent of people without recognizable neurologic or psychiatric dysfunction" (Wells and Duncan, 1980: 226). "EEG studies of such specifically defined personality disorders [these include psychopathy, but they are anything but specifically defined] are mostly lacking [*sic*]. There have been numerous EEG reports of individuals exhibiting criminal behavior and prisoners, but definitive diagnostic criteria have generally not been employed" (Niedermeyer and Lopes da Silva, 1982: 450). "Terminological differences and varying diagnostic criteria make it difficult to compare the work on personality disorders and psychopathy carried out at different centres [where EEG examinations are made]" (Kiloh et al., 1981: 201). "The EEG is of relatively little aid in the evaluation of psychological illness, because specific EEG abnormalities do not correlate with specific emotional disorders" (Solomon, 1980: 266).

Even in regard to so serious a matter, there is little that would elicit the confidence of the critical reader. Some psychiatrists writing on the etiology of psychopathy make much of the EEG; others do not as much as mention it. The latest edition of the text most often cited as the leading authoritative work on psychopathy cites eight references in the course of its brief discussion of EEG. Although over the past thirty years there have been several thousands of researches and publications worldwide on EEG, eight out of ten references in this book are at least 23 years old, four of these being 30 years or older, and one, 20 years old. Only one is fairly recent (Cleckley, 1976: 412-413).

Three psychiatrists conclude that "frequent electroencephalographic abnormalities have been reported" (Eaton et al., 1981: 132). No qualifications or reservations are made, and if one were to rely on that source alone one would not learn that a different authority, referring to the studies on the incidence of electroencephalographic abnormalities in psychopaths, expresses a view that makes the foregoing pronouncement virtually worthless: "Up to now the results were not uniform, sometimes even contradictory, and difficult to interpret" (Zerbin-Rudin, 1980: 70). Elliott (1978: 146) provides another example of a flatly stated position, leaving no room for skepticism: "From 50% to 80% of psychopaths exhibit abnormal EEG's." There is nothing in Elliott's discussion that would arouse even the slightest skepticism in the reader about the finality of the conclusion. Yet, in the very same volume, a different practitioner raises grave doubts as to whether or not psychopaths have been found to "exhibit" abnormal EEG records (Leaff, 1978: 80).

OTHER ASPECTS

Only a small display of the chaos surrounding the most important diagnosis and theory psychiatry has to offer in explanation of crime has been set forth. All other aspects are equally in disarray. Views on treatment range from total pessimism to optimism. Treatments range from psychotherapy to brain surgery. Prodigious amounts of drugs have been prescribed, but there is disagreement as to which drugs should be prescribed and their efficacy. Every aspect of therapy, in fact, is in dispute. Sharp controversy and confusion pervade the issues of prognosis, course, association with other mental disorders and diseases, correlation with various types of behavior and criminality, prediction of dangerousness, certifiability as to criminal insanity, and every other issue. There are, besides, marked international differences and disagreements on the diagnosis. The presentation given earlier in this chapter made the subject appear more orderly than it actually is because an attempt was made to squeeze some sensible meaning out of the dense and tortuous literature. To give one example, take the symptoms that were listed. Though some criticisms were made of them, much more could have been said. Specific examples were not given to show that there is vast disagreement about specific symptoms, some psychiatrists affirming and some denying the existence of this or that symptom and arguing about other aspects of it.

COMMENT

As has been pointed out, psychopathy is a psychiatric theory that has had great practical application in criminal justice. How could so unscientific a theory be supported and adopted by legislators, judges, administrators, and the general public as a basis for making fateful decisions about people? Those involved in making decisions about its incorporation into legislation are not, except in rare instances, competent to make an intellectually responsible appraisal of it. They have not shown themselves to be able to do the required investigation to get a valid picture of the credibility of the theory. Legislators and other decision makers are quite prone to appeal to authority and to form their opinions on the basis of what they are told by psychiatrists about it. Psychiatrists, on their part, have been quite aggressive in demanding acceptance of their expertise. Except rarely, psychiatrists, adumbrating their expertise and knowledge before boards, commissions, courts, legislators, and the general public, are not committed to portraying honestly their theory of crime and the limitations of their science. They show themselves rather to be either ignorant of the appalling state of their theories or disingenuous. Just recently, to draw one instance from among many, psychiatrists testified at hearings on the insanity defense held by House and Senate committees. Practically all psychiatrists, almost all of them professors, gave assurance that psychiatrists are in agreement, that diagnoses are reliable, and that any appearance of disagreement in forensic contexts was not attributable to the inadequacy of psychiatry but rather to the restrictions and distortions imposed by legal procedures (U.S. Congress, Senate, 1982a: 211, 234-235, 251; 1982b: 59). One psychiatrist was particularly adamant about it, and, referring specifically to reliability of diagnosis, affirmed: "We have studies to show that." His claim was that these studies show agreement among psychiatrists on the diagnoses of "severe, medically defined, mental illness" in 80 percent of their cases (U.S. Congress, House, 1982: 59). But he did not cite even one of the scores, perhaps hundreds, of studies over the past 30 years showing gross unreliability of diagnoses. The American Psychiatric Association also submitted an official statement to the same committee minimizing the disagreements among psychiatrists and blaming the law for making them appear worse than they are (U.S. Congress, House, 1982: 77-78).

The prospects of getting a psychiatric theory of criminal behavior that would meet the most minimal requirements for scientific recognition are wholly unpromising. The psychiatric literature does not reflect the requisite competence even to deal with the issues involved. Reference is not made to medical or psychiatric training, but to sophistication in scientific methodology, logic, the commitment to objectivity, and all the other elementary norms, values, skills, and virtues of scholarship. These are the respects in which the psychiatric literature examined exposes gross inadequacies.

The minds of psychiatrists have played an awful trick on them, and they cannot see it. They think that if one deviates in a disapproved, especially an "antisocial," direction, personality or mental disorder must be behind it—the evil-causes-evil fallacy. How often does one find psychiatrists probing the brain, the brain stem, the electroencephalogram, the neurological functioning, and the hormones of those who deviate singularly in the direction of being virtuous, generous, self-sacrificing, and saintly?

REFERENCES

ALLEN, J. R. and B. A. ALLEN (1978) Guide to Psychiatry: A Handbook in Psychiatry for Health Professionals. Garden City, NY: Medical Examination Publishing.
ARIETI, S. (1978) On Schizophrenia, Phobias, Depression, Psychotherapy and the Farther Shores of Psychiatry. New York: Brunner/Mazel.
AWAD, G. A. (1983) "The middle phase of psychotherapy with antisocial adolescents." American Journal of Psychotherapy 37 (April): 190-201.
BERMAN, S. (1979) "The psychodynamic aspects of behavior," in J. D. Noshpitz (ed.) Basic Handbook of Child Psychiatry, Vol. 2. New York: Basic Books.
CHAPMAN, A. H. (1976) Textbook of Clinical Psychiatry: An Interpersonal Approach. Philadelphia: J. B. Lippincott.
CLECKLEY, H. (1976) The Mask of Sanity. St. Louis, MO: Mosby.
CURRAN, D. et al. (1980) Psychological Medicine: An Introduction to Psychiatry. Edinburgh: Churchill, Livingstone.
EATON, M. T., Jr., et al. (1981) Psychiatry. Garden City, NY: Medical Examination Publishing.
ELLIOTT, F. A. (1978) "Neurological aspects of antisocial behavior," in W. H. Reid (ed.) The Psychopath: A Comprehensive Study of Antisocial Disorders and Behaviors. New York: Brunner/Mazel.
GLASER, D. [ed.] (1974) Handbook of Criminology. Chicago: Rand McNally.
GOLDBERG, M. (1973) A Guide to Psychiatric Diagnosis and Understanding for the Helping Professions. Chicago: Nelson-Hall.
GOODWIN, D. and S. B. GUZE (1979) Psychiatric Diagnosis. New York: Oxford University Press.
GREGORY, I. and D. J. SMELTZER (1977) Psychiatry: Essentials of Clinical Practice with Examination Questions, Answers, and Comments. Boston: Little, Brown.
HAKEEM, M. (1958) "A critique of the psychiatric approach to crime and correction." Law and Contemporary Problems 23 (Autumn): 650-682.
HALLECK, S. L. (1981) "Sociopathy: ethical aspects of diagnosis and treatment," pp. 157-176 in J. Masserman (ed.) Current Psychiatric Therapies, Vol. 20. New York: Grune & Stratton.
HIRE, F. R. et al. (1983) Introduction to Behavioral Science in Medicine. New York: Springer-Verlag.
HODGE, J. R. (1975) Practical Psychiatry for the Primary Physician. Chicago: Nelson-Hall.
IMBODEN, J. B. and J. C. URBAITIS (1978) Practical Psychiatry in Medicine. New York: Appleton-Century-Crofts.
KEYES, J. J. and C. K. HOFLING (1974) Basic Psychiatric Concepts in Nursing. Philadelphia: J. B. Lippincott.
KILOH, L. G. et al. (1981) Clinical Electroencephalography. London: Butterworth.
KOLB, L. C. and H.K.H. BRODIE (1982) Modern Clinical Psychiatry. Philadelphia: Saunders.
Law Enforcement Assistance Administration (LEAA), National Criminal Justice Reference Service (1979) The Etiology of Criminality: Nonbehavioral Science

Perspectives: A Definitive Bibliography. Washington, DC: Government Printing Office.

LEAFF, L. A. (1978) "The antisocial personality: psychodynamic implications," in W. H. Reid (ed.) The Psychopath: A Comprehensive Study of Antisocial Disorders and Behaviors. New York: Brunner/Mazel.

LION, J. R. (1978) "Nomenclature in psychiatry," in G. U. Balis et al. (eds.) The Psychiatric Foundations of Medicine, Vol. 3. Boston: Butterworth.

LUDWIG, A. M. (1980) Principles of Clinical Psychiatry. New York: Free Press.

MacDONALD, J. M. (1981) "The personality disorders," in R. C. Simons and H. Pardes (eds.) Understanding Human Behavior in Health and Illness. Baltimore: Williams & Wilkins.

MacKINNON, R. A. and R. MICHELS (1971) The Psychiatric Interview in Clinical Practice. Philadelphia: Saunders.

McLEILAN, A. T. et al. (1980) Letter to the editor. New England Journal of Medicine 302 (April 10): 870.

MARMOR, J. (1978) "Psychosocial roots of violence," in R. L. Sadoff (ed.) Violence and Responsibility: The Individual, the Family and Society. New York: Spectrum.

MENNINGER, K. (1973) Sparks (L. Freeman, ed.). New York: Crowell.

MERSKY, H. and W. L. TONGE (1974) Psychiatric Illness: Diagnosis, Management and Treatment for General Practitioners and Students. London: Bailliere Tindall.

MEZER, R. (1970) Dynamic Psychiatry in Simple Terms. New York: Springer.

MODLIN, H. C. (1983) "The antisocial personality." Bulletin of the Menninger Clinic 47 (March): 129-144.

MONROE, R. R. (1970) Episodic Behavioral Disorders: A Psychodynamic and Neurophysiologic Analysis. Cambridge, MA: Harvard University Press.

NIEDERMEYER, E. and F. LOPES da SILVA (1982) Electroencephalography: Basic Principles, Clinical Applications and Related Fields. Baltimore: Urban & Schwarzenberg.

OPPENHEIMER, H. (1971) Clinical Psychiatry: Issues and Challenges. New York: Harper & Row.

PFOHL, S. J. (1978) Predicting Dangerousness. Lexington, MA: D. C. Heath.

PLANANSKY, K. (1972) "Phenotypic boundaries and genetic specificity in schizophrenia," in A. R. Kaplan et al. (eds.) Genetic Factors in "Schizophrenia." Springfield, IL: Charles C Thomas.

RAPPEPORT, J. R. (1974) "Antisocial behavior," in S. Arieti (ed.) Handbook of Psychiatry, Vol. 3. New York: Basic Books.

REES, W.L.L. (1976) A Short Textbook of Psychiatry. Philadelphia: J. B. Lippincott.

ROBITSCHER, J. (1980) The Powers of Psychiatry. Boston: Houghton Mifflin.

ROCKWELL, D. A. (1978) "Social and familial correlates of antisocial disorders," in W. H. Reid (ed.) The Psychopath: A Comprehensive Study of Antisocial Disorders and Behaviors. New York: Brunner/Mazel.

ROTH, L. H. (1980) "Correctional psychiatry," in W. J. Curran et al. (eds.) Modern Legal Medicine, Psychiatry, and Forensic Science. Philadelphia: E. A. Davis.

SIM, M. (1981) Guide to Psychiatry. Edinburgh: Churchill, Livingstone.

SMYTHIES, J. R. and L. CORBETT (1976) Psychiatry for Students of Medicine. Chicago: Year Book Medical Publishers.

SOLOMON, S. (1980) "Science of human behavior: neurology," in H. I. Kaplan et al. (eds.) Comprehensive Textbook of Psychiatry, Vol. 1. Baltimore: Williams & Wilkins.

SPITZER, R. L. et al. (1977) "DSM-III: guiding principles," in V. M. Rakoff et al. (eds.) Psychiatric Diagnosis. New York: Brunner/Mazel.

TUCKER, G. T. and J. H. PINCUS (1980) "Child, adolescent and adult antisocial and dyssocial behavior," in H. I. Kaplan et al. (eds.) Comprehensive Textbook of Psychiatry, Vol. 3. Baltimore: Williams & Wilkins.

U.S. Congress, House, Committee on the Judiciary, Subcommittee on Criminal Justice (1982) Insanity Defense in Federal Courts (2nd session, 97th Congress). Washington, DC: Government Printing Office.

U.S Congress, Senate, Committee on the Judiciary, Subcommittee on Criminal Law (1982a) Limiting the Insanity Defense (2nd session, 97th Congress). Washington, DC: Government Printing Office.

――――(1982b) The Insanity Defense (2nd session, 97th Congress). Washington, DC: Government Printing Office.

VAILLANT, G. E. (1975) "Sociopathy as a human process." Archives of General Psychiatry 32 (February): 178-183.

――――and J. C. PERRY (1980) "Personality disorders," in H. I. Kaplan et al. (eds.) Comprehensive Textbook of Psychiatry, Vol. 2. Baltimore: Williams & Wilkins.

WELLS, C. E. and G. W. DUNCAN (1980) Neurology for Psychiatrists. Philadelphia: F. A. Davis.

WILLIS, J. H. (1976) Clinical Psychiatry. Oxford: Blackwell Scientific Publications.

WOLFGANG, M. E. and N. A. WEINER [eds.] (1982) Criminal Violence. Beverly Hills, CA: Sage.

WOODRUFF, R. A., D. W. GOODWIN, and S. B. GUZE (1974) Psychiatric Diagnosis. New York: Oxford University Press.

ZERBIN-RÜDIN, E. (1980) "Genetic factors in neurosis, psychopathy, and alcoholism," in H. M. van Praag (ed.) Handbook of Biological Psychiatry. New York: Marcel Dekker.

10

The Assumption that Crime Is a Product of Environments: Sociological Approaches

ALBERT K. COHEN

I have a problem in approaching the subject of this chapter: I don't know what it means. Is it conceivable—is it meaningful—that crime might *not* be "a product of environments"? Is the assumption that crime is a product of environments to be set off against the assumption—which Professor Hakeem addresses in Chapter 9—that crime is a product of individuals? Is this meant to be tantamount to setting off psychological and psychiatric explanations against sociological explanations? Because of the dubious logic and the ambiguities of all these notions, I think it best to approach the subject by discussing the nature of explanation in the social sciences and criminology, the meaning of environment, and where, as I understand it, environments fit in the process of explanation.[1]

MOTIVATION

We begin with a platitude: All crime is a function of some properties of the actor and some properties of the situation in which the actor acts. No person, no organism—for that matter, no object—can behave without reference to the stuff of which it is made and its organization. Anything the object does could have turned out different if it had been in some respect different. When we deal with the human actor, the relevant stuff is attitudes, reflexes, instincts, drives, values, traits, and the like; different theories recognize and assign importance to different elements. Again, whatever an object—any object: a sparrow, a child's balloon, a dump truck—does could have been different if something about the *situation* had been different. Something about the situation links up with, energizes, releases some potentiality of the object. When we deal with action we say it prompts, inhibits, permits, denies, tempts, provokes, guides, stimulates, repels, informs, elicits, attracts, and so on. In short, we have theories that identify those things about actors and those things about situations that make a difference with respect to the outcomes and that provide rules or, as we sometimes call them, models that relate these outcomes to particular combinations of these actor properties and situation properties. We commonly call these theories of motivation. They enable us to say something about the actor or the actor's situation or both: "*He* was hungry and *there* was an apple," and conclude, "*That's* why he did it." Although it makes no sense to say that an act depends more upon properties of the one side of the "motivational field" or the other, if both are essential to the product, one may meaningfully say that *differences* in outcomes—A steals and B does not, or A steals only now and then—are to be attributed to differences on only the actor side or the situation side. For example, Sutherland's theory of differential association does not make much of opportunities, provocations, or any other properties of the situation, not because he thought they had nothing to do with the production of crime, but because be believed that they did not help much to explain why some people committed crimes and others did not. His theory of criminal motivation is, in general, poorly developed and largely implicit, but it clearly emphasizes the actor side; the main explicit components are favorable and unfavorable definitions of crime and "the specific direction of motives, drives, rationalizations, and attitudes." (On the other hand, he denies the relevance of "general needs and values since non-criminal behavior is an expression of the same needs and values.")

Freudian theories of criminal motivation could not be more different from Sutherland's, but they too emphasize heavily the actor side of the motivational field. To find the motivation for the crime one has to look deep into the psyche of the individual. In most versions of Freudian theory the role of the situation is to precipitate or provide the occasion for the expression of a fully formed criminal impulse, an impulse that will almost inevitably find its expression sooner or later.

THE ORIGINS OF MOTIVATION

For "situation" in the foregoing paragraphs read "environment" or, at least, that aspect of the environment to which the human actor or other object responds directly. There is always, of course, a more extended or wider environment, the influence of which is mediated by the more immediate environment. On the level of motivation, the relevance of the environment, here called "situation," is logically inescapable. The theoretical issues have to do with the questions of (1) what aspects of the world "out there" influence action, (2) how they articulate with properties of the actor to determine the outcome, and (3) whether they may, for any particular category of actors or acts, be treated as constants and therefore ignored in accounting for differences. We have seen that, on the level of motivation, there are major theories that give little recognition to the environment in accounting for differences in criminal outcomes. The decisive determinants are the properties of the actor.

But where do the properties of the actor come from? How is it that we have an actor with such-and-such properties that, when brought into conjunction with such-and-such elements of the environment, will produce certain kinds of behavior? We are no longer dealing with theory of motivation. We are dealing with the *origins* of the actor's contribution to the motivational field. Our explanations may invoke the body, which may emphasize genetic determinants on the one hand and biological events, such as diet or injury, on the other. If the personality is conceived of as a system of action, the body is not part of the personality. It is, in the analytical sense, environment. Lombroso's and Sheldon's schemes would illustrate biological theories of the origins of criminal motivation. Or our explanations may invoke experience, the residual effects of past activity on those constituents of personality that enter into criminal motivation. We deal here with theories of learning and personality development. Again we may refer to Sutherland and Freud. Each has two theories: a theory of criminal motivation and a theory of where the motivation came from. Sutherland calls his theory of learning a theory of criminal behavior, and the variables of the theory—the modalities of association—are directly linked in the statement of the theory to criminal behavior. But this direct linkage is possible only because the theory of criminal motivation denies that differences in the situation make any very important difference in the outcome. Since the associations produce the attitudes, rationalizations, and so on that in turn are said to motivate the criminal behavior, and since one need not take much account of the situation, one can therefore proceed operationally from biography to behavioral outcome without stopping to consider motivation.

Freudian writers, on the other hand, go to great lengths to unravel the motives of criminals, probably for two reasons: first, because Freudian motives are so much more complex and obscure than the motives of Sutherland's criminals that laypersons cannot be expected to take them for granted—they need help in deciphering them; and second, because, in the therapeutic doctrine of psychoanalysis, insight into motivation is necessary for successful treatment. But Freudian theories of the origins of motivation are also complex and diverse, emphasizing in various degrees biologically given species attributes on the one hand and childhood experiences in the family on the other.

My purpose here is not exegesis of Sutherland or Freud. It is to make the point that the role of the environment depends on the questions we ask. In the Sutherland and Freud examples, environment does not figure prominently in accounting for variations in criminal motivation. In accounting for the actor's contribution to the motivational field, on the other hand, environment, for Sutherland, is everything. The constituents of motivation—favorable and unfavorable definitions of crime—are literally taken over from others in a process of interaction with others. The actor is close to being a *tabula rasa* who receives the imprint of his or her cultural environment. In Freud, some constituents of motivation—notably the id—are derived from the internal biological environment; others, notably the ego and superego, are acquired in the process of transacting business with the social environment.

INTERACTION PROCESS

The approach to explanation that I have been explicating—through analysis of the motivation of the responsible offender—is the conventional way, but it is not the only way. Somebody, it seems, has done something criminal. "Why," we ask, "did he [or she] do it?" In answering that question we quite naturally focus on either the characteristics or the circumstances of *that* person. Suppose that, instead, we begin by noting that an act has been committed and we ask, "Why did it happen?" We are interested in everything in the context of that act that helps to explain it. This would include *all the people* who contributed to the production of the act. We make no a priori assumptions that the contributions of some person or persons to it are more important than somebody else's contribution. We do take for granted that there will be some particular person who did it, whose act it is. We recognize, however, that determining the authorship of an act is itself an instance of the social construction of reality. However obvious that authorship may appear to be, it is, in fact, a species of ownership. It exists in the fact that it is attributed to somebody by others around him or her. Usually the person to whom it is attributed will be somebody who was involved in a particularly intimate way with the physical production of the act. Indeed, the criteria for making such an attribution commonly include the existence of such an involvement, and there is usually such consensus on those criteria that it does not occur to anybody that he or she is doing anything more than taking a reading, an objective and the only possible reading, of "the facts." Those criteria are, however, cultural. They vary somewhat among social systems, and sometimes agency may be very much in contention, not because the facts are in dispute but because the criteria—the law, so to speak—are uncertain. Thus, given agreement on the facts, we may debate whether the act was committed by A, by B, by both A and B as distinct but parallel or convergent authors, or by a single collective entity such as a corporation of which A and B are "members," or whether it was an "act of God"— that is, an "accident." If A recruited and paid B to poison C and B did poison C and C died, did A kill C? A and B? B only? To questions such as these, different cultures will provide different answers, and the same culture may change its answers over time. It was obvious until not very long ago that corporations could not kill people, much less murder them. Now they can do both. If, during a shootout with robbers, a bullet from a police officer's gun strikes another police officer or an innocent bystander and that person dies, who killed the dead person? Under the doctrine (in our legal system) of felony murder, it was probably the robber. The last example strongly suggests that the attribution of agency in everyday life and in court is never a matter of analyzing causality alone. It is also, to some degree, a matter of pinning down responsibility, of assigning blame, so that we may know whom to punish. The two will likely be in some way connected, but the magnitude of blame need not be correlated with the magnitude of the contribution to causality. To some degree the concept of victim-precipitated crime (Wolfgang, 1958: 252) takes cognizance of this; it recognizes that what the victim did may have contributed as much to making the crime happen as what the offender did. It implies, furthermore, that knowing the victim's motivation may contribute as much to our understanding of the crime as knowing the offender's motivation.

We deal, however, with much more than provocation on the part of victims. Victims may contribute by being rash or ignorant or naive enough to expose themselves to victimization. They may be victims because they are members of despised minorities or because they are puny or defenseless or have no friends to back them up or because they are forced to walk or take the subway home from work. They could be victims because they are too kind and helpful for their own good. The occurrence of the crime could turn on any of these or other attributes of the victims, but these have not concerned criminology to the degree that victim-precipitation has, probably because victim-precipitation always connotes some measure of blameworthiness. Criminologists, not only lawyers, are prone to assign causality where they perceive blame. But the scene that engenders the crime may include other actors as well: friendly or unfriendly audiences; people who, knowingly or unknowingly, provide information or helpful distractions; people who promise asylum, alibis, markets for the proceeds. What made it happen may also include the time, the place, the flow of traffic, the built environment, the available means of transportation, the availability of necessary hardware. All of these elements interact and out of this interaction is born a crime. The task of theory, focusing on the *event* rather than the legally culpable *agent*, is to develop conceptual schemes that can code the multifarious constituents of the scene and the ways that they interact into a manageable number of abstract concepts that lend themselves, in turn, to the construction of verifiable propositions about criminogenic interaction processes. Motivation will, of course, figure here, but it will be the motivation of whoever participates in this interaction process. No special magic attaches to the motivation of the offender.

Where now, in the context of this interaction process model, is the environment? This scene—let us call it a "local interactional field"—may contain many actors. From the standpoint of any one actor, the other actors are environmental, but this does not seem to be a particularly helpful locution. It says only that each actor receives feedback and inputs from the others. It is perhaps better to think of the interaction process itself as a game, or analogous to a game. Like a game, it is a coherent structure of action that runs its course; unlike a game, this system or structure is an entity, and how it evolves depends not only upon its internal organization, its membership, and the rules that govern it, but upon a world "out there." The interaction process that culminates in a robbery, a conspiracy in restraint of trade, a drug deal, or any one of the manifold crimes that made up the Watergate affair occurs within some larger setting—a setting that provides opportunities and imposes constraints on the interaction process. In short, for every entity around which one can draw a boundary, there is an "out there" that is environment relative to that entity. The setting we now speak of is the environment of the interactional field.

REVIEW

We have by now attended to several different kinds of questions. One takes the form: Why did this person commit this crime? The question is asked about people whose contribution to the crime meets the legal criteria of agency and responsibility. The question really asks, Why did this person do whatever he did that makes him legally responsible for the event? We now know that this is not the same as asking, Why did it happen? The question is about motivation. It is usually regarded as a psychological question.

Another kind of question asks, also of particular persons, How did he or she get that way? That is, How did he or she become the sort of person who, placed in a certain kind of situation, produced behavior that qualifies him or her, under the law, as a criminal? We deal here with questions that fall under the domains of learning theory and personality development, which are also usually taken to be psychological.

A third kind of question does not locate the act in the life space of a particular actor but takes the act itself as the point of reference and investigates the interaction process that brought it about. There is some uncertainty about what discipline this "belongs" to; people seem to be content to call it social psychological. It appears to me that the interactional field is a small social system and that the stuff of which it is constituted, interaction, is what sociology claims to be all about; I would myself be disposed to call it microsociological. Be that as it may, theory of interaction process is remarkably underdeveloped.

THE SOCIOLOGICAL LEVEL
OF EXPLANATION

There is another kind of question. Every act, including every criminal act, is located somewhere in a social system. Every *kind* of act is *distributed* somehow in a social system. Social systems are extended and differentiated in space and time; acts are therefore located and distributed in both dimensions. We must then ask, What is it *about a system* that accounts for the kinds of crime we find in it and how these crimes are distributed in space and time? This is, of course, the quintessentially sociological question. What we are being asked to explain is a property or, if you will, a product of a social system (how rape, for example, varies by age, race, or time of year) and the answer must consist of identifying other properties of the system (structural, cultural, demographic) and describing how they articulate and interact to produce the product. The systems can be of any scale—families, gangs, factories, neighborhoods, cities, countries—and what is constitutive of one system may be environment relative to another. The relevant theory here is a theory about how social systems work.

It should be clear that the different sorts of theory I have identified and the explanations they provide are not necessarily in conflict. Many different theories may provide explanations of why A shot B, but they are all answers to the same question. Unless they are all saying the same thing in somewhat different words (which would not be unusual), they cannot all be right. But the different sorts of theory I have talked about here are theories about different things. Different questions, different answers.

However, it does not follow that the different sorts of theory are entirely independent of one another. If, for example, we have a theory of motivation that accounts for criminal motivation by feelings of relative deprivation, unresolved psychological complexes, an unconscious need to be punished, or the availability of certain kinds of opportunities, then it necessarily follows that how crime is distributed in a social system will correspond to an identical distribution of the respective motivational fields. A distribution of motivational fields different from that would be bad news for the theory. When the two distributions match closely, it is evidence for the theory. This does not, however, answer the sociological question: What is it about the social system that accounts for the criminal product? If one assumes that criminal actors are distributed as they are because a certain kind of motivational field is distributed in the same way, the sociological task will be to analyze the workings of the social system to show how they produce such a distribution of motivational fields. If the motivational theory minimizes the properties of the actor and emphasizes the presence of opportunity in the actor's milieu, then the sociological task is to explain the distribution of opportunity. This is not a reduction to the psychological level, because the sociological explanation is an analysis of the way *the social system* works and of how systems that work that way engender characteristic distributions of the ingredients of criminal motivation. The relevant theory is social system theory.

If our starting point is a theory that predicts crime directly from a theory of learning or personality development, then the distribution of crime must correspond to the distribution of those persons who are products of the learning and developmental histories that, according to the theory, are necessary to produce crime. This implies, on the level of sociological analysis, an account of how the workings of the social system produce histories of that kind and assure that those who experience them wind up distributed in the way that they are. Again, there is no reductionism here. The question falls outside the jurisdiction of psychology. The actual disciplinary affiliations of the people who work on the respective levels is beside the point. The reference to the disciplines is to a distinction in jobs to be done, not to the credentials of the people who do them.

Finally, the interaction process perspective requires that the distribution of crime correspond to the distribution of the interactional fields called for by the theory. The sociological task is to account for that distribution. This entails accounting for whatever, according to the theory, are the ingredients and circumstances necessary to engender and sustain the interaction process that produces the crime. It must account for the convergence, in time and space, of the necessary cast of characters, including those who eventually turn out to be "offender" and "victim." (As Von Hentig points out, this may not be decided until late in the interaction process. It may be touch and go who is going to be conned or murdered, as the criminal law codes these things.) And it must include also the convergence with this cast of characters of whatever other circumstances—opportunities, reference objects, information— that the theory recognizes as having something to do with the outcome. To account for the convergence of the several constituents is to account for how they came to be *what* they are—what we call socialization in human—and how they came to be *where* they are, which we call mobility when speaking of humans, distribution when speaking of objects other than human. The social system within which a distribution of motivational fields, or biographies, or of interactional fields is to be found may be thought of as the environment common to all members of the distribution.

SOCIOLOGICAL ANALYSIS AND DIFFERENTIAL ASSOCIATION THEORY

Let us look at some of the better known theories of crime from this perspective. Differential association theory predicts crime from certain kinds of associational histories. If the theory is valid, the distribution of crime must correspond to the distribution of the products of the predicted histories, and we are faced with the following question: How is the social system organized to produce that distribution? One might consider how the routine functioning of the system generates combinations of affinity and propinquity that bring people together, how it affects the possibility of deliberate (but also inadvertent) supervision and control over interaction and communication, how it moves people about with the effect, intended or not, of promoting or preventing certain kinds of association. Certainly one would want to consider the implications of Homans's (1950) proposition that people who interact in the external system will interact also in the internal system, which is to say that, where social arrangements require people to interact with one another in order to accomplish the tasks and ensure the viability of the organization, these people will tend also to form relationships of a more intimate and personal character, which will be expressed in still more interaction and shared activities. To be more accurate, we are concerned here not with associations with people but with the *definitions of crime* that people present in what they say and what they do. The extent to which people feel free to display their definitions of crime to those with whom they interact—for example, how safe they will feel in doing so—will itself be constrained by various features of the setting of the interaction. That being so, it follows that sociological analysis will also examine the social production of these features of the setting. These are a few examples of avenues of inquiry one might explore in sociological analysis premised on the validity of differential association theory.

SOCIOLOGICAL ANALYSIS
AND ANOMIE THEORY

Merton's "Social Structure and Anomie" (1957) provides an interesting contrast to Sutherland's theory. Merton begins by asking the sociological question: Why is deviance distributed as it is in American society, and why do different societies exhibit different rates and distributions? What is it *about these societies* that produces these results? He answers these questions in terms of the distribution of culture goals, regulatory norms, and institutionalized means among the positions of the system. Although this is cited as a preeminently sociological theory, two things are worth noting. First, the theory is clearly premised upon a theory of human motivation that in turn appears to be a simplified version of the structure of the unit act according to Talcott Parsons: Action consists of the selection of those means, available in the situation of action, that are logically suited to the accomplishment of the actor's goals, the choice of means being constrained, however, by normative rules. Given this basis in psychology, the statement of anomie theory follows with a certain inevitability. Second, the theory goes only a short way toward answering the question, What is it about American society—or any other society— that accounts for the way in which various patterns of attachment to goals and regulative norms and of accessibility of institutionalized means (that is, variously composed motivational fields) are distributed within the system? More specifically, it does not tell us very much about what features of the polity, the economy, the family—whatever structures are relevant—and of their interaction generate the observed distributions of motivational fields. In short, in terms of the scheme set forth in this chapter, Merton has laid the groundwork for an explanation of deviance on the sociological level, but the task, for the most part, still lies ahead.

SOCIOLOGICAL ANALYSIS
AND BIOLOGICAL THEORIES

Those biological theories that explain crime by the effects of the inherited biological constitution on the actor's motivation to crime provide an especially instructive example of the distinctiveness of the speaking of humans, production in speaking of objects other than sociological level of explanation. I have said that in these theories biology is environment relative to personality and therefore to action, although many people like to think of the actor as everything that is contained within a single human integument: bones, vessels, glands, ideas, habits, self-conceptions. These people will feel uncomfortable with the idea of biology as environment. It is not important to debate this matter of nomenclature here and now. Regardless of one's preferences in this regard, the question still arises, In what sense may one speak of the sociology of crime when crime on the individual level is regarded as a product of biological structure? Well, the sociology of crime is inquiry into the ways in which the properties of the social system determine the nature and distribution of crime within the system. If crime is a product of inherited biology, the distribution of crime in the social system must correspond to the distribution of the genetic determinants of criminal behavior. The distribution of those genetic determinants depends, in turn, upon how human beings who carry different sorts of genetic material are moved around in the system, the probability of their sexual union, the further probabilities of live births and survival to various ages. These depend upon the economy, the family system, stratification, mobility, health care, and so on—that is, upon the organization and functioning of the social system. The social system is, then, environment relative to that distribution. I am saying that, even if we start with a biological theory, we are still left with a sociological question: Why is crime distributed as it is? We are also left with a task for sociological analysis.

SOCIOLOGICAL ANALYSIS AND LABELING THEORY

Labeling theory consists of two families of theory. For one, deviance consists of the fact of being successfully labeled as a deviant or criminal. The "criminal," in this type of theory, is somewhat analogous to the victim in conventional theory; he or she is somebody to whom something happens. In many versions of labeling theory, the criminal *is* a victim—the victim of the criminal justice system. Attention tends to focus on the motivation of the agent of social control and the resources available to him or her in the situation. On the side of the potential labelee, attention tends to focus on those characteristics that make him or her attractive or vulnerable as a candidate for labeling and the resources in the situation available to him or her for resisting labeling. The explanatory schema of the labeling event—the arrest, the indictment, the conviction—perhaps fits best under our category of interactional field. Explanation on the sociological level tends to focus upon the ways in which the structure and functioning of the social system, and especially of the bureaucracies of the criminal justice system, generate motivation on the part of agents of social control to round people up and label them and also the social distribution of power to implement labeling on the one hand and to resist it on the other.

The other family of labeling theories takes the explanation of rule breaking as its object, but sees labeling as the crucial experience in shaping the motivation to commit crimes. Crime and deviance are reactive to efforts to control crime and deviance. The labeling event sets off an interaction process that, in one way or another—by narrowing opportunity, by shaping self-conception, by channeling associations, by alienating the actor from the conventional reference world—leads to criminality or heightened criminality. I call this a "family" of theories because each conception of the process that mediates the labeling event and the consequent criminality defines a somewhat different model of the evolution of criminality and directs attention to a different set of variables and interactions.

Both families suggest strategies for the construction of theories of the social distribution of crime. Both direct the investigator to look for the ways in which the organization of the criminal justice system, of the larger society of which it is a part, and of the exchanges between them generate histories of actors as criminal labelees. The second family (and each of its branches) suggests inquiry into the ways that the organization of the system promotes the convergence and sequencing of those constituents of the interaction process that mediate the effect of labeling on conduct. For example, societies may differ in the extent to which they provide the conditions that make it possible for people to move away from where they are known and conceal their pasts; they may differ with respect to the role of government in encouraging or requiring employers to hire people with known criminal records.

CONTROL THEORY AND
SOCIOLOGICAL ANALYSIS

According to Hirschi, crime is the product of the weakness of bonds to society—of attachment, commitment, involvement, and belief. Like most other American criminological theories, Hirschi's is formulated on what I have called the psychological level. It is an attempt to answer the question, What are the differences between individuals A and B that explain the differences in the ways they behave? All of the bonds are checks on the normal propensity to criminal actions. They create anxiety on the part of the actors that if they misbehave, they will lose something of value—close ties to other people or the accomplishment of long-range goals—or they consume the actors' time and other resources, or they function as internalized moral censors. Each actor is the locus of a unique set of bonds. Tests of the theory consist, essentially, of correlations between individual measurements on criminality or delinquency and the corresponding measurements on strength of bonds.

We continue our argument along what is now a familiar course. Suppose that it can be demonstrated that, as control theory predicts, high crime rates are correlated with weak bonds. Now what has control theory to say to the questions: Why do blacks have weaker bonds (and therefore higher crime rates) than whites? Or Americans than Japanese? Or Soviets than East Germans? Control theory has very little to say to these questions. This is not a defect of control theory. Control theory tries to explain individual differences in criminal behavior in terms of individual differences in social bonds. It is not a theory about the societal origins of social bonds. There are, to be sure, theories or "models" that try to integrate control theory with other theories in such manner that variables derived from one theory account for the variables that derive from another theory, which account, in turn, for the dependent variable, crime. So, for example, differences in feelings of frustration about one's life chances as measured, perhaps by the magnitude of the disjunction between aspirations and expectations (all this derived from anomie theory) may be found, or alleged, to account for differences in strength of social bonds and indirectly, therefore, for crime. But note that all the measurements pertain to attributes of the individuals we are comparing or their respective backgrounds or situations. The combined theories still do not carry us beyond the local fields as they are directly experienced by the subjects. They do not help us to answer the questions we are now asking. These are sociological questions—questions about how the way that the system is built and runs produces the system map of attachments, commitments, involvements, and beliefs.

CONVERGING THEORIES

Lofland

I would like now to mention three important contributions to criminological theory that are substantively worlds apart but that converge on the same conception of the relationship among levels of explanation.

Lofland's *Deviance and Identity*, published in 1969 (see especially pp. 29-31), sets forth "three levels of explanation." The difference between the first two appears to me to be rather subtle and, for our purposes, not very important. At any rate, Lofland is clearly talking at times of what I have called the psychological, and at other times of the macrosociological levels of explanation. His conceptual scheme defines a local field consisting of (1) what the *actor* brings with him or her, in terms of such things as skills, self-esteem, and the ways in which he or she defines events, (2) a complement of *others* who play some sort of role in the development of the action, (3) the properties of the *place* where events transpire, and (4) hardware, which means most tangible objects that might have some significance as facilitators or inhibitors of action. These elements are defined in such a way that they come close to including everything in the immediate context of the deviant that might affect its outcome. "Bracketing together others, places, hardware, and actor as elements of a proximate system, there can be raised the question: Upon what does a given variation in each of them depend?" The answer to this lies in "social organizational" sources and determinants, and this, for all practical purposes, appears to be the equivalent of what I have called the "sociological" level of explanation.

For example, "actors" and "others," in short, all the human members of the "proximate system," are products of their biographies. On Lofland's (1969: 31) third level, therefore, "there is the question of the determinants of the type of social organization in which given persons could experience given kinds of biographies." Or again, having noted, in the context of his discussion of "others," that certain kinds of crime typically occur between strangers, he goes on to say that the explanation of such crimes "requires some understanding of the kind of social order in which it is possible for persons to be physically proximate but personally unknown," (Lofland, 1969: 81), and suggests what some of the characteristics of such a social order might be.

Another feature of Lofland's scheme should be noted. The organizational sources of the composition of the local fields that produce deviance are only analytically distinct from those that produce conformity. For example: "The social sources of hardware for many deviant acts are the *same* as the social sources of hardware for the conduct of normal activity" (Lofland, 1969: 71-72). In other words, in looking for the system-level determinants of deviance and conformity, we are looking at much the same concrete activities and arrangements, but we are looking at them from the point of view of their bearing upon, their contribution to, the part they play in the social machineries that produce deviance and conformity.

Cohen and Felson

When all is said and done, however, Lofland's *primary* concern in *Deviance and Identity* remains the individual actor and his or her deviance. Cohen and Felson (1979; Felson, 1983) approach the subject of crime at the social system level. Their primary concerns are the distribution of crime and changes in crime rates over time. A crime occurs when there are brought together a likely offender, a suitable target, and the absence of a capable guardian. Differences in crime rates in space and time are the result of differences in the patterning of routine activities, those same activities that account for noncriminal behavior. The patterning of routine activities influences the distribution of crime by producing, at the various locations within the system, the necessary convergences among likely offenders, suitable targets, and absence of capable guardians. Cohen and Felson's own attempts to explain crime rate changes focus on the ways in which changes in routine activities produce changes in capable guardians and suitable targets, and therefore criminal opportunities. For example, a decrease in the number of households without capable guardians is partly the result of an increase in the number of people going off to work or play and leaving households unattended; this, in turn, is partly a result of an increase in the number of divorced persons and of married women who work; and these in turn are the result of various demographic and economic changes.

In short, Cohen and Felson provide us with an extremely simple conceptual scheme to identify what is essential on the level of the immediate determinants of the individual offense; they have nothing to say about the subtleties of motivation or the dynamics of interaction among the three elements of the conceptual scheme; and the explanation of the social distribution of crime focuses on the ways in which system-level properties generate the social distribution of only two of those determinants, omitting that determinant that has traditionally been the favorite preoccupation of criminological theory, the "likely offender." They do, however, suggest that "the routine activity approach might in the future be applied to the analysis of offenders and their inclinations as well. For example, the structure of primary group activity may affect the likelihood that cultural transmission or social control of criminal inclinations will occur, while the structure of the community may affect the tempo of criminogenic peer group activity" (Cohen and Felson, 1979: 605). The important point for our purposes is that they develop a strategy for explaining crime on the social system level, that the strategy rests upon and clearly presupposes assumptions on the psychological and microsociological levels, and that the explanations cannot themselves be derived from those assumptions. For example, that one essential element of the local interactional field is the presence of a suitable target is one assumption; but from that assumption it is not possible to derive a description of how changes in marriage and divorce rates and the sex composition of the labor force produce changes in the production and distribution of suitable targets. That is a task for sociological analysis.

Colvin and Pauly

Is it possible to frame a successful theory of crime or delinquency that accounts for the dependent variable as the product, in the main at least, of a single, fundamental property of the macrosystem? A paper by Colvin and Pauly (1983) is of great interest for our purposes because it attempts such a theory and because it employs a methodology of theory construction that is thoroughly consistent with what I have been espousing in this chapter. Colvin and Pauly begin by reviewing several current theories of juvenile delinquency, recognizing that all of them have merit, but criticizing all of them because they do not go significantly beyond what I have called the psychological and microsociological levels of explanation. That is, they all identify certain sets of circumstances as the determinants of delinquent acts, but they do not explain or try to explain how these determinants are distributed in the social system. Colvin and Pauly's "integrated, structural-Marxist" theory does not reject but rather incorporates elements of these theories. It is a Marxist theory in that it finds the explanation for these psychological and microsociological-level determinants in capitalism. Capitalism is one way of organizing the social relations of production. One aspect of the social relations of production is the relationship of authority and the structure of social control in the work place. Experience with authority and control in the work place is a profound socialization experience with consequences that have ramifications throughout one's life. Even within a capitalistic framework, however, variations in the exigencies of technology and the market produce marked variations in the structure of control. These variations, in turn, engender in the participants different attitudes toward authority, ranging from respect and willing compliance to hostility and alienation. The more coercive the control, the more intense the alienation.

Workers, tenuously or firmly bonded to authority, reproduce in their roles as parents the authority structures that to them have become most natural. Their children, in turn, form positive or alienative bonds to parents and to authority, of which parents are the first representatives. Children's experiences in the home influence their placement in school and the kind of control structures they will encounter there; the effect is likely to be reinforcement of the initial positive or alienative bonds and attitudes toward authority. These outcomes in turn influence children's peer group affiliations, which, in conjunction with community opportunity structures, generate both qualitative and quantitative variations in delinquent activity. This is not a theory of adult criminality, but a structural-Marxist theory of crime would presumable emphasize the same system properties and link them in similar manner to psychological and microsociological determinants.

This theory makes use of control theory and other theories to explain delinquent motivation and why children differ with respect to delinquency. But it makes use of system-level analysis to explain why the circumstances that engender delinquent motivation arise at all and why they are more prevalent in some sectors of the population than in others. It fails, however, to address certain questions. I raise these questions because they have implications for my main concern in this chapter, the methodology of theory construction. It is clear that there are crime and delinquency in noncapitalistic, including socialist, societies; that there is great variation in these respects within both kinds of societies; and that it is probable that some capitalistic societies—such as Japan—have less crime than some socialist countries—such as the Soviet Union. What are the implications?

First, it is possible that crime in American society is indeed a product of capitalism, in the manner described by Colvin and Pauly, and that crime in other societies, including socialist societies, is produced by mechanisms other than those recognized by Marxist theories. In this case, the Marxist theories are not in fact general theories of cross-sectional applicability.

Second, it is possible that, if crime can flourish elsewhere without benefit of capitalism, it can flourish *with* capitalism but not *because* of it—in other words, that the Marxist theory of crime does not explain crime even in the United States.

Third, it is conceivable that Colvin and Pauly are right, that the kinds of mechanisms they describe do indeed account for crime and delinquency in American society, but that they also account for them in socialist societies. That is to say, the most criminogenic features of the social relations of production—that is, coercive control structures— may not be uniquely associated with capitalism but exist also under some kinds of socialism, where they have the same alienative effect as under capitalism. However, it is still the case that crime varies widely within both types of society. These "within" variations could result from the fact that under the rubrics of both capitalism and socialism are economies that vary greatly in the respects that bear upon the production of coercion and alienation in the work place; they could result from the fact that members of both classes of society vary with respect to *other* features of the culture or social organization that independently affect the production of crime and delinquency; they could result from the fact that variations with respect to noneconomic properties of the system exert an effect upon the production of crime and delinquency through their effect on the social relations of production and therefore on the quality of experience in the work place.

I do not intend this to be a critique of Marxist theory, nor do I mean to derogate Colson and Pauly's work, which I find original and seminal.

The purpose of my critique is to make a very general point: that it is highly unlikely that any single structural feature of a social system, no matter how profound and pervasive its consequences, is likely, taken by itself, to account satisfactorily for crime and delinquency. However we conceptualize the constituents of the local fields that generate criminal acts—that is, the variables that must be considered in accounting for such acts—there are enough of them and they are different enough that a thoroughgoing analysis of their structural origins is likely to entail the study of something like the total social system. Some properties of the system will turn out to be more important than others; the social relations of production might well turn out to be the most important of all. But we should not expect theory to take the form of an invariant relationship between some one dominant system attribute and crime or delinquency.

CONCLUSION

To return to my theme: The assumption that crime is the product of the environment does not need to be proved. The antithesis—the assumption that crime is *not* the product of the environment—is meaningless. Whether we are interested in the occurrence of a crime, the involvement of some person in the crime as actor or victim, a career in crime or victimization, the distribution of crime within a society, or intersocietal differences in crime rates, the object of explanation does not arise by spontaneous generation, nor do actors squeeze out acts from their own insides like toothpaste out of a tube. Every behaving entity, human and nonhuman, including those that are sometimes described as "closed systems," behaves as it does because it has certain properties of its own and these interact with the properties of the relevant environment. This is true of a personality, a dyad, an interactional field, a collectivity, or some set of people defined by their occupancy of the same location in a social system.

However, to say of something—crime or anything else—that it is the product of its environment is an empty truism and not very helpful. In fact, it can be argued that it is true by definition. The environment of x is anything that lies outside the boundaries of x and makes a difference to the behavior of x. If it makes no difference, it is not environment.

Explaining consists, in a sense, of discovering what is the environment for any particular purpose. It consists, that is to say, of abstracting, from everything that goes on out there, that which is relevant for the purpose at hand and tracing the connections and pathways through which its influence makes itself felt. Maybe it is even better to say that it consists of *constructing* the relevant environment. Every theory considered in this chapter not only "takes the environment into account," it is a set of rules for constructing, from the materials "out there," environments that can produce crime.

NOTE

1. Much of what follows is an extension of some ideas contained in Cohen (1983).

REFERENCES

COHEN, A. K. (1983) "Crime causation: sociological theories," pp. 342-353 in S. H. Kadish et al. (eds.) Encyclopedia of Crime and Justice, Vol. 1. New York: Free Press.
COHEN, L. E. and M. FELSON (1979) "Social change and crime rate trends: a routine activities approach." American Sociological Review 44 (August): 588-608.
COLVIN, M. and J. PAULY (1983) "A critique of criminology: toward an integrated structural-Marxist theory of delinquency production." American Journal of Sociology 89 (November): 513-551.
FELSON, M. (1983) "Ecology of crime," pp. 665-670 in S. H. Kadish et al. (eds.) Encyclopedia of Crime and Justice, Vol. 1. New York: Free Press.
HOMANS, G. C. (1950) The Human Group. New York: Harcourt Brace Jovanovich.
LOFLAND, J. (1969) Deviance and Identity. Englewood Cliffs, NJ: Prentice-Hall.
MERTON, R. K. (1957) "Social structure and anomie," pp. 131-194 in R. K. Merton (ed.) Social Theory and Social Structure. New York: Free Press.
WOLFGANG, M. E. (1958) Patterns in Criminal Homicide. Philadelphia: University of Pennsylvania Press.

About the Authors

Albert K. Cohen received his B.A. from Harvard, his M.A. from Indiana University, where he worked under Edwin H. Sutherland, and his Ph.D. from Harvard. His principal teaching posts have been at Indiana University and the University of Connecticut, where he is now University Professor of Sociology. He is author of *Delinquent Boys: The Culture of the Gang* and *Deviance and Control,* and numerous papers on crime, delinquency, and deviance. He has served as President of the Society for the Study of Social Problems and is now Vice-President of the American Society of Criminology.

Delbert S. Elliott is currently the Director of the Behavioral Research Institute in Boulder, Colorado, and a Professor of Sociology at the University of Colorado. His publications include "An Integrated Theoretical Perspective on Delinquent Behavior" (*Journal of Research in Crime and Delinquency,* 1979), with Suzanne Ageton and Rachelle Canter, and *Explaining Delinquency and Drug Use* (Sage, 1985), with David Huizinga and Suzanne Ageton. He is also the Principal Investigator for the ongoing National Youth Survey, a major longitudinal study of delinquency and substance use.

Don C. Gibbons is Professor of Sociology and Urban Studies at Portland State University. He is the author of a number of books and articles in criminology, including *Society, Crime, and Criminal Behavior; Delinquent Behavior;* and *The Criminological Enterprise.* His current research interests include the study of forcible rape, mundane crime, and the impact of changes in urban social structure upon crime.

Jack P. Gibbs is Centennial Professor of Sociology at Vanderbilt University. His interests include the sociology of deviance, social control, the sociology of law, human ecology, and the methodology of theory construction. He is the author of *Norms, Deviance, and Social Control:*

Conceptual Matters (Elsevier, 1981) and editor of *Social Control: Views from the Social Sciences* (Sage, 1982). He has served as President of the Pacific Sociological Association, and is now one of two nominees for the presidency of the American Sociological Association. He received his Ph.D. in sociology from the University of Oregon.

John Hagan is Professor of Sociology and Law at the University of Toronto. He is currently studying the sanctioning of securities violators and the entry and advancement of women and men in the legal profession. He is an Associate Editor of the *American Sociological Review,* an International Consulting Editor for the *American Journal of Sociology,* and serves on the editorial boards of several other American and Canadian journals. His recent books include *Modern Criminology* (McGraw-Hill, 1985) and *The Disreputable Pleasures* (2nd ed., McGraw-Hill Ryerson, 1984).

Michael Hakeem is Professor Emeritus of Sociology at the University of Wisconsin—Madison. He received his doctorate in sociology from the Ohio State University. He recently retired after forty years of teaching at the Ohio State University, the University of Iowa, and the University of Wisconsin, where he was for many years Special Departmental Adviser in Correctional Administration in the Department of Sociology. He has served as a Sociologist and Sociologist-Actuary in the Division of the Criminologist of the Illinois State Prison System, where he did research on parole prediction. He has done research on criminally insane offenders for the Ohio State Division of Mental Hygiene. He has published in the areas of parole prediction, psychiatric criminology, and the criminality of military veterans. He has taught courses in general sociology, criminology, juvenile delinquency, correctional institutions, probation and parole, social problems, and the family. At present, he is pursuing interests in educational philosophy and in issues and problems in the teaching of scientific thinking.

Robert F. Meier is Professor and Chair of the Department of Sociology at Washington State University. His most recent books include *Major Forms of Crime* (Sage, 1984) and *Sociology of Deviant Behavior,* with Marshall B. Clinard (6th ed., Holt, Rinehart and Winston, 1985). His interests include processes of deviance and social control, and he has published on social control, white-collar and corporate criminality, deterrence, and criminological theory.

James F. Short, Jr., is Professor of Sociology and Director of the Social Research Center at Washington State University. He currently serves as Associate Editor of the Annual Review of Sociology, and he was Editor of the American Sociological Review from 1972-1974. He has also served in editorial capacities for several other journals and books. He was President of the American Sociological Association in 1984, having previously been elected as a Council-at-Large member (1968-1970), and as Secretary of that Association (1977-1980). He was Co-Director of Research for the National Commission on the Causes and Prevention of Violence (1968-1969). His books include *Suicide and Homicide: Some Economic, Sociological and Psychological Aspects of Agression* (with A. F. Henry), *Group Process and Gang Delinquency* (with F. L. Strodtbeck), *Delinquency, Crime, and Society,* and *The State of Sociology: Problems and Prospects.*

Charles R. Tittle is Professor of Sociology and Chairman, Department of Sociology and Social Psychology, Florida Atlantic University, Boca Raton, Florida. His interests focus on the effects of sanctions in the maintenance of social order, deviant behavior and social status, and criminological theory. His current work involves explication, modeling, testing, and modification of Sutherland's theory of differential association.

Ernest van den Haag is the John M. Olin Professor of Jurisprudence and Public Policy at Fordham University. He formerly served as Visiting Professor of Criminal Justice at the Graduate School of Criminal Justice, State University of New York at Albany, and as Professor of Law at New York Law School and Professor of Social Philosophy at New York University. His two most recent books are *Punishing Criminals: Concerning a Very Old and Painful Question* (Basic Books, 1975) and *The Death Penalty: A Debate,* with John P. Conrad (Plenum, 1983).

About the Authors

James F. Short, Jr., is Professor of Sociology and Director of the Social Research Center at Washington State University. He currently serves as Associate Editor of the Annual Review of Sociology, and he was Editor of the American Sociological Review from 1972-1974. He has also served in editorial capacities for several other journals and books. He was President of the American Sociological Association in 1984, having previously been elected as a Council-at-Large member (1968-1970), and as Secretary of that Association (1977-1980). He was Co-Director of Research for the National Commission on the Causes and Prevention of Violence (1968-1969). His books include *Suicide and Homicide: Some Economic, Sociological and Psychological Aspects of Agression* (with A. F. Henry), *Group Process and Gang Delinquency* (with F. L. Strodtbeck), *Delinquency, Crime, and Society,* and *The State of Sociology: Problems and Prospects.*

Charles R. Tittle is Professor of Sociology and Chairman, Department of Sociology and Social Psychology, Florida Atlantic University, Boca Raton, Florida. His interests focus on the effects of sanctions in the maintenance of social order, deviant behavior and social status, and criminological theory. His current work involves explication, modeling, testing, and modification of Sutherland's theory of differential association.

Ernest van den Haag is the John M. Olin Professor of Jurisprudence and Public Policy at Fordham University. He formerly served as Visiting Professor of Criminal Justice at the Graduate School of Criminal Justice, State University of New York at Albany, and as Professor of Law at New York Law School and Professor of Social Philosophy at New York University. His two most recent books are *Punishing Criminals: Concerning a Very Old and Painful Question* (Basic Books, 1975) and *The Death Penalty: A Debate,* with John P. Conrad (Plenum, 1983).

Waynesburg College Library
Waynesburg, Pa. 15370